ABOUT THIS PUBLICATION

FOR SERVICE ASSISTANCE

Customer Service Department
704.898.0770

North Carolina General Statues is published by The Muliti-Media Group of Greater Charlotte in Charlotte, North Carolina. Copyright 2015 by the Multi-Media Group of Greater Charlotte. This book or parts thereof may not be reproduced in any form, stored in a retrieval system, or transmitted in any form by any means—electronic, mechanical, photocopy, recording or otherwise—without prior written permission of the publisher, except as provided by United States of America copyright law.

The records required by U.S. Code 2257(a) through (c) and the pertinent regulations 28 C.F.R. Cli. 1, Part 75 with respect to this publication and all materials associated with such records are maintained by The Multi-Media Group of Greater Charlotte, Publisher and available for review by Attorney General.

www.visionbooks.org

Copyright © 2015 by MMGGC
All rights reserved!

TID: 4993984
ISBN (10) digit: 150233657X
ISBN (13) digit: 978-1502336576

123-4-56789-01234-Paperback
123-4-56789-01234-Hardback

First Edition

090520140547

Printed in the United States of America

2015 EDITION

North Carolina Criminal Law And Procedure-Pamphlet # 12

Printed In conjunction with the Administration of the Courts

North Carolina Criminal Law and Procedure
Pamphlet Reference Guide

Chapters	Pamphlet
Chapter 1 Civil Procedure	1
Chapter 1 Civil Procedure (Continue)	2
Chapter 1A Rules of Civil Procedure	2
Chapter 1B Contribution.	2
Chapter 1C Enforcement of Judgments.	2
Chapter 1D Punitive Damages.	2
Chapter 1E Eastern Band of Cherokee Indians.	2
Chapter 1F North Carolina Uniform Interstate Depositions and Discovery Act.	2
Chapter 2 - Clerk of Superior Court [Repealed and Transferred.]	3
Chapter 3 - Commissioners of Affidavits and Deeds [Repealed.]	3
Chapter 4 - Common Law	3
Chapter 5 - Contempt [Repealed.]	3
Chapter 5A - Contempt	3
Chapter 6 - Liability for Court Costs	3
Chapter 7 - Courts [Repealed and Transferred.]	3
Chapter 7A – Judicial Department	3
Chapter 7A – Continuation (Judicial Department)	4
Chapter 7A – Continuation (Judicial Department)	5
Chapter 7B - Juvenile Code	5
Chapter 8 - Evidence	6
Chapter 8A - Interpreters for Deaf Persons [Recodified.]	6
Chapter 8B - Interpreters for Deaf Persons	6
Chapter 8C - Evidence Code	6
Chapter 9 - Jurors	6
Chapter 10 - Notaries [Repealed.]	6
Chapter 10A - Notaries [Recodified.]	6
Chapter 10B - Notaries	6
Chapter 11 - Oaths	6
Chapter 12 - Statutory Construction	6
Chapter 13 - Citizenship Restored	6
Chapter 14 - Criminal Law	7
Chapter 14 –Criminal Law (Continuation)	8
Chapter 15 - Criminal Procedure	9
Chapter 15A - Criminal Procedure Act (Continuation)	10
Chapter 15A - Criminal Procedure Act (Continuation)	11
Chapter 15B - Victims Compensation	11
Chapter 15C - Address Confidentiality Program	11
Chapter 16 - Gaming Contracts and Futures	11
Chapter 17 - Habeas Corpus	11

Chapter 17A - Law-Enforcement Officers [Recodified.]	11
Chapter 17B - North Carolina Criminal Justice Education and Training System [Recodified.] Chapter 17C - North Carolina Criminal Justice Education and Training Standards Commission	11 11
Chapter 17D - North Carolina Justice Academy	11
Chapter 17E - North Carolina Sheriffs' Education and Training Standards Commission	11
Chapter 18 - Regulation of Intoxicating Liquors [Repealed.]	12
Chapter 18A - Regulation of Intoxicating Liquors [Repealed.]	12
Chapter 18B - Regulation of Alcoholic Beverages	12
Chapter 18C - North Carolina State Lottery	12
Chapter 19 - Offenses against Public Morals	12
Chapter 19A - Protection of Animals	12
Chapter 20 - Motor Vehicles	13
Chapter 20 - Motor Vehicles (Continuation)	14
Chapter 20 - Motor Vehicles (Continuation)	15
Chapter 20 - Motor Vehicles (Continuation)	16
Chapter 21 - Bills of Lading	17
Chapter 22 - Contracts Requiring Writing	17
Chapter 22A - Signatures	17
Chapter 22B - Contracts Against Public Policy	17
Chapter 22C - Payments to Subcontractors	17
Chapter 23 - Debtor and Creditor	17
Chapter 24 – Interest	17
Chapter 25 – Uniform Commercial Code	18
Chapter 25 – Uniform Commercial Code (Continuation)	19
Chapter 25A – Retail Installment Sales Act	20
Chapter 25B - Credit	20
Chapter 25C - Sales of Artwork	20
Chapter 26 - Suretyship	20
Chapter 27 - Warehouse Receipts [Repealed.]	20
Chapter 28 - Administration [Repealed.]	20
Chapter 28A - Administration of Decedents' Estates	20
Chapter 28B - Estates of Absentees in Military Service	20
Chapter 28C - Estates of Missing Persons	20
Chapter 29 - Intestate Succession	21
Chapter 30 - Surviving Spouses	21
Chapter 31 - Wills	21
Chapter 31A - Acts Barring Property Rights	21
Chapter 31B - Renunciation of Property and Renunciation of Fiduciary Powers Act	21
Chapter 31C - Uniform Disposition of Community Property Rights at Death Act	21
Chapter 32 - Fiduciaries	21
Chapter 32A - Powers of Attorney	21
Chapter 33 - Guardian and Ward [Repealed and Recodified.]	21

Chapter 33A - North Carolina Uniform Transfers to Minors Act	21
Chapter 33B - North Carolina Uniform Custodial Trust Act	21
Chapter 34 - Veterans' Guardianship Act	22
Chapter 35 - Sterilization Procedures	22
Chapter 35A - Incompetency and Guardianship	22
Chapter 36 - Trusts and Trustees [Repealed.]	22
Chapter 36A - Trusts and Trustees	22
Chapter 36B - Uniform Management of Institutional Funds Act [Repealed.]	22
Chapter 36C - North Carolina Uniform Trust Code	22
Chapter 36D - North Carolina Community Third Party Trusts, Pooled Trusts	23
Chapter 36E - Uniform Prudent Management of Institutional Funds Act	23
Chapter 37 - Allocation of Principal and Income [Repealed.]	23
Chapter 37A - Uniform Principal and Income Act	23
Chapter 38 - Boundaries	23
Chapter 38A - Landowner Liability	23
Chapter 39 - Conveyances	23
Chapter 39A - Transfer Fee Covenants Prohibited	23
Chapter 40 - Eminent Domain [Repealed.]	23
Chapter 40A - Eminent Domain	23
Chapter 41 - Estates	23
Chapter 41A - State Fair Housing Act	23
Chapter 42 - Landlord and Tenant	23
Chapter 42A - Vacation Rental Act	23
Chapter 43 - Land Registration	23
Chapter 44 - Liens	24
Chapter 44A - Statutory Liens and Charges	24
Chapter 45 - Mortgages and Deeds of Trust	24
Chapter 45A - Good Funds Settlement Act	24
Chapter 46 - Partition	24
Chapter 47 - Probate and Registration	25
Chapter 47A - Unit Ownership	25
Chapter 47B - Real Property Marketable Title Act	25
Chapter 47C - North Carolina Condominium Act	25
Chapter 47D - Notice of Settlement Act [Expired.]	25
Chapter 47E - Residential Property Disclosure Act	25
Chapter 47F - North Carolina Planned Community Act	25
Chapter 47G - Option to Purchase Contracts	25
Chapter 47H - Contracts for Deed	25
Chapter 48 - Adoptions +	26
Chapter 48A - Minors	26
Chapter 49 - Bastardy	26
Chapter 49A - Rights of Children	26
Chapter 50 - Divorce and Alimony	26
Chapter 50A - Uniform Child-Custody Jurisdiction and	

Enforcement Act	26
Chapter 50B - Domestic Violence	26
Chapter 50C - Civil No-Contact Orders	26
Chapter 51 - Marriage	26
Chapter 52 - Powers and Liabilities of Married Persons	27
Chapter 52A - Uniform Reciprocal Enforcement of Support Act [Repealed.]	27
Chapter 52B - Uniform Premarital Agreement Act	27
Chapter 52C - Uniform Interstate Family Support Act	27
Chapter 53 - Banks	27
Chapter 53A - Business Development Corporations and North Carolina Capital Resource Corporations	28
Chapter 53B - Financial Privacy Act	28
Chapter 54 - Cooperative Organizations	28
Chapter 54A - Capital Stock Savings and Loan Associations [Repealed.]	28
Chapter 54B - Savings and Loan Associations	29
Chapter 54C - Savings Banks	29
Chapter 55 - North Carolina Business Corporation Act	30
Chapter 55A - North Carolina Nonprofit Corporation Act	31
Chapter 55B - Professional Corporation Act	31
Chapter 55C - Foreign Trade Zones	31
Chapter 55D - Filings, Names, and Registered Agents for Corporations, Nonprofit Corporations, and Partnerships	31
Chapter 56 - Electric, Telegraph and Power Companies [Repealed.]	31
Chapter 57 - Hospital, Medical and Dental Service Corporations [Recodified.]	31
Chapter 57A - Health Maintenance Organization Act [Recodified.]	31
Chapter 57B - Health Maintenance Organization Act [Recodified.]	31
Chapter 57C - North Carolina Limited Liability Company Act.	31
Chapter 58 - Insurance.	32
Chapter 58 - Insurance (Continuation)	33
Chapter 58 - Insurance (Continuation)	34
Chapter 58 - Insurance (Continuation)	35
Chapter 58 - Insurance (Continuation)	36
Chapter 58 - Insurance (Continuation)	37
Chapter 58 - Insurance (Continuation)	38
Chapter 58A - North Carolina Health Insurance Trust Commission [Recodified.]	38
Chapter 59 - Partnership.	39
Chapter 59B - Uniform Unincorporated Nonprofit Association Act.	39
Chapter 60 - Railroads and Other Carriers [Repealed and Transferred.]	39
Chapter 61 - Religious Societies	39
Chapter 62 - Public Utilities	39

Chapter 62 - Public Utilities (Continuation)	40
Chapter 62A - Public Safety Telephone Service And Wireless Telephone Service	40
Chapter 63 - Aeronautics	40
Chapter 63A - North Carolina Global TransPark Authority	40
Chapter 64 - Aliens	40
Chapter 65 – Cemeteries	40
Chapter 66 - Commerce and Business	41
Chapter 67 - Dogs	41
Chapter 68 - Fences and Stock Law	41
Chapter 69 - Fire Protection	41
Chapter 70 - Indian Antiquities, Archaeological Resources and Unmarked Human Skeletal Remains Protection	42
Chapter 71 - Indians [Repealed.]	42
Chapter 71A - Indians	42
Chapter 72 - Inns, Hotels and Restaurants	42
Chapter 73 - Mills	42
Chapter 74 - Mines and Quarries	42
Chapter 74A - Company Police [Repealed.]	42
Chapter 74B - Private Protective Services Act [Repealed.]	42
Chapter 74C - Private Protective Services	42
Chapter 74D - Alarm Systems	42
Chapter 74E - Company Police Act	42
Chapter 74F - Locksmith Licensing Act	42
Chapter 74G - Campus Police Act	42
Chapter 75 - Monopolies, Trusts and Consumer Protection	42
Chapter 75A - Boating and Water Safety	43
Chapter 75B - Discrimination in Business	43
Chapter 75C - Motion Picture Fair Competition Act	43
Chapter 75D - Racketeer Influenced and Corrupt Organizations	43
Chapter 75E - Unlawful Activities in Connection With Certain Corporate Transactions	43
Chapter 76 - Navigation	43
Chapter 76A - Navigation and Pilotage Commissions	43
Chapter 77 - Rivers, Creeks, and Coastal Waters	43
Chapter 78 - Securities Law [Repealed.]	43
Chapter 78A - North Carolina Securities Act	43
Chapter 78B - Tender Offer Disclosure Act [Repealed.]	43
Chapter 78C - Investment Advisers	43
Chapter 78D - Commodities Act	43
Chapter 79 - Strays [Repealed.]	43
Chapter 80 - Trademarks, Brands, etc.	44
Chapter 81 - Weights and Measures [Recodified.]	44
Chapter 81A - Weights and Measures Act of 1975.	44
Chapter 82 - Wrecks [Repealed.]	44
Chapter 83 - Architects [Recodified.]	44

Chapter 83A - Architects	44
Chapter 84 - Attorneys-at-Law	44
Chapter 84A - Foreign Legal Consultants	44
Chapter 85 - Auctions and Auctioneers [Repealed.]	44
Chapter 85A - Bail Bondsmen and Runners [Recodified.]	44
Chapter 85B - Auctions and Auctioneers	44
Chapter 85C - Bail Bondsmen and Runners [Recodified.]	44
Chapter 86 - Barbers [Recodified.]	44
Chapter 86A - Barbers	44
Chapter 87 - Contractors	44
Chapter 88 - Cosmetic Art [Repealed.]	44
Chapter 88A - Electrolysis Practice Act	44
Chapter 88B - Cosmetic Art	45
Chapter 89 - Engineering and Land Surveying [Recodified.]	45
Chapter 89A - Landscape Architects	45
Chapter 89B - Foresters	45
Chapter 89C - Engineering and Land Surveying	45
Chapter 89D - Landscape Contractors	45
Chapter 89E - Geologists Licensing Act	45
Chapter 89F - North Carolina Soil Scientist Licensing Act	45
Chapter 89G - Irrigation Contractors	45
Chapter 90 - Medicine and Allied Occupations	45
Chapter 90 - Medicine and Allied Occupations (Continuation)	46
Chapter 90 - Medicine and Allied Occupations (Continuation)	47
Chapter 90 - Medicine and Allied Occupations (Continuation)	48
Chapter 90A - Sanitarians and Water and Wastewater Treatment Facility Operators	48
Chapter 90B - Social Worker Certification and Licensure Act	48
Chapter 90C - North Carolina Recreational Therapy Licensure Act	48
Chapter 90D - Interpreters and Transliterators	48
Chapter 91 - Pawnbrokers [Repealed.]	48
Chapter 91A - Pawnbrokers Modernization Act of 1989	48
Chapter 92 - Photographers [Deleted.]	48
Chapter 93 - Certified Public Accountants	48
Chapter 93A - Real Estate License Law	49
Chapter 93B - Occupational Licensing Boards	49
Chapter 93C - Watchmakers [Repealed.]	49
Chapter 93D - North Carolina State Hearing Aid Dealers and Fitters Board.	49
Chapter 93E - North Carolina Appraisers Act	49
Chapter 94 - Apprenticeship	49
Chapter 95 - Department of Labor and Labor Regulations	49
Chapter 95 - Department of Labor and Labor Regulations (Continuation)	50
Chapter 96 - Employment Security	50
Chapter 97 - Workers' Compensation Act	50
Chapter 97 - Workers' Compensation Act (Continuation)	51

Chapter 98 - Burnt and Lost Records	51
Chapter 99 - Libel and Slander	51
Chapter 99A - Civil Remedies for Criminal Actions	51
Chapter 99B - Products Liability	51
Chapter 99C - Actions Relating to Winter Sports Safety and Accidents	51
Chapter 99D - Civil Rights	51
Chapter 99E - Special Liability Provisions	51
Chapter 100 - Monuments, Memorials and Parks	51
Chapter 101 - Names of Persons	51
Chapter 102 - Official Survey Base	51
Chapter 103 - Sundays, Holidays and Special Days	51
Chapter 104 - United States Lands	51
Chapter 104A - Degrees of Kinship	51
Chapter 104B - Hurricanes or Other Acts of Nature	51
Chapter 104C - Atomic Energy, Radioactivity and Ionizing Radiation [Repealed and Recodified.]	51
Chapter 104D - Southern States Energy Compact	51
Chapter 104E - North Carolina Radiation Protection Act	51
Chapter 104F - Southeast Interstate Low-Level Radioactive Waste Management Compact [Repealed]	51
Chapter 104G - North Carolina Low-Level Radioactive Waste Management Authority Act of 1987 [Repealed]	51
Chapter 105 - Taxation	51
Chapter 105 - Taxation (Continuation)	52
Chapter 105 - Taxation (Continuation)	53
Chapter 105 - Taxation (Continuation)	54
Chapter 105A - Setoff Debt Collection Act	55
Chapter 105B - Defaulted Student Loan Recovery Act	55
Chapter 106 - Agriculture	55
Chapter 106 - Agriculture (Continue)	56
Chapter 106 - Agriculture (Continue)	57
Chapter 107 - Agricultural Development Districts [Repealed.]	57
Chapter 108 - Social Services [Repealed and Recodified.]	57
Chapter 108A - Social Services	57
Chapter 108B - Community Action Programs	58
Chapter 108C Medicaid and Health Choice Provider Requirements.	58
Chapter 108D Medicaid Managed Care for Behavioral Health Services.	58
Chapter 109 - Bonds [Recodified.]	58
Chapter 110 - Child Welfare	58
Chapter 111 - Aid to the Blind	58
Chapter 112 - Confederate Homes and Pensions [Repealed.]	58
Chapter 113 - Conservation and Development	58
Chapter 113 - Conservation and Development (Continuation)	59

Chapter 113A - Pollution Control and Environment	59
Chapter 113A - Pollution Control and Environment (Continuation)	60
Chapter 113B - North Carolina Energy Policy Act of 1975	60
Chapter 114 - Department of Justice	60
Chapter 115 - Elementary and Secondary Education [Repealed.]	60
Chapter 115A - Community Colleges, Technical Institutes, and Industrial Education Centers [Repealed.]	60
Chapter 115B - Tuition and Fee Waivers	60
Chapter 115C - Elementary and Secondary Education	60
Chapter 115C - Elementary and Secondary Education (Continuation)	61
Chapter 115C - Elementary and Secondary Education (Continuation)	62
Chapter 115C - Elementary and Secondary Education (Continuation)	63
Chapter 115D - Community Colleges	63
Chapter 115E - Private Educational Facilities Finance Act [Recodified]	63
Chapter 116 - Higher Education	63
Chapter 116 - Higher Education (Continuation)	63
Chapter 116A - Escheats and Abandoned Property [Repealed.]	64
Chapter 116B - Escheats and Abandoned Property	64
Chapter 116C - Continuum of Education Programs	64
Chapter 116D - Higher Education Bonds	64
Chapter 117 - Electrification	64
Chapter 118 - Firemen's and Rescue Squad Workers' Relief and Pension Funds [Recodified.]	64
Chapter 118A - Firemen's Death Benefit Act [Repealed.]	64
Chapter 118B - Members of a Rescue Squad Death Benefit Act [Repealed.]	64
Chapter 119 - Gasoline and Oil Inspection and Regulation	64
Chapter 120 - General Assembly	65
Chapter 120 - General Assembly (Continuation)	66
Chapter 120 - General Assembly (Continuation)	67
Chapter 120C - Lobbying	67
Chapter 121 - Archives and History	67
Chapter 122 - Hospitals for the Mentally Disordered [Repealed.]	67
Chapter 122A - North Carolina Housing Finance Agency	67
Chapter 122B - North Carolina Agricultural Facilities Finance Act [Repealed.]	67
Chapter 122C - Mental Health, Developmental Disabilities, and Substance Abuse Act of 1985	67
Chapter 122C - Mental Health, Developmental Disabilities, and Substance Abuse Act of 1985 (Continuation)	68
Chapter 122D - North Carolina Agricultural Finance Act	68

Chapter 122E - North Carolina Housing Trust and Oil Overcharge Act	68
Chapter 123 - Impeachment	69
Chapter 123A - Industrial Development [Repealed.]	69
Chapter 124 - Internal Improvements	69
Chapter 125 - Libraries	69
Chapter 126 - State Personnel System	69
Chapter 127 - Militia [Repealed.]	69
Chapter 127A - Militia	69
Chapter 127B - Military Affairs	69
Chapter 127C - Advisory Commission on Military Affairs	69
Chapter 128 - Offices and Public Officers	69
Chapter 128 - Offices and Public Officers (Continuation)	70
Chapter 129 - Public Buildings and Grounds	70
Chapter 130 - Public Health [Repealed.]	70
Chapter 130A - Public Health	70
Chapter 130A - Public Health (Continuation)	71
Chapter 130A - Public Health (Continuation)	72
Chapter 130B - Hazardous Waste Management Commission [Repealed.]	72
Chapter 131 - Public Hospitals [Repealed.]	72
Chapter 131A - Health Care Facilities Finance Act	72
Chapter 131B - Licensing of Ambulatory Surgical Facilities [Repealed.]	72
Chapter 131C - Charitable Solicitation Licensure Act [Repealed.]	72
Chapter 131D - Inspection and Licensing of Facilities	72
Chapter 131E - Health Care Facilities and Services	72
Chapter 131E - Health Care Facilities and Services (Continuation)	73
Chapter 131F - Solicitation of Contributions	73
Chapter 132 - Public Records	73
Chapter 133 - Public Works	74
Chapter 134 - Youth Development [Recodified.]	74
Chapter 134A - Youth Services [Repealed.]	74
Chapter 135 - Retirement System for Teachers and State Employees; Social Security; Health Insurance Program for Children	74
Chapter 135 - Retirement System for Teachers and State Employees; Social Security; Health Insurance Program for Children	75
Chapter 136 - Transportation	75
Chapter 136 - Transportation (Continuation)	76
Chapter 137 - Rural Rehabilitation [Repealed.]	76
Chapter 138 - Salaries, Fees and Allowances	76
Chapter 138A - State Government Ethics Act	76
Chapter 139 - Soil and Water Conservation Districts	76

Chapter 140 - State Art Museum; Symphony and Art Societies	76
Chapter 140A - State Awards System	76
Chapter 141 - State Boundaries	76
Chapter 142 - State Debt	76
Chapter 143 - State Departments, Institutions, and Commissions	77
Chapter 143 - State Departments, Institutions, and Commissions (Continuation)	78
Chapter 143 - State Departments, Institutions, and Commissions (Continuation)	79
Chapter 143 - State Departments, Institutions, and Commissions (Continuation)	80
Chapter 143A - State Government Reorganization	80
Chapter 143B - Executive Organization Act of 1973	80
Chapter 143B - Executive Organization Act of 1973 (Continuation)	81
Chapter 143B - Executive Organization Act of 1973 (Continuation)	82
Chapter 143C - State Budget Act	83
Chapter 143D - The State Governmental Accountability and Internal Control Act	83
Chapter 144 - State Flag, Official Governmental Flags, Motto, and Colors	83
Chapter 145 - State Symbols and Other Official Adoptions.	83
Chapter 146 - State Lands	83
Chapter 147 - State Officers	83
Chapter 148 - State Prison System	84
Chapter 149 - State Song and Toast	84
Chapter 150 - Uniform Revocation of Licenses [Repealed.]	84
Chapter 150A - Administrative Procedure Act [Recodified.]	84
Chapter 150B - Administrative Procedure Act	84
Chapter 151 - Constables [Repealed.]	84
Chapter 152 - Coroners	84
Chapter 152A - County Medical Examiner [Repealed.]	84
Chapter 152A - County Medical Examiner [Repealed.] (Continuation)	85
Chapter 153 - Counties and County Commissioners [Repealed.]	85
Chapter 153A - Counties	85
Chapter 153B - Mountain Resources Planning Act	85
Chapter 153C - Uwharrie Regional Resources Act	85
Chapter 154 - County Surveyor [Repealed.]	85
Chapter 155 - County Treasurer [Repealed.]	85
Chapter 156 - Drainage	85
Chapter 156 – Drainage (Continuation)	86

Chapter 157 - Housing Authorities and Projects	86
Chapter 157A - Historic Properties Commissions [Transferred.]	86
Chapter 158 - Local Development	86
Chapter 159 - Local Government Finance	86
Chapter 159 - Local Government Finance (Continuation)	87
Chapter 159A - Pollution Abatement and Industrial Facilities Financing Act [Unconstitutional.]	87
Chapter 159B - Joint Municipal Electric Power and Energy Act	87
Chapter 159C - Industrial and Pollution Control Facilities Financing Act	87
Chapter 159D - The North Carolina Capital Facilities Financing Act	87
Chapter 159E - Registered Public Obligations Act	87
Chapter 159F - North Carolina Energy Development Authority [Repealed.]	87
Chapter 159G - Water Infrastructure	87
Chapter 159H - [Reserved.]	87
Chapter 159I - Solid Waste Management Loan Program and Local Government Special Obligation Bonds	87
Chapter 160 - Municipal Corporations [Repealed And Transferred.]	87
Chapter 160A - Cities and Towns	88
Chapter 160A - Cities and Towns (Continuation)	89
Chapter 160B - Consolidated City-County Act	89
Chapter 160C - Baseball Park Districts [Repealed.]	90
Chapter 161 - Register of Deeds	90
Chapter 162 - Sheriff	90
Chapter 162A - Water and Sewer Systems	90
Chapter 162B Continuity of Local Government in Emergency.	90
Chapter 163 Elections and Election Laws.	90
Chapter 163 Elections and Election Laws. (Continuation)	91
Chapter 164 Concerning the General Statutes of North Carolina.	92
Chapter 165 Veterans.	92
Chapter 166 Civil Preparedness Agencies [Repealed.]	92
Chapter 166A North Carolina Emergency Management Act.	92
Chapter 167 State Civil Air Patrol [Repealed.]	92
Chapter 168 Persons with Disabilities.	92
Chapter 168A Persons With Disabilities Protection Act.	92

Chapter 18

Regulation of Intoxicating Liquors.

§§ 18-1 through 18-152. Repealed by Session Laws 1971, c. 872, s. 3.

Chapter 18A

Regulation of Intoxicating Liquors.

§§ 18A-1 through 18A-69. Repealed by Session Laws 1981, c. 412, s. 1, effective January 1, 1982.

Chapter 18B.

Regulation of Alcoholic Beverages.

Article 1.

General Provisions.

§ 18B-100. Purpose of Chapter.

This Chapter is intended to establish a uniform system of control over the sale, purchase, transportation, manufacture, consumption, and possession of alcoholic beverages in North Carolina, and to provide procedures to insure the proper administration of the ABC laws under a uniform system throughout the State. This Chapter shall be liberally construed to the end that the sale, purchase, transportation, manufacture, consumption, and possession of alcoholic beverages shall be prohibited except as authorized in this Chapter.

Except as provided in this Chapter, local ordinances establishing different rules on the manufacture, sale, purchase, transportation, possession, consumption, or other use of alcoholic beverages, or requiring additional permits or fees, are prohibited. (1937, c. 49, s. 1; 1971, c. 872, s. 1; 1981, c. 412, s. 2.)

§ 18B-101. Definitions.

As used in this Chapter, unless the context requires otherwise:

(1) "ABC law" or "ABC laws" means any statute or statutes in this Chapter or in Article 2C of Chapter 105, and the rules issued by the Commission under the authority of this Chapter.

(2) "ABC permit" or "permits" means any written or printed authorization issued by the Commission pursuant to the provisions of this Chapter, other than a purchase-transportation permit. Unless the context clearly requires otherwise, as in the provisions concerning applications for permits, "ABC permit" or "permit" means a presently valid permit.

(3) "ABC system" means a local board and all ABC stores operated by it, its law-enforcement branch, and all its employees.

(4) "Alcoholic beverage" means any beverage containing at least one-half of one percent (0.5%) alcohol by volume, including malt beverages, unfortified wine, fortified wine, spirituous liquor, and mixed beverages.

(5) "ALE Section" means the Alcohol Law Enforcement Section of the Department of Public Safety.

(5a) "Bailment surcharge" means the charge imposed on each case of liquor shipped from a Commission warehouse as provided in G.S. 18B-208. This bailment surcharge is in addition to the bailment charge imposed by G.S. 18B-804(b)(2).

(6) "Commission" means the North Carolina Alcoholic Beverage Control Commission established under G.S. 18B-200.

(6a) "Finance officer" means the local board employee, other than a general manager, who is responsible for keeping the accounts of the local board, receiving and depositing receipts, disbursing funds, and any other duties assigned by the local board or Commission.

(7) "Fortified wine" means any wine, of more than sixteen percent (16%) and no more than twenty-four percent (24%) alcohol by volume, made by fermentation from grapes, fruits, berries, rice, or honey; or by the addition of pure cane, beet, or dextrose sugar; or by the addition of pure brandy from the same type of grape, fruit, berry, rice, or honey that is contained in the base wine and produced in accordance with the regulations of the United States.

(7a) "General manager" means the local board employee who is responsible for the oversight of daily operations of the ABC system and any other duties assigned by the local board or Commission. The board may designate only one employee to be the general manager.

(7b) "Historic ABC establishment" means a restaurant or hotel that meets all of the following requirements:

a. Is on the national register of historic places or located within a State historic district.

b. Is a property designed to attract local, State, national, and international tourists located on a State Route (SR) and with a property line located within 1.5 miles of the intersection of a designated North Carolina scenic byway as defined in G.S. 136-18(31).

c. Is located within 15 miles of a national scenic highway.

d. Is located in a county in which the on-premises sale of malt beverages or unfortified wine is authorized in two or more cities in the county.

(7c) "Keg" means a portable container designed to hold and dispense 7.75 gallons or more of malt beverage.

(8) "Local board" means a city or county ABC board, or local board created pursuant to the provisions of G.S. 18B-703. A local board is an independent local political subdivision of the State. Nothing in this Chapter shall be construed as constituting a local board the agency of a city or county or of the Commission.

(8a) "Lottery law" or "lottery laws" means any provision of Chapter 18C of the General Statutes and the rules issued by the Lottery Commission under the authority of Chapter 18C of the General Statutes.

(9) "Malt beverage" means beer, lager, malt liquor, ale, porter, and any other brewed or fermented beverage except unfortified or fortified wine as defined by this Chapter, containing at least one-half of one percent (0.5%), and not more than fifteen percent (15%), alcohol by volume. Any malt beverage containing more than six percent (6%) alcohol by volume shall bear a label clearly indicating the alcohol content of the malt beverage.

(10) "Mixed beverage" means either of the following:

a. A drink composed in whole or in part of spirituous liquor and served in a quantity less than the quantity contained in a closed package.

b. A premixed cocktail served from a closed package containing only one serving.

(11) "Nontaxpaid alcoholic beverage" means any alcoholic beverage upon which the taxes imposed by the United States, this State, or any other territorial jurisdiction in which the alcoholic beverage was purchased have not been paid.

(12) "Person" means an individual, firm, partnership, association, corporation, limited liability company, other organization or group, or other combination of individuals acting as a unit.

(12a) "Premises" means all areas, whether inside or outside the licensed premises, where the permittee has control of the property through a lease, deed, or other legal process.

(13) "Sale" means any transfer, trade, exchange, or barter, in any manner or by any means, for consideration.

(13a) (See note) "Special ABC area" means an area that meets the following requirements:

Either:

a. The area has fewer than 500 permanent residents, and the area:

1. Is located in a county that borders another state, that has at least one city that has approved the operation of an ABC store, and in which the sale of unfortified wine and malt beverages is permitted countywide or in one city; and

2. Contains more than 500 contiguous acres made up of privately-owned land and land owned by an association or a club that is exempt from income tax on its membership income under Article 4 of Chapter 105 of the General Statutes, has more than 200 members, was created for municipal and recreational purposes, and, for three or more years, has levied assessments or dues and provided municipal services; or

b. The area has more than 500 permanent residents, and the area:

1. Is located in a county:

I. Where ABC stores have heretofore been established but in which the sale of mixed beverages has not been approved;

II. That borders on a county that has approved the sale of alcoholic beverages countywide and contains an international airport; and

III. Borders on a county where ABC stores have heretofore been established by petition pursuant to law; and

2. Contains more than 500 contiguous acres made up of privately-owned land and land owned by an association or a club that is exempt from income tax on its membership income under Article 4 of Chapter 105 of the General Statutes, has more than 200 members, was created for municipal and recreational purposes, and, for three or more years, has levied assessments or dues and provided municipal services; or

c. The area is an area of a county where the following requirements are met:

1. The county borders on the Atlantic Ocean and has a seaport supporting oceangoing vessels;

2. ABC stores have been established in the county and the sale of mixed beverages is allowed in six or more municipalities;

3. The population of the county, according to the 2000 census, exceeds 52,000;

4. The tourism economy of the county is made up of more than 3,000 tourism-related jobs; and

5. Tourism expenditures within the county exceed two hundred million dollars ($200,000,000) annually.

(14) "Spirituous liquor" or "liquor" means distilled spirits or ethyl alcohol, including spirits of wine, whiskey, rum, brandy, gin and all other distilled spirits

and mixtures of cordials, liqueur, and premixed cocktails, in closed containers for beverage use regardless of their dilution.

(14a) "Tourism ABC establishment" means a restaurant or hotel that meets both of the following requirements:

a. Is located on property, a property line of which is located within 1.5 miles of the end of an entrance or exit ramp of a junction on a national scenic parkway designed to attract local, State, national, and international tourists between the State line and Milepost 460.

b. Is located in a county in which the on-premises or off-premises sale of malt beverages or unfortified wine is authorized in at least one city.

(14b) "Tourism resort" means:

a. Any restaurant and lodging facility, whether public or private, owned and operated as a resort property offering food, beverage, lodging, and meeting facilities to travelers and tourists and featuring one or more golf courses and two or more tennis courts along with other recreational and sporting activities, or

b. Any restaurant, whether public or private, owned and operated as a resort property offering food and beverage to travelers and tourists and featuring an equestrian center and two or more tennis courts along with other recreational and sporting activities.

Receipts from sporting and recreational activities of a tourism resort shall be at least twenty-five percent (25%) of total gross receipts. Receipts from the sale of alcoholic beverages shall not exceed fifty percent (50%) of total gross receipts. A tourism resort open to the public shall advertise at least quarterly in a regional or national travel or sports industry publication, or in the State travel guide published by the North Carolina Department of Commerce.

(15) "Unfortified wine" means any wine of sixteen percent (16%) or less alcohol by volume made by fermentation from grapes, fruits, berries, rice, or honey; or by the addition of pure cane, beet, or dextrose sugar; or by the addition of pure brandy from the same type of grape, fruit, berry, rice, or honey that is contained in the base wine and produced in accordance with the regulations of the United States. (1981, c. 412, s. 2; 1981 (Reg. Sess., 1982), c. 1262, s. 2; c. 1285, s. 1; 1983, c. 435, s. 41; 1985, c. 69; 1987, c. 443, s. 1; 1989, c. 629, s. 1; 1989 (Reg. Sess., 1990), c. 1024, s. 5; 1991 (Reg. Sess.,

1992), c. 920, ss. 1, 10; 1993, c. 415, ss. 1, 2; 1995, c. 466, s. 1; 1997-443, s. 16.27(b); 1999-461, s. 1; 1999-462, ss. 1, 13; 2001-515, s. 1; 2004-135, s. 1; 2004-203, s. 23; 2005-276, s. 31.1(x); 2005-277, s. 1; 2005-344, s. 10.1(a); 2005-392, s. 1; 2005-435, s. 25(a); 2006-253, s. 2; 2006-264, s. 95; 2010-122, s. 1; 2011-145, s. 19.1(g), (gg).)

§ 18B-102. Manufacture, sale, etc., forbidden except as expressly authorized.

(a) General Prohibition. - It shall be unlawful for any person to manufacture, sell, transport, import, deliver, furnish, purchase, consume, or possess any alcoholic beverages except as authorized by the ABC law.

(b) Violation a Class 1 Misdemeanor. - Unless a different punishment is otherwise expressly stated, any person who violates any provision of this Chapter shall be guilty of a Class 1 misdemeanor. In addition the court may impose the provisions of G.S. 18B-202 and of G.S. 18B-503, 18B-504, and 18B-505. (1923, c. 1, s. 1; C.S., s. 3411(a); 1937, c. 49, s. 24; c. 411; 1939, c. 158, s. 501; 1941, c. 339, ss. 1, 3, 4; 1945, c. 780; c. 903, ss. 1, 3, 10; 1971, c. 872, s. 1; 1973, c. 476, s. 193; c. 1014; 1975, c. 329; c. 411, s. 2; 1977, 2nd Sess., c. 1138, s. 1; 1979, c. 683, s. 1; 1981, c. 412, s. 2; 1989, c. 800, s. 1; 1993, c. 539, s. 310; 1994, Ex. Sess., c. 14, s. 29; c. 24, s. 14(c).)

§ 18B-102.1. Direct shipments from out-of-state prohibited.

(a) It is unlawful for any person who is an out-of-state retail or wholesale dealer in the business of selling alcoholic beverages to ship or cause to be shipped any alcoholic beverage directly to any North Carolina resident who does not hold a valid wholesaler's permit under Article 11 of this Chapter.

(b) The Commission shall mail a notice by certified mail ordering a person who violates the provisions of subsection (a) of this section to cease and desist any shipments of alcoholic beverages to North Carolina residents. If the offender cannot produce a receipt or otherwise show that applicable State taxes have been paid on the shipped alcohol within 30 days after this notice has been deposited by certified mail addressed to the out-of-state retail or wholesale dealer either at the address shown on the shipment or the last known address of that dealer in any legal registry, such as a registry with the Secretary of State for incorporation of a business, or within 30 days after personal service of the notice on the out-of-state retail or wholesale dealer, it shall be presumptive evidence of his intent to ship alcoholic beverages directly to a North Carolina resident who does not hold a valid wholesaler's permit issued by the Commission.

(c) This section shall not apply to producers of beverage alcohol holding a basic permit from the Bureau of Alcohol, Tobacco and Firearms.

(d) Upon determination by the Commission that a holder of a basic permit from the Bureau of Alcohol, Tobacco and Firearms has made an illegal shipment to consumers in North Carolina, the Commission shall notify the Bureau of Alcohol, Tobacco and Firearms in writing and by certified mail and request the Bureau to take appropriate action.

(e) Whoever violates the provisions of this section shall be guilty of a Class I felony and shall pay a fine of not more than ten thousand dollars ($10,000). (1997-348, s. 1.)

§ 18B-103. Exemptions.

The following activities shall be permitted:

(1) The use of ethyl alcohol for scientific, chemical, pharmaceutical, mechanical, and industrial purposes;

(2) The use of ethyl alcohol by persons authorized to obtain it tax free, as provided by federal law;

(3) The use of ethyl alcohol in the manufacture and preparation of any product unfit for use as a beverage;

(4) The use of alcoholic beverages by licensed physicians, druggists, or dental surgeons for medicinal or pharmaceutical purposes; or the use of alcoholic beverages by medical facilities established and maintained for the treatment of patients addicted to the use of alcohol or drugs;

(5) The use of grain alcohol by college, university or State laboratories, and by manufacturers of medicine, for compounding, mixing, or preserving medicines or medical preparations, or for surgical purposes;

(5a) The manufacture, possession, and consumption of alcoholic beverages for the purpose of conducting scientific, chemical, pharmaceutical, mechanical, industrial, and educational research in connection with teaching, research, or extension programs conducted by, or under the supervision of, an instructor at an accredited community college, public or private college or university, or an extension agent in connection with educational programs and activities offered by the North Carolina Cooperative Extension Service;

(6) The manufacture, importation, and possession of denatured alcohol produced and used as provided by federal law;

(7) The manufacture or sale of cider or vinegar;

(8) The possession and use of unfortified wine or fortified wine for sacramental purpose by any organized church or ordained minister, including in public school buildings when the use of those buildings is approved by the local school board;

(9) The possession and use of alcohol acquired for controlled-drinking programs as authorized under G.S. 20-139.1(g);

(10) The use of spirituous liquor in the manufacture of flavors or flavoring extracts that are unfit for beverage use;

(11) Under the direct supervision of an instructor during a culinary class that is part of an established culinary curriculum at an accredited college or university, the delivery to or possession or consumption by a student who is less than 21 years of age, when the student is required to taste or imbibe the alcoholic beverage during a culinary class conducted pursuant to the curriculum. (1923, c. 1, ss. 4, 19, 20; C.S., s. 3411(d), (s), (t); 1935, c. 1141; 1971, c. 872, s. 1; c. 1233; 1981, c. 412, s. 2; c. 747, s. 36; 1981 (Reg. Sess., 1982), c. 1262, s. 3; 1983, c. 435, s. 6; 1985, c. 566, s. 2; 1993, c. 127, s. 1; 2004-199, s. 8; 2009-539, s. 1.)

§ 18B-104. Administrative penalties.

(a) Penalties. - For any violation of the ABC laws, the Commission may take any of the following actions against a permittee:

(1) Suspend the permittee's permit for a specified period of time not longer than three years;

(2) Revoke the permittee's permit;

(3) Fine the permittee up to five hundred dollars ($500.00) for the first violation, up to seven hundred fifty dollars ($750.00) for the second violation, and up to one thousand dollars ($1,000) for the third violation; or

(4) Suspend the permittee's permit under subdivision (1) and impose a fine under subdivision (3).

(b) Compromise. - In any case in which the Commission is entitled to suspend or revoke a permit, the Commission may accept from the permittee an offer in compromise to pay a penalty of not more than five thousand dollars ($5,000). The Commission may either accept a compromise or revoke a permit, but not both. The Commission may accept a compromise and suspend the permit in the same case.

(c) Fines and Penalties to Treasurer. - The clear proceeds of fines and penalties assessed pursuant to this section shall be remitted to the Civil Penalty and Forfeiture Fund in accordance with G.S. 115C-457.2.

(d) Effect on Licenses. - Suspension or revocation of a permit includes automatic suspension or revocation of any related State or local revenue license.

(e) Effect on Other Permits. - Unless some other disposition is ordered by the Commission, revocation or suspension of a permit under subsection (a) includes automatic revocation or suspension, respectively, of any other ABC permit held by the same permittee for the same establishment. (1939, c. 158, s. 514; 1943, c. 400, s. 6; 1945, c. 903, s. 1; 1947, c. 1098, ss. 2, 3; 1949, c. 974, ss. 7, 14; 1953, c. 1207, ss. 2-5; 1957, cc. 1048, 1440; 1963, c. 426, ss. 4, 5, 10, 12; c. 460, s. 1; 1971, c. 872, s. 1; 1973, c. 476, s. 193; 1977, c. 669, s. 1; 1981, c. 412, s. 2; 1998-215, s. 27.)

§ 18B-105. Advertising.

(a) General Rule. - No person shall advertise alcoholic beverages in this State except in compliance with the rules of the Commission.

(b) Rule-making Authority. - The Commission shall have the authority to adopt rules to:

(1) Prohibit or regulate advertising of alcoholic beverages by permittees in newspapers, pamphlets, and other print media;

(2) Prohibit or regulate advertising by on-premises permittees of brands or prices of alcoholic beverages via newspapers, radio, television, and other mass media;

(3) Prohibit deceptive or misleading advertising of alcoholic beverages;

(4) Require all advertisements of alcoholic beverages to disclose fully the identity of the advertiser and of the product being advertised;

(5) Prohibit advertisements of alcoholic beverages on the premises of a permittee, or regulate the size, number, and appearance of those advertisements;

(6) Prohibit or regulate advertisement of prices of alcoholic beverages on the premises of a permittee;

(7) Prohibit or regulate alcoholic beverage advertisements on billboards;

(8) Prohibit alcoholic beverage advertisements on outdoor signs, or regulate the nature, size, number, and appearance of those advertisements;

(9) Prohibit or regulate advertising of alcoholic beverages by mail;

(10) Prohibit or regulate contests, games, or other promotions which serve or tend to serve as advertisement for a specific brand or brands of alcoholic beverages; and

(11) Prohibit or regulate any advertising of alcoholic beverages which is contrary to the public interest. (1923, c. 1, s. 3; C.S., s. 3411(c); 1933, cc. 216,

229; 1945, c. 903, s. 1; 1947, c. 1098, ss. 2, 3; 1957, c. 1048; 1963, c. 426, s. 10; c. 460, s. 1; 1971, c. 872, s. 1; 1981, c. 412, s. 2.)

§ 18B-106. Alcoholic beverages for use on oceangoing ships.

(a) Delivery Permitted. - Alcoholic beverages for use outside the United States on oceangoing vessels shall be delivered as follows:

(1) Spirituous liquor may be imported into this State under United States customs bonds, held in United States customs bonded warehouses, and transferred between those warehouses. Spirituous liquors may only be released from customs bonds for delivery to an officer or agent of an oceangoing vessel who has obtained a permit from the Commission for that purpose.

(2) Malt beverages, unfortified wine, and fortified wine may be sold and delivered by any wholesaler or retailer licensed in this State to an officer or agent of an oceangoing vessel. The Commission may require the officer or agent to obtain a permit before purchasing alcoholic beverages under this subdivision.

(b) Definition. - "Oceangoing vessel" means a ship which plies the high seas in interstate or foreign commerce, in the transport of freight or passengers, or both, for hire exclusively.

(c) Rules. - The Commission may issue rules relating to applications for permits and otherwise regulate the importation, sale, and delivery of alcoholic beverages under this section to insure that those beverages are used only on oceangoing vessels outside the United States. (1981, c. 412, s. 2.)

§ 18B-107. Alcoholic beverages for use in air commerce.

(a) Purchase and Storage. - The Commission may issue permits authorizing air carriers offering regularly scheduled or chartered flights in foreign, interstate, or intrastate commerce to purchase malt beverages, unfortified wine, and fortified wine from any wholesaler or retailer licensed in this State, and to transport those alcoholic beverages. The Commission may also authorize air carriers to store, at facilities approved by the Commission, alcoholic beverages to be sold or served pursuant to subsection (b).

(b) Sale. - Air carriers may sell and serve alcoholic beverages anywhere in this State to passengers while in transit aboard any aircraft. At airports which service airplanes boarding at least 150,000 passengers annually, air carriers may serve complimentary alcoholic beverages to their passengers in air carrier passenger rooms approved by the Commission. Alcoholic beverages may not be sold in such a room unless a permit has been issued under Article 10 authorizing sale there. (1981, c. 412, s. 2.)

§ 18B-108. Sales on trains.

Alcoholic beverages may be sold on railroad trains in this State upon compliance with Article 2C of Chapter 105 of the General Statutes. Malt beverages, unfortified wine, and fortified wine may be sold and delivered by any wholesaler or retailer licensed in this State to an officer or agent of a rail line that carries at least 60,000 passengers annually. (1981, c. 412, s. 2; c. 747, s. 37; 1985, c. 114, s. 5; 2000-140, s. 39; 2006-227, s. 8.)

§ 18B-109. Direct shipment of alcoholic beverages into State.

(a) General Prohibition. - Except as provided in G.S. 18B-1001.1, no person shall have any alcoholic beverage mailed or shipped to him from outside this State unless he has the appropriate ABC permit.

(b) Armed Forces Installation and Indian Country Lands. - No person shall have malt beverages or unfortified wine shipped directly from a point outside this State to an installation of the Armed Forces of the United States within this State if those alcoholic beverages are for resale on the installation or to the Eastern Band of Cherokee Indians for resale on Indian Country lands within this State under the jurisdiction of the Eastern Band of Cherokee Indians.

(c) Wine Shipper Permittees. - It is unlawful for a wine shipper permittee to ship any wines except in compliance with this Chapter and Articles 2C and 5 of Chapter 105 of the General Statutes.

(d) On-Premises Purchases. - A person who purchases wine while visiting the premises of a winery, whether located within or outside the State, may authorize the winery to ship by common carrier, or may personally ship by common carrier, the purchased wine directly to addresses in the State in amounts that can be personally transported in accordance with the laws of this State and of the state in which the winery is located. A winery shipping wine pursuant to this subsection is not required to have a wine shipper permit. (1923, c. 1, s. 2; C.S., s. 3411(b); 1971, c. 872, s. 1; 1975, c. 654, s. 4; 1981, c. 412, s. 2; 2003-402, s. 4; 2011-183, s. 19; 2011-333, s. 1.)

§ 18B-110. Emergency.

When the Governor finds that an emergency, as that term is defined in G.S. 166A-19.3, exists anywhere in this State, the Governor may

(1) Order the closing of all ABC stores; and

(2) Order the cessation of all sales, transportation, manufacture, and bottling of alcoholic beverages.

The Governor's order shall apply in those portions of the State designated in the order, for the duration of the state of emergency. Any order by the Governor under this section shall be directed to the Chairman of the Commission and to the Secretary of Public Safety. (1969, c. 869, ss. 4, 5; 1971, c. 872, s. 1; 1977, c. 70, s. 21; 1977, 2nd Sess., c. 1138, s. 16; 1981, c. 412, s. 2; 2011-145, s. 19.1(g); 2012-12, s. 2(cc).)

§ 18B-111. Nontaxpaid alcoholic beverages.

No person may possess, transport, or sell nontaxpaid alcoholic beverages except as authorized by the ABC law. (1981 (Reg. Sess., 1982), c. 1262, s. 4.)

§ 18B-112. Tribal alcoholic beverage control.

(a) Application of This Chapter. - The Eastern Band of Cherokee Indians, a federally recognized Indian tribe and sovereign nation, shall be exempt from the provisions of this Chapter, except for those made applicable by this section. The Eastern Band of Cherokee Indians tribe shall adopt by ordinance the provisions of this Chapter which are made applicable to the tribe by this section, and such ordinance shall be approved by the Secretary of the United States Department of the Interior and published in the Federal Register accordingly. The Eastern Band of Cherokee Indians shall hold lawful tribal elections as set out in G.S. 18B-600(a), and if the result of such election authorizes the activity upon which a vote was held, the activity shall be deemed authorized by this section. For the purposes of this section, the tribal alcoholic beverage control commission shall possess the same powers and authority conveyed upon the North Carolina Alcoholic Beverage Control Commission by any section of this Chapter made applicable to the tribe by this section.

(b) Compliance Required. - The Eastern Band of Cherokee Indians shall comply with the following provisions of this Chapter to the extent they apply to or can be made applicable to the tribe:

(1) The following provisions of Article 1. - General Provisions.

a. G.S. 18B-101(4), (7), (7c), (9), (10), (11), (12), (12a), (13), (14)(14a), (14b), and (15).

b. G.S. 18B-102.1.

c. G.S. 18B-104.

d. G.S. 18B-105, except that this section shall not apply to any establishment where gaming is permitted under a State compact and pursuant to federal law.

e. G.S. 18B-109(b).

f. G.S. 18B-110.

g. G.S. 18B-111.

h. G.S. 18B-112.

(2) Article 1A. - Compensation for Injury Caused by Sales to Underage Persons, to the extent it applies to retail establishments or the tribal alcoholic beverage control commission if it operates ABC stores, or any other permitted establishment, at retail pursuant to the provisions of this section.

(3) Article 3. - Sale, Possession, and Consumption, except for G.S. 18B-308 and G.S. 18B-309.

(4) Article 4. - Transportation.

(5) Article 5. - Enforcement, except for G.S. 18B-500 and G.S. 18B-501.

(6) Article 9. - Issuance of Permits, except for G.S. 18B-902(g) and (h) and G.S. 18B-906.

(7) Article 10. - Retail Activity, except for G.S. 18B-1001.1, 18B-1001.2, and 18B-1001.3.

Any provision of this Chapter which has not been made applicable to the Eastern Band of Cherokee Indians by this section shall act as a bar to engaging in any activity authorized by that Article or section.

(c) Alcoholic Beverages Which May Be Sold. - No alcoholic beverage may be sold on Indian Country lands under the jurisdiction of the Eastern Band of Cherokee Indians pursuant to this section which has not been approved for sale in this State by the North Carolina Alcoholic Beverage Control Commission.

(d) Establishment of a Tribal Commission. - In accordance with the provisions of 18 U.S.C. § 1161, the Eastern Band of Cherokee Indians is authorized to establish a tribal alcoholic beverage control commission to regulate the purchase, possession, consumption, sale, and delivery of alcoholic beverages at retail on any land designated as Indian Country pursuant to 18 U.S.C. § 1151 under the jurisdiction of the Eastern Band of Cherokee Indians. The tribal commission shall have exclusive authority to issue retail permits to retail establishments located wholly on Indian Country lands under the jurisdiction of the Eastern Band of Cherokee Indians and to regulate the purchase, possession, consumption, sale, and delivery of alcoholic beverages at retail outlets and premises. Permits issued by the tribal commission pursuant to this section shall be deemed issued by the State for the purposes of sales and delivery of beer and wine by wholesalers to the retail outlets located on Indian Country lands. The fees generated by the tribal alcoholic beverage control commission for the issuance of retail permits may be retained by the Eastern Band of Cherokee Indians to offset costs of operating the tribal alcoholic beverage control commission.

(e) Establishment of Rules. - The tribal alcoholic beverage control commission shall adopt the rules of the North Carolina Alcoholic Beverage Control Commission regulating retail outlet activity.

(f) Authority of the North Carolina Alcoholic Beverage Control Commission. - The North Carolina Alcoholic Beverage Control Commission shall have the authority to enter into agreements with the tribal alcoholic beverage control commission to provide for the sale, delivery, and distribution of spirituous liquor to the tribal alcoholic beverage control commission. The tribal alcoholic beverage control commission shall purchase spirituous liquor for resale by the tribal alcoholic beverage control commission exclusively from the North Carolina Alcoholic Beverage Control Commission at the same price and on the same basis that such spirits are purchased by local boards. To the extent there is a conflict between the tribal alcoholic beverage control commission's authority or purpose and the North Carolina Alcoholic Beverage Control Commission's authority or purpose, the North Carolina Alcoholic Beverage Control Commission shall prevail.

(g) Discrimination. - The tribal alcoholic beverage control commission shall not discriminate against non-Indians in the application of the tribal ABC law. Non-Indians shall be entitled to apply for and receive ABC permits in the same manner as an Indian on Indian Country lands under the jurisdiction of the Eastern Band of Cherokee Indians.

(h) Resolution of Contested Cases. - If the tribal alcoholic beverage control commission levies a fine or suspends or revokes a permit pursuant to the provisions of G.S. 18B-104 for a violation of the provisions applicable to the Eastern Band of Cherokee Indians in this section, the permittee shall have the right of appeal of an agency final decision of the tribal commission to the tribal courts. Any further appeal shall be to the appellate courts of the tribe. All fines paid to the tribal commission in satisfaction of any penalty assessed by the tribal commission may be retained by the Eastern Band of Cherokee Indians to offset costs of operating the tribal alcoholic beverage control commission.

(i) Failure to Comply With Laws of This State. - If the Eastern Band of Cherokee Indians fails to adopt the provisions of this Chapter, made applicable to the tribe by this section, by ordinance; fails to amend tribal ordinances to comply with amendments to the provisions of this Chapter, made applicable to the tribe by this section, within six months of passage of such amendments; or fails to comply with the provisions of this Chapter, made applicable to the tribe by this section, as required by 18 U.S.C. § 1161, the North Carolina Alcoholic Beverage Control Commission is authorized to terminate and prohibit future delivery of any alcoholic beverages from any person to the tribal alcoholic beverage control commission until the Eastern Band of Cherokee Indians complies with the provisions of this Chapter made applicable to the tribe by this section and 18 U.S.C. § 1161.

(j)   Conflict of Laws. - If any provision of this section or its application conflicts with federal law, the conflict of laws shall be resolved in favor of the federal law unless compliance with the federal law abrogates a right reserved to the State under the Constitution of the United States. (2011-333, s. 3.)

§ 18B-113. Reserved for future codification purposes.

§ 18B-114. Reserved for future codification purposes.

§ 18B-115. Reserved for future codification purposes.

§ 18B-116. Reserved for future codification purposes.

§ 18B-117. Reserved for future codification purposes.

§ 18B-118. Reserved for future codification purposes.

§ 18B-119. Reserved for future codification purposes.

Article 1A.

Compensation for Injury Caused by Sales to Underage Persons.

§ 18B-120. Definitions.

As used in this Article:

(1)   "Aggrieved party" means a person who sustains an injury as a consequence of the actions of the underage person, but does not include the

underage person or a person who aided or abetted in the sale or furnishing to the underage person.

(2) "Injury" includes, but is not limited to, personal injury, property loss, loss of means of support, or death. Damages for death shall be determined under the provisions of G.S. 28A-18-2(b). Nothing in G.S. 28A-18-2(a) or subdivision (1) of this section shall be interpreted to preclude recovery under this Article for loss of support or death on account of injury to or death of the underage person or a person who aided or abetted in the sale or furnishing to the underage person.

(3) "Underage person" means a person who is less than the age legally required for purchase of the alcoholic beverage in question.

(4) "Vehicle" shall have the same meaning as prescribed by G.S. 20-4.01(49). (1983, c. 435, s. 37.)

§ 18B-121. Claim for relief created for sale to underage person.

An aggrieved party has a claim for relief for damages against a permittee or local Alcoholic Beverage Control Board if:

(1) The permittee or his agent or employee or the local board or its agent or employee negligently sold or furnished an alcoholic beverage to an underage person; and

(2) The consumption of the alcoholic beverage that was sold or furnished to an underage person caused or contributed to, in whole or in part, an underage driver's being subject to an impairing substance within the meaning of G.S. 20-138.1 at the time of the injury; and

(3) The injury that resulted was proximately caused by the underage driver's negligent operation of a vehicle while so impaired. (1983, c. 435, s. 37.)

§ 18B-122. Burden of proof and admissibility of evidence.

The plaintiff shall have the burden of proving that the sale or furnishing of the alcoholic beverage to the underage person, as defined, was, under the circumstances, negligent. Proof of the sale or furnishing of the alcoholic beverage to an underage person, as defined, without request for identification shall be admissible as evidence of negligence. Proof of good practices (including but not limited to, instruction of employees as to laws regarding the sale of alcoholic beverages, training of employees, enforcement techniques, admonishment to patrons concerning laws regarding the purchase or furnishing of alcoholic beverages, or detention of a person's identification documents in accordance with G.S. 18B-129 and inquiry about the age or degree of intoxication of the person), evidence that an underage person misrepresented his age, or that the sale or furnishing was made under duress is admissible as evidence that the permittee was not negligent. (1983, c. 435, s. 37.)

§ 18B-123. Limitation on damages.

The total amount of damages that may be awarded to all aggrieved parties pursuant to any claims for relief under this Article is limited to no more than five hundred thousand dollars ($500,000) per occurrence. When all claims arising out of an occurrence exceed five hundred thousand dollars ($500,000), each claim shall abate in the proportion it bears to the total of all claims. (1983, c. 435, s. 37.)

§ 18B-124. Joint and several liability.

The liability of the negligent driver or owner of the vehicle that caused the injury and the permittee or ABC board which sold or furnished the alcoholic beverage shall be joint and several, with right of contribution but not indemnification. (1983, c. 435, s. 37.)

§ 18B-125. Exceptions.

This Article does not create a claim for relief against the following:

(1) One who holds only a brown bagging permit, a special occasions permit, or a limited special occasions permit;

(2) One who holds only a special one-time permit under G.S. 18B-1002;

(3) One who holds only permits listed in G.S. 18B-1100;

(4) One who holds any combination of the permits listed in this section. (1983, c. 435, s. 37.)

§ 18B-126. Statute of limitations.

The statute of limitations is as provided in G.S. 1-54. (1983, c. 435, s. 37.)

§ 18B-127. Duty of clerk of superior court.

When execution on a judgment on a cause of action under G.S. 18B-121 is returned unsatisfied, in whole or in part, the clerk of superior court to whom such return is made shall transmit to the Commission certified copies of the judgment, the execution and return and any other proceedings upon the judgment. (1983, c. 435, s. 37.)

§ 18B-128. Common-law rights not abridged.

The creation of any claim for relief by this Article may not be interpreted to abrogate or abridge any claims for relief under the common law, but this Article does not authorize double recovery for the same injury. (1983, c. 435, s. 37.)

§ 18B-129. No liability for refusal to sell or for holding documents.

(a) No permittee or his agent or employee may be held liable for damages resulting from the refusal to sell or furnish an alcoholic beverage to a person who fails to show proper identification as described in G.S. 18B-302(d), or who appears to be an underage person.

(b) No permittee or his agent or employee may be held civilly liable if the permittee or his agent or employee holds a customer's identification documents for a reasonable length of time in a good faith attempt to determine whether the customer is of legal age to purchase an alcoholic beverage, provided the permittee or his agent or employee informs the customer of the reason for his actions. (1983, c. 435, s. 37.)

§§ 18B-130 through 18B-199. Reserved for future codification purposes.

Article 2.

State Administration.

§ 18B-200. North Carolina Alcoholic Beverage Control Commission.

(a) Creation of Commission; compensation. - The North Carolina Alcoholic Beverage Control Commission is created to consist of a chairman and two associate members. The chairman shall devote his full time to his official duties and receive a salary fixed by the General Assembly in the Current Operations Appropriations Act. The associate members shall be compensated for per diem, subsistence and travel as provided in Chapter 138 of the General Statutes.

(b) Appointment of Members. - Members of the Commission shall be appointed by the Governor to serve at his pleasure.

(c) Vacancy. - The Governor shall fill any vacancy on the Commission by appointing a successor to serve at the Governor's pleasure. If the chairman's seat becomes vacant, the Governor may designate either the new member or an existing member of the Commission as the chairman.

(d) Employees. - The Commission may authorize the chairman to employ, discharge, and otherwise supervise subordinate personnel of the Commission. The Commission shall appoint at least one employee to make investigations, hold hearings requested under G.S. 18B-1205, and represent the Commission in contested case hearings or perform any other duties authorized by Chapter 150B. (1937, c. 49, ss. 2, 3; c. 411; 1939, c. 185, s. 5; 1941, c. 107, s. 5; 1963, c. 916, s. 1; 1965, c. 1102, ss. 1, 2; 1969, c. 294, ss. 1, 2; 1971, c. 872, s. 1; 1979, c. 336; 1981, c. 412, s. 2; 1983, c. 717, s. 4; 1983 (Reg. Sess., 1984), c. 1034, s. 164; 1987, c. 827, s. 1; 1993, c. 415, s. 3.)

§ 18B-201. Conflict of interest; gifts.

(a)   Financial Interests Restricted. - No person shall be appointed to or employed by the Commission, a local board, or the ALE Section if that person or a member of that person's family related to that person by blood or marriage to the first degree has or controls, directly or indirectly, a financial interest in any commercial alcoholic beverage enterprise, including any business required to have an ABC permit. The Commission may exempt from this provision any person, other than a Commission member, when the financial interest in question is so insignificant or remote that it is unlikely to affect the person's official actions in any way. Exemptions may be granted only to individuals, not to groups or classes of people, and each exemption shall be in writing, be available for public inspection, and contain a statement of the financial interest in question.

(b)   Self-dealing. - The provisions of G.S. 14-234 shall apply to the Commission and local boards.

(c)   Dealing for Family Members. - Neither the Commission nor any local board shall contract or otherwise deal in any business matter so that a member, member's spouse or any person related to the member by blood to a degree of first cousin or closer in any way financially benefits, directly or indirectly, from the transaction unless:

(1)   The member who financially benefits from the transaction or whose spouse or relative financially benefits from the transaction abstains from participating in any way, including voting, in the decision;

(2)   The minutes of the meeting at which the final decision is reached specifically note the member who is financially benefited or whose spouse or relative is financially benefited and the amount involved in each transaction;

(3) The next annual audit of the Commission or local board specifically notes the member and the amount involved in each transaction occurring during the year covered by the audit; and

(4) If the transaction is by a local board, the Commission is notified at least two weeks before final board approval of the transaction.

(d) Gifts Generally. - The provisions of G.S. 133-32 shall apply to the Commission and local boards.

(e) Conflicts of Interest for the Commission. - The provisions of Article 4 of Chapter 138A of the General Statutes shall apply to the Commission.

(f) Conflicts of Interest for Local Boards. - Except as permitted under subsection (h) of this section, a local ABC board member shall not knowingly use the local ABC board member's position on the board in any way that will result in financial benefit to the local ABC board member, the local ABC board member's spouse, any person related to the local ABC board member by blood to a degree of first cousin or closer, or any business with which the local ABC board member is associated.

(g) For purposes of subsection (f) of this section, "business with which associated" shall have the same meaning as in G.S. 138A-3(3). For purposes of this section, "financial benefit" shall mean a direct pecuniary gain or loss, or a direct pecuniary loss to a business competitor.

(h) Notwithstanding subsection (f) of this section, a local ABC board member may participate in an action of the local ABC board under any of the following circumstances except as specifically limited:

(1) The financial benefit that accrues to the local ABC board member, the local ABC board member's spouse or any person related to the local ABC board member by blood to a degree of first cousin or closer, or a business with which the local ABC board member is associated is one that is accrued as a member of a profession, occupation, or general class and is no greater than that which could reasonably be foreseen to accrue to all members of that profession, occupation, or general class.

(2) The financial benefit derived by a local ABC board member, the local ABC board member's spouse or any person related to the local ABC board member by blood to a degree of first cousin or closer, or a business with which

the local ABC board member is associated is one that would be enjoyed to an extent no greater than that which other citizens of the State would or could enjoy.

(3) The financial benefit derived by a local ABC board member, the local ABC board member's spouse or any person related to the local ABC board member by blood to a degree of first cousin or closer, or a business with which the local ABC board member is so remote, tenuous, insignificant, or speculative that a reasonable person would conclude under the circumstances that the local ABC board member's ability to protect the public interest and perform the local ABC board member's duties would not be compromised.

(4) When an action affects or would affect the local ABC board member's compensation as a local ABC board member.

(5) Before the local ABC board member participated in the action, the board member requested and received from the ABC Commission a written advisory opinion that authorized the participation. In authorizing the participation under this subdivision, the ABC Commission shall consider the need for the local ABC board member's particular contribution, such as special knowledge of the subject matter and the effective functioning of the local ABC board.

(6) When action is ministerial only and does not require the exercise of discretion.

(7) When the local ABC board records in its minutes that it cannot obtain a quorum in order to take the action because the local ABC board member is disqualified from acting, the local ABC board member may be counted for purposes of a quorum but shall otherwise abstain from taking any further action.

(i) Nothing in this section shall allow participation in an action prohibited by G.S. 14-234 or G.S. 133-32.

(j) A local board member shall not improperly use or improperly disclose any confidential information.

(k) A local board member shall have an affirmative duty to promptly disclose in writing to the local board any conflict of interest or potential conflict of interest. (1981, c. 412, s. 2; 1993, c. 415, s. 4; 2010-122, s. 2; 2011-145, s. 19.1(q).)

§ 18B-202. Discharge upon conviction.

In addition to imposing any other penalty authorized by law, a judge may remove from office or discharge from employment any Commission or local board member or employee, or any ALE agent, who is convicted of a violation of any provision of this Chapter or of any felony and may declare that person ineligible for membership or employment with the Commission, any local board, or the ALE Section, for a period of not longer than three years. Conviction of a crime under this Chapter or of any felony shall also be grounds for the Commission to remove from office or discharge from employment any local board member or employee. In addition to imposing any other penalty authorized by law, a judge may prohibit an individual convicted of a violation of this Chapter, or of any felony, from participating in any contract to enforce the ABC laws for a local board if that individual is a designated officer of an agency which holds a contract to enforce the ABC laws for a local board. A judge may also prohibit an individual convicted of a violation of this Chapter, or of any felony, from being designated as an officer that enforces the ABC law under a contract with any local board for a period of not longer than three years. (1981, c. 412, s. 2; 2010-122, s. 3; 2011-145, s. 19.1(q).)

§ 18B-203. Powers and duties of the Commission.

(a) Powers. - The Commission shall have authority to:

(1) Administer the ABC laws;

(2) Provide for enforcement of the ABC laws, in conjunction with the ALE Section;

(3) Set the prices of alcoholic beverages sold in local ABC stores as provided in Article 8;

(4) Require reports and audits from local boards as provided in G.S. 18B-205;

(5) Determine what brands of alcoholic beverages may be sold in this State;

(6) Contract for State ABC warehousing, as provided in G.S. 18B-204;

(7) Dispose of damaged alcoholic beverages, as provided in G.S. 18B-806;

(8) Remove for cause any member or employee of a local board;

(9) Supervise or disapprove purchasing by any local board and inspect all records of purchases by local boards;

(10) Approve or disapprove rules adopted by any local board;

(11) Approve or disapprove the opening and location of ABC stores, as provided in Article 8;

(12) Issue ABC permits, and impose sanctions against permittees;

(13) Provide for the testing of alcoholic beverages, as provided in G.S. 18B-206;

(14) Fix the amount of bailment charges and bailment surcharges to be assessed on liquor shipped from a Commission warehouse;

(15) Collect bailment charges and bailment surcharges from local boards;

(16) Notwithstanding any law to the contrary, enter into contracts for design and construction of a warehouse or warehouses and supervise work and materials used in the construction, as provided in G.S. 18B-204;

(17) Provide for the distribution of spirituous liquor to installations of the Armed Forces of the United States within this State for resale on the installation and to the Eastern Band of Cherokee Indians for resale on Indian Country lands within this State under the jurisdiction of the Eastern Band of Cherokee Indians.

(18) Provide for the distribution and posting of warning signs to local ABC boards regarding the dangers of alcohol consumption during pregnancy as required under G.S. 18B-808;

(19) Recognize the holder of a wine importer permit or nonresident wine vendor permit as a primary American source of supply for the wine of a winery. To be considered a primary American source of supply, a wine importer must establish that it has lawfully purchased the wine from the winery, or from an

agent of the winery, and by written contract or otherwise has been authorized by the winery to distribute the wine to wholesalers in the United States.

(20) Promulgate rules to establish performance standards for local boards. Performance standards established pursuant to this subdivision shall include, but not be limited to, standards that address enforcement of ABC laws, store appearance, operating efficiency, solvency, and customer service.

(21) Promulgate rules to establish mandatory training requirements for local board members, finance officers, and general managers. If personal attendance is required, the Commission shall not require more than four hours of training and shall provide up to two hours of training at convenient locations around the State in conjunction with ethics training.

(22) Provide for the purchase of spirituous liquor from another ABC board by mixed beverage permittees when an ABC system becomes insolvent, closes, or is closed by the Commission and the county or municipality in which the system is located has approved the sale of mixed beverages.

(b) Implied Powers. - The Commission shall have all other powers which may be reasonably implied from the granting of the express powers stated in subsection (a), or which may be incidental to, or convenient for, performing the duties given to the Commission. (1937, c. 49, s. 4; cc. 237, 411; 1945, c. 954; 1949, c. 974, s. 9; 1961, c. 956; 1963, c. 426, s. 12; c. 916, s. 2; c. 1119, s. 1; 1965, c. 1063; c. 1102, s. 3; 1967, c. 222, s. 2; c. 1240, s. 1; 1971, c. 872, s. 1; 1973, c. 28; c. 473, s. 1; c. 476, s. 133; c. 606; c. 1288, s. 1; cc. 1369, 1396; 1975, cc. 240, 453, 640; 1977, c. 70, ss. 15.1, 15.2, 16; c. 176, ss. 2, 6; 1977, 2nd Sess., c. 1138, ss. 3, 4, 18; 1979, c. 384, s. 1; c. 445, s. 5; c. 482; c. 801, s. 4; 1981, c. 412, s. 2; c. 747, s. 38; 1981 (Reg. Sess., 1982), c. 1285, s. 2; 1987, c. 136, s. 1; 2003-339, s. 1; 2006-227, s. 10; 2010-122, s. 4; 2011-145, s. 19.1(q); 2011-183, s. 20; 2011-333, s. 2.)

§ 18B-204. State warehouse.

(a) Contracting for Private Warehouse. - The Commission shall provide for the receipt, storage, and distribution of spirituous liquor by one of the following methods:

(1) By negotiated contract with a privately owned warehouse;

(2) By negotiated contract with privately owned warehouses in several regions of the State. The Commission shall choose locations for the warehouses to promote efficient distribution of spirituous liquor to all local boards, to maintain control of that liquor, and to insure the Commission's supervision of warehousing procedures; or

(3) By the construction of a warehouse, and by contracting for receipt, storage and distribution of spirituous liquor by an independent contractor, by negotiated contract or by the use of procedures for purchase and contract by State agencies, for the operation of that warehouse.

(b) Audits and Inspections. - Contracts entered into pursuant to this section shall provide the following:

(1) That an annual audited financial statement be prepared and submitted to the Commission by the person contracting with the Commission;

(2) That all warehouse records be available for inspection at all times by the Commission and the Department of Revenue; and

(3) That all warehouse accounts relating to the receipt, storage, or distribution of spirituous liquor be subject to audit by the State Auditor.

(c) Emergency or Temporary Operation. - If the independent operator of a warehouse changes, or if some other occurrence results in substantially impeded distribution of spirituous liquor from a warehouse, the Commission may operate that warehouse on an interim emergency or temporary basis.

(d) Rules. - The Commission may adopt rules regarding warehouse operations, and violations of those rules by a party with whom the Commission contracts shall be grounds for termination by the Commission of a contract entered into under this section. (1937, c. 49, s. 4; cc. 237, 411; 1945, c. 954; 1949, c. 974, s. 9; 1961, c. 956; 1963, c. 426, s. 12; c. 916, s. 2; c. 1119, s. 1; 1965, c. 1063; c. 1102, s. 3; 1967, c. 222, s. 2; c. 1240, s. 1; 1971, c. 872, s. 1; 1973, c. 28; c. 473, s. 1; c. 476, s. 133; c. 606; c. 1288, s. 1; cc. 1369, 1396; 1975, cc. 240, 453, 640; 1977, c. 70, ss. 15.1, 15.2, 16; c. 176, ss. 2, 6; 1977, 2nd Sess., c. 1138, ss. 3, 4, 18; 1979, c. 384, s. 1; c. 445, s. 5; c. 482; c. 801, s. 4; 1981, c. 412, s. 2; 1981 (Reg. Sess., 1982), c. 1285, s. 3; 1987, c. 136, s. 2.)

§ 18B-205. Accounts and reports required.

(a) Accounts and Reports. - The Commission may require local boards to submit quarterly mixed beverage reports, quarterly and annual audits, monthly sales records, and any other reports or audits relating to the operations of the local ABC systems.

(b) Accounting System. - The Commission may require local boards to use generally accepted accounting standards and a chart of accounts prescribed by the Commission in the operation of ABC stores, and to record all information necessary and useful to the Commission in auditing the operation of ABC systems and administering the ABC law.

(c) Audits. - The Commission may audit the operation of any local ABC store or board, and the books of those stores and boards shall remain open to the Commission for inspection. (1937, c. 49, s. 4; cc. 237, 411; 1945, c. 954; 1949, c. 974, s. 9; 1961, c. 956; 1963, c. 426, s. 12; c. 916, s. 2; c. 1119, s. 1; 1965, c. 1063; c. 1102, s. 3; 1967, c. 222, s. 2; c. 1240, s. 1; 1971, c. 872, s. 1; 1973, c. 28; c. 473, s. 1; c. 476, s. 133; c. 606; c. 1288, s. 1; cc. 1369, 1396; 1975, cc. 240, 453, 640; 1977, c. 70, ss. 15.1, 15.2, 16; c. 176, ss. 2, 6; 1977, 2nd Sess., c. 1138, ss. 3, 4, 18; 1979, c. 384, s. 1; c. 445, s. 5; c. 482; c. 801, s. 4; 1981, c. 412, s. 2.)

§ 18B-206. Standards for alcoholic beverages.

(a) Authority to Set Standards. - The Commission may set standards and adopt rules for malt beverages, unfortified wine, fortified wine, and spirituous liquor to protect the public against beverages containing harmful or impure substances, beverages containing an improper balance of substances as determined by the Commission, spurious or imitation beverages, and beverages unfit for human consumption. In setting standards and in issuing rules relating to them, the Commission may follow federal guidelines for standards of identity, labeling and advertising contained in Title 27 of the Code of Federal Regulations, or may adopt more restrictive standards.

(b) Effective Date of Standards. - A person possessing alcoholic beverages which do not meet a new standard set by the Commission shall have 60 days after the effective date of the standard to sell or otherwise dispose of those alcoholic beverages.

(c) Testing. - The Commission may test malt beverages, unfortified wine, fortified wine, and spirituous liquor possessed or offered for sale in this State to determine whether they meet the standards set by the Commission. If the Commission chooses to test an alcoholic beverage, that test may be performed by the Commission, the Commission may arrange for the State Chemist to perform the testing, or the Commission may have the testing performed in some other manner. The manufacturer of tested alcoholic beverages shall pay the costs of the test. In lieu of testing an alcoholic beverage, the Commission may rely on testing by a federal agency or an agency of another state or may accept test results from a federal agency, an agency of another state, or the manufacturer of the alcoholic beverage or his authorized agent. A manufacturer who submits test results shall also submit a fee of ten dollars ($10.00) for each test result to cover administrative costs. (1939, c. 158, s. 514; 1943, c. 400, s. 6; 1949, c. 974, s. 14; 1953, c. 1207, ss. 2-4; 1957, c. 1440; 1963, c. 426, ss. 4, 5; 1971, c. 872, s. 1; 1977, c. 70, s. 20.4; 1981, c. 412, s. 2.)

§ 18B-207. Rules.

The Commission shall have authority to adopt, amend, and repeal rules to carry out the provisions of this Chapter. Those rules shall become effective when adopted and filed pursuant to the provisions of Chapter 150B of the General Statutes. (1937, c. 49, s. 4; cc. 237, 411; 1945, c. 954; 1949, c. 974, s. 9; 1961, c. 956; 1963, c. 426, s. 12; c. 916, s. 2; c. 1119, s. 1; 1965, c. 1063; c. 1102, s. 3; 1967, c. 222, s. 2; c. 1240, s. 1; 1971, c. 872, s. 1; 1973, c. 28; c. 473, s. 1; c. 476, s. 133; c. 606; c. 1288, s. 1; cc. 1369, 1396; 1975, cc. 240, 453, 640; 1977, c. 70, ss. 15.1, 15.2, 16; c. 176, ss. 2, 6; 1977, 2nd Sess., c. 1138, ss. 3, 4, 18; 1979, c. 384, s. 1; c. 445, s. 5; c. 482; c. 801, s. 4; 1981, c. 412, s. 2; 1987, c. 827, s.1.)

§ 18B-208. ABC Commission bonds and funds.

(a) Issuance of Bonds. - As a means of raising the funds needed from time to time in the design, acquisition, construction, equipping, maintenance and operation of a warehouse under G.S. 18B-204(a)(3), the Commission may, with the approval of the Governor, at one time or from time to time issue negotiable revenue bonds of the Commission. The issuance of revenue bonds shall not directly or indirectly or contingently obligate the State to levy or to pledge any form of taxation or to make any appropriation for their payment. Revenue bonds issued pursuant to this subsection shall be repaid from the bailment surcharge as provided in subsection (b). These bonds and the income from them are exempt from all taxation within the State.

(b) Special Fund. - A special fund in the office of the State Treasurer, the ABC Commission Fund, is created. On and after November 1, 1982, all moneys derived from the collection of bailment charges and bailment surcharges shall be deposited in the ABC Commission Fund for the purpose of carrying out the provisions of this Chapter. The ABC Commission Fund shall be subject to the provisions of the State Budget Act except that no unexpended surplus of this fund shall revert to the General Fund. The Commission shall fix the level of the bailment surcharges at an amount calculated to cover operating expenses of the Commission and the retirement of bonds issued for construction of a Commission warehouse and offices. Upon payment of the bonds issued pursuant to this section, the Commission shall reduce the bailment surcharge to an amount no greater than necessary to pay operating expenses of the Commission as authorized by the General Assembly.

All moneys credited to the ABC Commission Fund shall be used to carry out the intent and purposes of the ABC law in accordance with plans approved by the North Carolina ABC Commission and the Director of the Budget, and all these funds are appropriated, reserved, set aside, and made available until expended for the administration of the ABC law. (1981 (Reg. Sess., 1982), c. 1285, s. 4; 1983, c. 761, s. 133; 1987, c. 832, s. 1; 1989, c. 800 s. 6; 2006-203, s. 13.)

§§ 18B-209 through 18B-299. Reserved for future codification purposes.

Article 3.

Sale, Possession, and Consumption.

§ 18B-300. Purchase, possession and consumption of malt beverages and unfortified wine.

(a) Generally. - Except as otherwise provided in this Chapter, the purchase, consumption, and possession of malt beverages and unfortified wine by individuals 21 years old and older for their own use is permitted without restriction.

(a1) Consumption on Premises During Time of Permit Revocation or Suspension. - It shall be unlawful to consume or for a permittee or his agent or employee to allow the consumption of malt beverages or unfortified wine on the premises of any business during the period of time that any on-premises permit issued to the business authorizing the sale and consumption of malt beverages or unfortified wine has been suspended or revoked by the Commission. The prohibition in this subsection does not apply to the premises upon which the business was located at the time the permit was suspended or revoked if the business ceases to operate in that location and the owner of the property is not the permittee, provided that the permittee is not engaged in any other business or other activity on the premises during the period of suspension or revocation.

(b) Consumption at Off-Premises Establishment. - It shall be unlawful to consume, or for a permittee to allow the consumption of, malt beverages or unfortified wine on any premises having only an off-premises permit for the kind of alcoholic beverage being consumed.

(c) Local Ordinance. - A city or county may by ordinance:

(1) Regulate or prohibit the consumption of malt beverages and unfortified wine on the public streets in that city or county by persons who are not occupants of motor vehicles and on property owned, occupied, or controlled by that city or county;

(2) Regulate or prohibit the possession of open containers of malt beverages and unfortified wine on public streets in that city or county by persons who are not occupants of motor vehicles and on property owned, occupied, or controlled by that city or county; and

(3) Regulate or prohibit the possession of malt beverages and unfortified wine on public streets, alleys, or parking lots which are temporarily closed to regular traffic for special events.

For the purposes of this subsection, an open container means a container whose seal has been broken or a container other than the manufacturer's unopened original container. As provided by G.S. 18B-102(a), possession or consumption of alcoholic beverages is unlawful except as authorized by the ABC law. (1939, c. 158, s. 503; 1971, c. 872, s. 1; 1973, c. 1452, ss. 1-3; 1977, c. 176, ss. 2, 3; c. 693; 1979, c. 19, s. 2; c. 445, s. 4; c. 893, s. 11; 1981, c. 412, s. 2; 1983, c. 435, s. 32; 1985, c. 141, s. 1; 1995, c. 144, s. 1; c. 366, s. 2; 2001-79, s. 1; 2013-392, s. 1.)

§ 18B-301. Possession and consumption of fortified wine and spirituous liquor.

(a) Possession at Home. - It shall be lawful, without an ABC permit, for any person at least 21 years old to possess for lawful purposes any amount of fortified wine and spirituous liquor at his home or a temporary residence, such as a hotel room.

(b) Possession on Other Property. - It shall be lawful, without an ABC permit, for a person to possess for his personal use and the use of his guests not more than eight liters of fortified wine or spirituous liquor, or eight liters of the two combined, at the following places:

(1) The residence of any other person with that person's consent;

(2) Any other property not primarily used for commercial purposes and not open to the public at the time the alcoholic beverage is possessed, if the owner or other person in charge of the property consents to that possession and consumption;

(3) An establishment with a brown-bagging permit as defined in G.S. 18B-1001(7).

(c) Special Occasions. - It shall be lawful for a person to possess, without a permit and not for sale, any amount of fortified wine or spirituous liquor for a private party, private reception, or private special occasion, at the following places:

(1) His home or a temporary residence, such as a hotel room;

(2) Any other property not primarily used for commercial purposes, which is under his exclusive control and supervision, and which is not open to the public during the event;

(3) The licensed premises of any business for which the Commission has issued a special occasions permit under G.S. 18B-1001(8), if he is the host of that private function and has the permission of the permittee.

(d) Consumption. - It shall be lawful for a person to consume fortified wine and spirituous liquor in any place where it is lawful for him to possess those alcoholic beverages under subsections (a) through (c).

(e) Incident to Sale. - It shall be lawful to possess fortified wine and spirituous liquor at any place, such as an ABC store, where possession is a necessary incident to lawful sale. Consumption at such a place shall be unlawful unless the establishment has a permit authorizing consumption on the premises as well as sale.

(f) Unlawful Possession or Use. - As illustration, but not limitation, of the general prohibition stated in G.S. 18B-102(a), it shall be unlawful for:

(1) Any person to consume fortified wine, spirituous liquor, or mixed beverages or to offer such beverages to another person:

a. On the premises of an ABC store, or

b. Upon any property used or occupied by a local board, or

c. On any public road, street, highway, or sidewalk.

(2) Any person to display publicly at an athletic contest fortified wine, spirituous liquor, or mixed beverages;

(3) Any person to permit any fortified wine, spirituous liquor, or mixed beverages to be possessed or consumed upon any premises not authorized by this Chapter;

(4) Any person to possess or consume any fortified wine, spirituous liquor, or mixed beverages upon any premises where such possession or consumption is not authorized by law, or where the person has been forbidden to possess or consume that beverage by the owner or other person in charge of the premises;

(5) Any person to possess on any of the premises described in subsections (a) through (c) a greater amount of fortified wine or spirituous liquor than authorized by this Chapter;

(6) Any permittee, other than a mixed beverage or culinary permittee, to possess spirituous liquor or mixed beverages on his licensed premises.

(7) Any person to possess on his person or consume malt beverages or unfortified wine upon any property owned or leased by a local board of education and used by the local board of education for school purposes. Provided, however, the prohibition in G.S. 18B-102(a) and this subdivision shall not apply on property owned by a local board of education which was leased for 99 years or more to a nonprofit auditorium authority created prior to 1991 whose governing board is appointed by a city board of aldermen, a county board of commissioners, or a local school board. (1905, c. 498, ss. 6-8; Rev., ss. 3526, 3534; C.S., s. 3371; 1937, c. 49, ss. 12, 16, 22; c. 411; 1955, c. 999; 1967, c. 222, ss. 1, 8; c. 1256, s. 3; 1969, c. 1018; 1971, c. 872, s. 1; 1973, c. 1226; 1977, c. 176, s. 1; 1977, 2nd Sess., c. 1138, ss. 8-12, 18; 1979, c. 384, s. 3; c. 609, s. 2; c. 718; c. 893, s. 10; 1981, c. 412, s. 2; c. 747, s. 39; 1983, c. 917, s. 1; 1985, c. 566, s. 1; 1991, c. 459, s. 1; 1993, c. 508, s. 1; 1995, c. 372, s. 1.)

§ 18B-302. Sale to or purchase by underage persons.

(a) Sale. - It shall be unlawful for any person to:

(1) Sell malt beverages or unfortified wine to anyone less than 21 years old; or

(2) Sell fortified wine, spirituous liquor, or mixed beverages to anyone less than 21 years old.

(a1) Give. - It shall be unlawful for any person to:

(1) Give malt beverages or unfortified wine to anyone less than 21 years old; or

(2) Give fortified wine, spirituous liquor, or mixed beverages to anyone less than 21 years old.

(b) Purchase, Possession, or Consumption. - It shall be unlawful for:

(1) A person less than 21 years old to purchase, to attempt to purchase, or to possess malt beverages or unfortified wine; or

(2) A person less than 21 years old to purchase, to attempt to purchase, or to possess fortified wine, spirituous liquor, or mixed beverages; or

(3) A person less than 21 years old to consume any alcoholic beverage.

(c) Aider and Abettor.

(1) By Underage Person. - Any person who is under the lawful age to purchase and who aids or abets another in violation of subsection (a), (a1), or (b) of this section shall be guilty of a Class 2 misdemeanor.

(2) By Person over Lawful Age. - Any person who is over the lawful age to purchase and who aids or abets another in violation of subsection (a), (a1), or (b) of this section shall be guilty of a Class 1 misdemeanor.

(d) Defense. - It shall be a defense to a violation of subsection (a) of this section if the seller:

(1) Shows that the purchaser produced a driver's license, a special identification card issued under G.S. 20-37.7, a military identification card, or a passport, showing his age to be at least the required age for purchase and bearing a physical description of the person named on the card reasonably describing the purchaser; or

(2) Produces evidence of other facts that reasonably indicated at the time of sale that the purchaser was at least the required age.

(3) Shows that at the time of purchase, the purchaser utilized a biometric identification system that demonstrated (i) the purchaser's age to be at least the required age for the purchase and (ii) the purchaser had previously registered with the seller or seller's agent a drivers license, a special identification card issued under G.S. 20-377.7, a military identification card, or a passport showing the purchaser's date of birth and bearing a physical description of the person named on the document.

(e) Fraudulent Use of Identification. - It shall be unlawful for any person to enter or attempt to enter a place where alcoholic beverages are sold or consumed, or to obtain or attempt to obtain alcoholic beverages, or to obtain or attempt to obtain permission to purchase alcoholic beverages, in violation of subsection (b) of this section, by using or attempting to use any of the following:

(1) A fraudulent or altered drivers license.

(2) A fraudulent or altered identification document other than a drivers license.

(3) A drivers license issued to another person.

(4) An identification document other than a drivers license issued to another person.

(5) Any other form or means of identification that indicates or symbolizes that the person is not prohibited from purchasing or possessing alcoholic beverages under this section.

(f) Allowing Use of Identification. - It shall be unlawful for any person to permit the use of the person's drivers license or any other form of identification of any kind issued or given to the person by any other person who violates or attempts to violate subsection (b) of this section.

(g) Conviction Report Sent to Division of Motor Vehicles. - The court shall file a conviction report with the Division of Motor Vehicles indicating the name of the person convicted and any other information requested by the Division if the person is convicted of any of the following:

(1) A violation of subsection (e) or (f) of this section.

(2) A violation of subsection (c) of this section.

(3) A violation of subsection (b) of this section, if the violation occurred while the person was purchasing or attempting to purchase an alcoholic beverage.

(4) A violation of subsection (a1) of this section.

Upon receipt of a conviction report, the Division shall revoke the person's license as required by G.S. 20-17.3.

(h) Handling in Course of Employment. - Nothing in this section shall be construed to prohibit an underage person from selling, transporting, possessing or dispensing alcoholic beverages in the course of employment, if the employment of the person for that purpose is lawful under applicable youth employment statutes and Commission rules.

(i) Purchase, Possession, or Consumption by 19 or 20-Year Old. - A violation of subdivision (b)(1) or (b)(3) of this section by a person who is 19 or 20 years old is a Class 3 misdemeanor.

(j) Notwithstanding any other provisions of law, a law enforcement officer may require any person the officer has probable cause to believe is under age 21 and has consumed alcohol to submit to an alcohol screening test using a device approved by the Department of Health and Human Services. The results of any screening device administered in accordance with the rules of the Department of Health and Human Services shall be admissible in any court or administrative proceeding. A refusal to submit to an alcohol screening test shall be admissible in any court or administrative proceeding.

(k) Notwithstanding the provisions in this section, it shall not be unlawful for a person less than 21 years old to consume unfortified wine or fortified wine during participation in an exempted activity under G.S. 18B-103(4), (8), or (11). (1933, c. 216, s. 8; 1959, c. 745, s. 1; 1967, c. 222, s. 3; 1969, c. 998; 1971, c. 872, s. 1; 1973, c. 27; 1977, 2nd Sess., c. 1138, s. 2; 1979, c. 683, s. 2; 1981, c. 412, s. 2; c. 747, ss. 40, 41; 1983, c. 435, ss. 32, 35; c. 740, ss. 1, 2; Ex. Sess., c. 5; 1985, c. 141, ss. 2-3; 1993, c. 539, s. 311; 1994, Ex. Sess., c. 24, s. 14(c); 1999-406, s. 7; 2001-461, ss. 2, 3; 2001-487, s. 42(b); 2005-350, s. 6(a); 2006-253, s. 26; 2007-537, s. 1.)

§ 18B-302.1. Penalties for certain offenses related to underage persons.

(a) A violation of G.S. 18B-302(a) or (a1) is a Class 1 misdemeanor. Notwithstanding the provisions of G.S. 15A-1340.23, if the court imposes a sentence that does not include an active punishment, the court must include among the conditions of probation a requirement that the person pay a fine of at least two hundred fifty dollars ($250.00) as authorized by G.S. 15A-1343(b)(9) and a requirement that the person complete at least 25 hours of community service, as authorized by G.S. 15A-1343(b1)(6). If the person has a previous conviction of this offense in the four years immediately preceding the date of the current offense, and the court imposes a sentence that does not include an active punishment, the court must include among the conditions of probation a requirement that the person pay a fine of at least five hundred dollars ($500.00) as authorized by G.S. 15A-1343(b)(9) and a requirement that the person complete at least 150 hours of community service, as authorized by G.S. 15A-1343(b1)(6).

(b) A violation of G.S. 18B-302(c)(2) is a Class 1 misdemeanor. Notwithstanding the provisions of G.S. 15A-1340.23, if the court imposes a sentence that does not include an active punishment, the court must include among the conditions of probation a requirement that the person pay a fine of at least five hundred dollars ($500.00) as authorized by G.S. 15A-1343(b)(9) and a requirement that the person complete at least 25 hours of community service, as authorized by G.S. 15A-1343(b1)(6). If the person has a previous conviction of this offense in the four years immediately preceding the date of the current offense, and the court imposes a sentence that does not include an active punishment, the court must include among the conditions of probation a requirement that the person pay a fine of at least one thousand dollars ($1,000) as authorized by G.S. 15A-1343(b)(9) and a requirement that the person complete at least 150 hours of community service, as authorized by G.S. 15A-1343(b1)(6).

(c) In addition to the punishments imposed under this section, the court may impose the provisions of G.S. 18B-202 and of G.S. 18B-503, 18B-504, and 18B-505. (1999-433, s. 1; 2007-537, s. 2.)

§ 18B-302.2. Medical treatment; limited immunity.

Notwithstanding any other provision of law, a person under the age of 21 shall not be prosecuted for a violation of G.S. 18B-302 for the possession or consumption of alcoholic beverages if law enforcement, including campus safety police, became aware of the possession or consumption of alcohol by the person solely because the person was seeking medical assistance for another individual. This section shall apply if, when seeking medical assistance on behalf of another, the person did all of the following:

(1) Acted in good faith, upon a reasonable belief that he or she was the first to call for assistance.

(2) Used his or her own name when contacting authorities.

(3) Remained with the individual needing medical assistance until help arrived. (2013-23, s. 3.)

§ 18B-303. Amounts of alcoholic beverages that may be purchased.

(a) Purchases Allowed. - Without a permit, a person may purchase at one time:

(1) Not more than 80 liters of malt beverages, except draft malt beverages in kegs for off-premises consumption. For purchase of a keg or kegs of malt beverages for off-premises consumption, the permit required by G.S. 18B-403.1(a) must first be obtained;

(2) Any amount of draft malt beverages by a permittee in kegs for on-premise consumption;

(3) Not more than 50 liters of unfortified wine;

(4) Not more than eight liters of either fortified wine or spirituous liquor, or eight liters of the two combined.

(b) Unlawful Purchase. - Except as provided in subsection (c) and in Article 11, it shall be unlawful for any person to purchase, or for any person to sell, an amount of alcoholic beverages greater than that stated in subsection (a).

(c) Greater Amounts. - Amounts of alcoholic beverages greater than those listed in subdivisions (a)(3) and (a)(4) may be purchased with a purchase-transportation permit under G.S. 18B-403. (1905, c. 498, ss. 6-8; Rev., ss. 3526, 3534; C.S., s. 3371; 1937, c. 49, ss. 12, 16, 22; c. 411; 1955, c. 999; 1967, c. 222, ss. 1, 8; c. 1256, s. 3; 1969, c. 1018; 1971, c. 872, s. 1; 1973, c. 1226; 1977, c. 176, s. 1; 1977, 2nd Sess., c. 1138, ss. 8-12, 18; 1979, c. 384, s. 3; c. 609, s. 2; c. 718; c. 893, s. 10; 1981, c. 412, s. 2; 1989, c. 553, s. 1; 1993, c. 508, s. 2; 2001-262, s. 5; 2006-253, s. 3.2.)

§ 18B-304. Sale and possession for sale.

(a)   Offense. - It shall be unlawful for any person to sell any alcoholic beverage, or possess any alcoholic beverage for sale, without first obtaining the applicable ABC permit and revenue licenses.

(b)   Prima Facie Evidence. - Possession of the following amounts of alcoholic beverages, without a permit authorizing that possession, shall be prima facie evidence that the possessor is possessing those alcoholic beverages for sale:

(1)   More than 80 liters of malt beverages, other than draft malt beverages in kegs;

(2)   More than eight liters of spirituous liquor; or

(3)   Any amount of nontaxpaid alcoholic beverages. (1913, c. 44, s. 2; 1915, c. 97, s. 8; 1923, c. 1, ss. 2, 6, 10; C.S., ss. 3379, 3411(b), (f), (j); 1937, c. 49, ss. 13, 15; 1945, c. 635; 1949, c. 1251, s. 2; 1951, c. 850; 1955, c. 560; 1957, c. 984; c. 1235, s. 1; 1963, c. 932; 1967, c. 222, ss. 4, 6; 1969, c. 789; 1971, c. 872, s. 1; 1975, c. 654, s. 4; 1977, c. 176, ss. 1-3; 1981, c. 412, s. 2; c. 747, s. 42; 1989, c. 553, s. 2; 1993, c. 508, s. 3.)

§ 18B-305. Other prohibited sales.

(a)   Sale to Intoxicated Person. - It shall be unlawful for a permittee or his employee or for an ABC store employee to knowingly sell or give alcoholic beverages to any person who is intoxicated.

(b)   Discretion for Seller. - Any person authorized to sell alcoholic beverages under this Chapter may, in his discretion, refuse to sell to anyone. It shall be unlawful for any person to knowingly buy alcoholic beverages for someone who has been refused the right to purchase under this subsection.

(c)   Notwithstanding subsection (b) of this section, no permittee may refuse to sell alcoholic beverages to a person solely based on that person's race, religion, color, national origin, sex, or disability. (1937, c. 49, ss. 11, 15; c. 411; 1971, c. 872, s. 1; 1977, 2nd Sess., c. 1138, s. 5; 1981, c. 412, s. 2; 1999-462, s. 5.)

§ 18B-306. Making wines and malt beverages for private use.

An individual may make, possess, and transport native wines and malt beverages for his own use and for the use of his family and guests. Native wines shall be made principally from honey, grapes, or other fruit or grain grown in this State, or from wine kits containing honey, grapes, or other fruit or grain concentrates, and shall have only that alcoholic content produced by natural fermentation. Malt beverages may be made by use of malt beverage kits containing grain extracts or concentrates. Wine kits and malt beverage kits may be sold in this State. No ABC permit is required to make beverages pursuant to this section. (1971, c. 872, s. 1; 1973, c. 1218; 1981, c. 412, s. 2; c. 747, s. 43; 1985, c. 114, s. 6.)

§ 18B-307. Manufacturing offenses.

(a) Offenses. - It shall be unlawful for any person, except as authorized by this Chapter, to:

(1) Sell or possess equipment or ingredients intended for use in the manufacture of any alcoholic beverage, except equipment and ingredients provided under a Brew on Premises permit or a Winemaking on Premises permit; or

(2) Knowingly allow real or personal property owned or possessed by him to be used by another person for the manufacture of any alcoholic beverage, except pursuant to a Brew on Premises permit or a Winemaking on Premises permit.

(b) Unlawful Manufacturing. - Except as provided in G.S. 18B-306, it shall be unlawful for any person to manufacture any alcoholic beverage, except at an establishment with a Brew on Premises permit or a Winemaking on Premises permit, without first obtaining the applicable ABC permit and revenue licenses.

(c) Second Offense of Manufacturing. - A second offense of unlawful manufacturing of alcoholic beverage shall be a Class I felony. (1905, c. 498, s. 2; Rev., s. 3533; 1923, c. 1, ss. 4, 6, 26; C.S., ss. 3407, 3411(d), (f), (z); 1937,

c. 49, s. 13; 1945, c. 635; 1951, c. 850; 1955, c. 560; 1957, c. 984; c. 1235, s. 1; 1969, c. 789; 1971, c. 872, s. 1; 1979, c. 699, s. 1; 1981, c. 412, s. 2; c. 747, s. 44; 1997-467, s. 1; 2006-222, s. 2.2; 2006-227, s. 2.)

§ 18B-308. Sale and consumption at bingo games.

It shall be unlawful to sell or consume, or for the owner or other person in charge of the premises to allow the sale or consumption of, any alcoholic beverage in any room while a raffle or bingo game is being conducted in that room under Part 2 of Article 37 of Chapter 14 of the General Statutes. (1905, c. 498, ss. 6-8; Rev., ss. 3526, 3534; C.S., s. 3371; 1937, c. 49, ss. 12, 16, 22; c. 411; 1955, c. 999; 1967, c. 222, ss. 1, 8; c. 1256, s. 3; 1969, c. 1018; 1971, c. 872, s. 1; 1973, c. 1226; 1977, c. 176, s. 1; 1977, 2nd Sess., c. 1138, ss. 8-12, 18; 1979, c. 384, s. 3; c. 609, s. 2; c. 718; c. 893, s. 10; 1981, c. 412, s. 2; 1983, c. 896, s. 4.)

§ 18B-309. Alcoholic beverage sales in Urban Redevelopment Areas.

(a)   A food business as defined in G.S. 18B-1000(3), a retail business as defined in G.S. 18B-1000(7), or an eating establishment as defined in G.S. 18B-1000(2) that holds an ABC permit under this Chapter and is located in a part of a city that has been designated as an Urban Redevelopment Area under Article 22 of Chapter 160A of the General Statutes shall not have alcoholic beverage sales in excess of fifty percent (50%) of the business's total annual sales. The city council, or its designee, shall file a certified copy of the official action and original documents, including a map or similar information, designating the area as an Urban Redevelopment Area. The Commission shall make this information available to any permittee who makes a request for this information to the Commission.

(b)   Upon request of a city, the Commission shall investigate the total annual alcohol sales and total sales of a business as defined in this section. The Commission shall report the results of such an investigation to the city council, and the report shall contain only the percentage of annual alcohol sales in proportion to the business's total annual sales. A city may request an investigation of a particular business by the Commission only once in each calendar year. These audits may be conducted by the Commission only upon the request of the city council.

(c) Businesses covered by this section shall maintain full and accurate monthly records of their finances, separately indicating each of the following:

(1) Amounts expended by the business for the purchase of alcoholic beverages and the quantity of alcoholic beverages purchased;

(2) Amounts collected from the sale of alcoholic beverages sold; and

(3) Amounts collected from the sale of food, nonalcoholic beverages, and all other items sold by the business.

Records of purchases of alcoholic beverages and sales of alcoholic beverages shall be filed separate and apart from all other records maintained on the premises, and all records related to alcoholic beverages, including original invoices, shall be maintained on the premises for three years and shall be open for inspection and audit pursuant to G.S. 18B-502. (1999-322, s. 1; 2001-515, s. 3(a).)

§§ 18B-310 through 18B-399. Reserved for future codification purposes.

Article 4.

Transportation.

§ 18B-400. Amounts that may be transported.

A person may transport at one time the same amount of alcoholic beverages that he is allowed to buy under G.S. 18B-303(a). Greater amounts of fortified wine, unfortified wine and spirituous liquor may be transported with a purchase-transportation permit under G.S. 18B-403. The Commission may also authorize a distillery representative, in the course of his business, to transport and possess up to 10 gallons of spirituous liquor. (1923, c. 1, s. 25; C.S., s. 3411(y);

1937, c. 49, ss. 14, 16; c. 411; 1967, c. 222, ss. 1, 7; c. 1256, s. 3; 1969, c. 598, ss. 2, 3; c. 1018; 1971, c. 872, s. 1; 1977, c. 176, s. 1; c. 586; 1979, c. 607, s. 1; 1981, c. 412, s. 2; 1985, c. 757, s. 163.)

§ 18B-401. Manner of transportation.

(a)   Opened Containers. - It shall be unlawful for a person to transport fortified wine or spirituous liquor in the passenger area of a motor vehicle in other than the manufacturer's unopened original container. It shall be unlawful for a person who is driving a motor vehicle on a highway or public vehicular area to consume in the passenger area of that vehicle any malt beverage or unfortified wine. Violation of this subsection shall constitute a Class 3 misdemeanor.

(b)   Taxis. - It shall be unlawful for a person operating a for-hire passenger vehicle as defined in G.S. 20-4.01(27)b, to transport fortified wine or spirituous liquor unless the vehicle is transporting a paying passenger who owns the alcoholic beverage being transported. Not more than eight liters of fortified wine or spirituous liquor, or combination of the two, may be transported by each passenger. A violation of this subsection shall not be grounds for suspension of the driver's license for illegal transportation of intoxicating liquors under G.S. 20-16(a)(8).

(c)   Definitions. - The definitions in Chapter 20 of the General Statutes apply in interpreting this section. If the seal on a container of alcoholic beverages has been broken, it is opened within the meaning of this section. For purposes of this section, "passenger area of a motor vehicle" means the area designed to seat the driver and passengers and any area within the reach of a seated driver or passenger, including the glove compartment. In the case of a station wagon, hatchback or similar vehicle, the area behind the last upright back seat shall not be considered part of the passenger area. (1923, c. 1, s. 25; C.S., s. 3411(y); 1937, c. 49, ss. 14, 16; c. 411; 1967, c. 222, ss. 1, 7; c. 1256, s. 3; 1969, c. 598, ss. 2, 3; c. 1018; 1971, c. 872, s. 1; 1977, c. 176, s. 1; c. 586; 1979, c. 607, s. 1; 1981, c. 412, s. 2; c. 747, s. 45; 1983, c. 435, s. 7; 1989, c. 553, s. 3; 1993, c. 508, s. 4, c. 539, s. 312; 1994, Ex. Sess., c. 24, s. 14(c).)

§ 18B-402. Alcoholic beverages purchased out-of-State.

A person may bring into North Carolina alcoholic beverages purchased legally outside the jurisdiction of this State in the same amounts that may be legally transported within the State under G.S. 18B-400 or G.S. 18B-403, except that no more than four liters of spirituous liquor purchased outside this State may be brought into this State. (1923, c. 1, s. 25; C.S., s. 3411(y); 1937, c. 49, ss. 14, 16; c. 411; 1967, c. 222, ss. 1, 7; c. 1256, s. 3; 1969, c. 598, ss. 2, 3; c. 1018; 1971, c. 872, s. 1; 1977, c. 176, s. 1; c. 586; 1979, c. 607, s. 1; 1981, c. 412, s. 2; 1981 (Reg. Sess., 1982), c. 1262, s. 5.)

§ 18B-403. Purchase-transportation permit.

(a) Amounts. - With a purchase-transportation permit, a person may purchase and transport an amount of alcoholic beverages greater than the amount specified in G.S. 18B-303(a). A permit authorizes the holder to transport from the place of purchase to the destination within North Carolina indicated on the permit at one time the following amount of alcoholic beverages:

(1) A maximum of 100 liters of unfortified wine;

(2) A maximum of 40 liters of either fortified wine or spirituous liquor, or 40 liters of the two combined; or

(3) The amount of fortified wine or spirituous liquors specified on the purchase-transportation permit for a mixed beverage permittee.

(b) Issuance of Permit. - A purchase-transportation permit may be issued by:

(1) The local board chairman;

(2) A member of the local board;

(3) The general manager or supervisor of the local board; or

(4) The manager or assistant manager of an ABC store, if he is authorized to issue permits by the local board chairman.

(c) Disqualifications. - A purchase-transportation permit shall not be issued to a person who:

(1) Is not sufficiently identified or known to the issuer;

(2) Is known or shown to be an alcoholic or bootlegger;

(3) Has been convicted within the previous three years of an offense involving the sale, possession, or transportation of nontaxpaid alcoholic beverages; or

(4) Has been convicted within the previous three years of an offense involving the sale of alcoholic beverages without a permit.

(d) Form. - A purchase-transportation permit shall be issued on a printed form adopted by the Commission. The Commission shall adopt rules specifying the content of the permit form.

(e) Restrictions on Permit. - A purchase may be made only from the store named on the permit. One copy of the permit shall be kept by the issuing person, one by the purchaser, and one by the store from which the purchase is made. The purchaser shall display his copy of the permit to any law-enforcement officer upon request. A permit for the purchase and transportation of spirituous liquor may be issued only by an authorized agent of the local board for the jurisdiction in which the purchase will be made.

(f) Time. - A purchase-transportation permit is valid only until 9:30 P.M. on the date of purchase, which date shall be stated on the permit.

(g) Special Occasion Purchase-Transportation Permit. - When a person holds a special occasion for which a permit under G.S. 18B-1001(8) or (9) is required, the purchase-transportation permit issued to him may provide for the storage at and transportation to and from the site of the special occasion of unfortified wine, fortified wine, and spirituous liquor for a period of no more than 48 hours before and after the special occasion. The purchase-transportation permit authorizes that person to transport only the amounts of those alcoholic beverages authorized by subsection (a). The Commission may adopt rules to govern issuance of these extended purchase-transportation permits. (1969, c. 617, s. 1; 1971, c. 872, s. 1; 1973, c. 94; c. 819, s. 1; 1975, ss. 1-4; 1977, c. 176, ss. 1, 2, 4; 1979, c. 19, ss. 3, 4; c. 286, s. 1; c. 445, ss. 1, 3; c. 1076, ss. 1,

2, 3; 1981, c. 412, s. 2; 1981 (Reg. Sess., 1982), c. 1262, ss. 6-8; 1983, c. 457, s. 1.)

§ 18B-403.1. Purchase-transportation permit for keg or kegs of malt beverages.

(a) Purchase-Transportation. - A person who is not a permittee may purchase and transport for off-premises consumption a keg or kegs as defined in G.S. 18B-101(7c) after obtaining a purchase-transportation permit. Failure to obtain a purchase-transportation permit according to this section is a violation of G.S. 18B-303(b).

(b) Issuance. - A person holding a permit (permittee) pursuant to G.S. 18B-1001(2) shall issue a purchase-transportation permit for a keg or kegs of malt beverage to a purchaser. A copy of the purchase-transportation permit shall be maintained by the permittee for 90 days. Upon request by any person, the permittee shall maintain the permit for a requested period in excess of 90 days.

(c) Form. - A purchase-transportation permit shall be issued on a printed form adopted and provided by the Commission. The Commission shall adopt rules specifying the content of the permit form.

(d) Restrictions on Permit. - A purchase may be made only from the store named on the permit. One copy of the permit shall be kept by the purchaser and one by the permittee from whom the purchase is made. The purchaser shall display his copy of the permit to any law enforcement officer upon request.

(e) Violation. - The first violation of this section by a permittee shall result in a warning to the permittee. (2006-253, s. 3.1; 2010-122, s. 1.)

§ 18B-404. Additional provisions for purchase and transportation by mixed beverage permittees.

(a) Designated Employee. - A mixed beverages permittee may designate an employee to purchase and transport spirituous liquor as authorized by the permittee's permit.

(b)   Issuance. - If mixed beverages sales have been approved for an establishment under G.S. 18B-603(d1) or under G.S. 18B-603(e), or for an establishment located in a township in which mixed beverages have been approved the purchase-transportation permit for that establishment may be issued by the local board of any city located in the same county as the establishment, provided the city has approved the sale of mixed beverages. Otherwise a licensed establishment may obtain a mixed beverages purchase-transportation permit only from the local board for the jurisdiction in which it is located. If there is no ABC store within the establishment's jurisdiction, then the mixed beverages permittee shall obtain a mixed beverages purchase-transportation permit from the nearest and most convenient ABC store.

(c)   Designated Store. - A local board may designate a store within its system to make sales to mixed beverages permittees.

(d)   Size of Bottles. - A purchase-transportation permit for a mixed beverages permittee shall authorize the purchase and transportation only of 355 milliliter or larger containers. A purchase-transportation permit for a mixed beverages permittee who is also a guest room cabinet permittee may authorize the purchase and transportation of containers in sizes approved by the Commission. (1981, c. 412, s. 2; c. 747, ss. 46, 47; 1987, c. 136, s. 3; 1991, c. 459, s. 10; c. 565, ss. 5, 7; 1991 (Reg. Sess., 1992), c. 920, s. 2; 1999-462, s. 4; 2003-218, s. 3.)

§ 18B-405. Transportation by permittee.

The holder of a permit for the retail sale of malt beverages, unfortified wine, or fortified wine may transport in the course of his business any amount of the alcoholic beverage he is authorized to sell, without a purchase-transportation permit or a commercial transportation permit under G.S. 18B-1115. (1923, c. 1, s. 15; C.S., s. 3411(o); 1939, c. 158, s. 503; 1971, c. 872, s. 1; 1975, c. 411, s. 7; 1977, c. 70, s. 20; c. 176, s. 7; 1979, c. 286, s. 5; 1981, c. 412, s. 2; 1987, c. 136, s. 4.)

§ 18B-406. Unlawful transportation.

It shall be unlawful to transport a greater amount of alcoholic beverage than permitted by this Article, unless the transportation is authorized under Article 11. (1981, c. 412, s. 2.)

§§ 18B-407 through 18B-499. Reserved for future codification purposes.

Article 5.

Law Enforcement.

§ 18B-500. Alcohol law-enforcement agents.

(a) Appointment. - The Secretary of Public Safety shall appoint alcohol law-enforcement agents and other enforcement personnel. The Secretary of Public Safety may also appoint regular employees of the Commission as alcohol law-enforcement agents. Alcohol law-enforcement agents shall be designated as "alcohol law-enforcement agents". Persons serving as reserve alcohol law-enforcement agents are considered employees of the Alcohol Law Enforcement Section for workers' compensation purposes while performing duties assigned or approved by the Director of Alcohol Law Enforcement Section or the Director's designee.

(b) Subject Matter Jurisdiction. - After taking the oath prescribed for a peace officer, an alcohol law-enforcement agent shall have authority to arrest and take other investigatory and enforcement actions for any criminal offense. The primary responsibility of an agent shall be enforcement of the ABC laws, lottery laws, and Article 5 of Chapter 90 (The Controlled Substances Act); however, an agent may perform any law-enforcement duty assigned by the Secretary of Public Safety or the Governor.

(c) Territorial Jurisdiction. - An alcohol law-enforcement agent is a State officer with jurisdiction throughout the State.

(d) Service of Commission Orders. - Alcohol law-enforcement agents may serve and execute notices, orders, or demands issued by the Alcoholic Beverage Control Commission or the North Carolina State Lottery Commission for the surrender of permits or relating to any administrative proceeding. While serving and executing such notices, orders, or demands, alcohol law-enforcement agents shall have all the power and authority possessed by law-enforcement officers when executing an arrest warrant.

(e) Discharge. - Alcohol law-enforcement agents are subject to the discharge provisions of G.S. 18B-202.

(f) Repealed by Session Laws 1995, c. 507, s. 6.2(a).

(g) Shifting of Personnel From One District to Another. - The Director of the Alcohol Law Enforcement Section, under rules adopted by the Department of Public Safety may, from time to time, shift the forces from one district to another or consolidate more than one district force at any point for special purposes. Whenever an agent of the Alcohol Law Enforcement Section is transferred from one district to another for the convenience of the State or for reasons other than the request of the agent, the Department shall be responsible for transporting the household goods, furniture, and personal apparel of the agent and members of the agent's household. (1939, c. 158, s. 514; 1943, c. 400, s. 6; 1949, c. 974, ss. 11, 14; c. 1251, s. 4; 1951, c. 1056, s. 1; c. 1186, ss. 1, 2; 1953, c. 1207, ss. 2-4; 1957, c. 1440; 1961, c. 645; 1963, c. 426, ss. 1, 2, 4, 5, 12; 1967, c. 868; 1971, c. 872, s. 1; 1977, c. 70, s. 17; 1981, c. 412, s. 2; 1983, c. 629, s. 1; c. 768, ss. 25.1, 25.2; 1995, c. 466, s. 2; c. 507, s. 6.2(a); 2005-276, ss. 31.1(y), 31.1(z); 2005-344, ss. 10.1(b), 10.1(c); 2006-264, s. 35; 2011-145, s. 19.1(z); 2011-391, s. 43(j); 2012-83, s. 3.)

§ 18B-501. Local ABC officers.

(a) Appointment. - Except as provided in subsection (f), each local board shall hire one or more ABC enforcement officers. Local ABC enforcement officers shall be designated as "ABC Officers". The local board may designate one officer as the chief ABC officer for that board.

(b) Subject Matter Jurisdiction. - After taking the oath prescribed for a peace officer, a local ABC officer may arrest and take other investigatory and enforcement actions for any criminal offense; however, the primary responsibility of a local ABC officer is enforcement of the ABC laws and Article 5 of Chapter 90 (The Controlled Substances Act).

(c) Territorial Jurisdiction. - A local ABC officer has jurisdiction anywhere in the county in which he is employed except that a city ABC officer's territorial jurisdiction is subject to any limitation included in any local act governing that city ABC system. A local ABC officer may pursue outside his normal territorial jurisdiction anyone who commits an offense within that jurisdiction, as provided in G.S. 15A-402(d).

(d) Assisting Other Local Agencies. - The local ABC officers employed by a local board shall constitute a "law-enforcement agency" for purposes of G.S. 160A-288, and a local board shall have the same authority as a city or county governing body to approve cooperation between law-enforcement agencies under that section.

(e) Assisting State and Federal Enforcement. - A local ABC officer may assist State and federal law-enforcement agencies in the investigation of criminal offenses in North Carolina, under the following conditions:

(1) The local board employing the officer has adopted a resolution approving such assistance and stating the conditions under which it may be provided;

(2) The State or federal agency has made a written request for assistance from that local board, either for a particular investigation or for any investigation that might require assistance within a certain period of time;

(3) The local ABC officer is supervised by someone in the requesting agency; and

(4) As soon as practical after the assistance begins, an acknowledgement of the action is placed in the records of the local board.

A local ABC officer shall have territorial jurisdiction throughout North Carolina while assisting a State or federal agency under this section. While providing that assistance the officer shall continue to be considered an employee of the local board for purposes of salary, worker's compensation, and other benefits, unless a different arrangement is negotiated between the local board and the requesting agency.

(f) Contracts with Other Agencies. - Instead of hiring local ABC officers, a local board may contract to pay its enforcement funds to a sheriff's department, city police department, or other local law-enforcement agency for enforcement of the ABC laws within the law-enforcement agency's territorial jurisdiction. Enforcement agreements may be made with more than one agency at the same time. When such a contract for enforcement exists, the designated officers of the contracting law-enforcement agency shall have the same authority to inspect under G.S. 18B-502 that an ABC officer employed by that local board would have. An agency contracted to provide ABC law enforcement shall designate no more than five officers to conduct inspections pursuant to this section and G.S. 18B-502. If a city located in two or more counties approves the sale of some type of alcoholic beverage pursuant to the provisions of G.S. 18B-600(e4), and there are no local ABC boards established in the city and one of the counties in which the city is located, the local ABC board of any county in which the city is located may enter into an enforcement agreement with the city's police department for enforcement of the ABC laws within the entire city, including that portion of the city located in the county of the ABC board entering into the enforcement agreement.

(f1)   Accountability; Enforcement Reports. - To ensure accountability to the appointing authority and the Commission, every local board's ABC officers and those law enforcement agencies subject to an enforcement agreement entered into pursuant to subsection (f) of this section shall report to the local board, by the fifth business day of each month, on a form developed by the Commission, the following:

(1)   The number of arrests made for ABC law, Controlled Substance Act, or other violations, by category, at ABC permitted outlets.

(2)   The number of arrests made for ABC law, Controlled Substance Act, or other violations, by category, at other locations.

(3)   The number of agencies assisted with ABC law or controlled substance related matters.

(4)   The number of alcohol education and responsible server programs presented.

The local board shall submit a copy of the enforcement report to the appointing authority and the Commission not later than five business days after receipt of the enforcement report by the local board. The Commission shall publish this information, by local board and enforcement agency, on a public Internet Web site maintained by the Commission.

(g) Discharge. - Local ABC officers and the designated officers of agencies which contract with local boards for enforcement of the ABC laws are subject to the discharge and ineligibility provisions of G.S. 18B-202. (1949, c. 1251, s. 4; 1961, c. 645; 1963, c. 426, s. 2; 1967, c. 868; 1971, c. 872, s. 1; 1973, c. 29; 1977, c. 908; 1981, c. 412, s. 2; 1993, c. 193, s. 2; 1995, c. 466, ss. 3, 4; 2010-122, ss. 5, 6, 7(a).)

§ 18B-502. Inspection of licensed premises.

(a) Authority. - To procure evidence of violations of the ABC law, alcohol law-enforcement agents, employees of the Commission, local ABC officers, and officers of local law-enforcement agencies that have contracted to provide ABC enforcement under G.S. 18B-501(f) shall have authority to investigate the operation of each licensed premises for which an ABC permit has been issued, to make inspections that include viewing the entire premises, and to examine the books and records of the permittee. The inspection authorized by this section may be made at any time it reasonably appears that someone is on the premises. Alcohol law-enforcement agents are also authorized to be on the premises to the extent necessary to enforce the provisions of Article 68 of Chapter 143 of the General Statutes.

(b) Interference with Inspection. - Refusal by a permittee or by any employee of a permittee to permit officers to enter the premises to make an inspection authorized by subsection (a) shall be cause for revocation, suspension or other action against the permit of the permittee as provided in G.S. 18B-104. It shall be a Class 2 misdemeanor for any person to resist or obstruct an officer attempting to make a lawful inspection under this section. (1939, c. 158, s. 514; 1943, c. 400, s. 6; 1949, c. 974, ss. 11, 14; c. 1251, s. 4; 1951, c. 1056, s. 1; c. 1186, ss. 1, 2; 1953, c. 1207, ss. 2-4; 1957, c. 1440; 1961, c. 645; 1963, c. 426, ss. 1, 2, 4, 5, 12; 1967, c. 868; 1971, c. 872, s. 1; 1977, c. 70, s. 17; 1981, c. 412, s. 2; 1993, c. 539, s. 313; 1994, (Ex. Sess.), c. 24, s. 14(c); 1998-212, s. 19.11(f).)

§ 18B-503. Disposition of seized alcoholic beverages.

(a) Storage. - A law-enforcement officer who seizes alcoholic beverages as evidence of an ABC law violation shall provide for the storage of those alcoholic beverages until the commencement of the trial or administrative hearing relating to the violation, unless some other disposition is authorized under this section.

(b) Disposition Before Trial. - After giving notice to each defendant, to any other known owner, and to the Commission, a judge may order any of the following dispositions of alcoholic beverages seized as evidence of an ABC law violation:

(1) The destruction of any malt beverages except that amount needed for evidence at trial.

(2) The sale of any alcoholic beverages other than malt beverages or nontaxpaid alcoholic beverages, and other than any alcoholic beverages needed for evidence at trial, if the trial is likely to be delayed for more than 90 days, or if the quantity or nature of the alcoholic beverages is such that storage is impractical or unduly expensive.

(3) The destruction of the alcoholic beverages if storage or sale is not practical.

(4) Continued storage of the alcoholic beverages.

(c) Disposition After Trial. - After the criminal charge is resolved, a judge may order the following dispositions of seized alcoholic beverages:

(1) If the owner or possessor of the alcoholic beverages is found guilty of a criminal charge relating to those alcoholic beverages, the judge may order the sale or destruction of any alcoholic beverages that were held until trial.

(2) If the owner or possessor of the alcoholic beverages is found not guilty, or if charges are dismissed or otherwise resolved in favor of the owner or possessor, the judge shall order the alcoholic beverages returned to that owner or possessor, except as provided in subdivision (3).

(3) If the owner or possessor of the alcoholic beverages is found not guilty, or if charges are otherwise resolved in favor of the owner or possessor, but possession of the alcoholic beverages by that owner or possessor would be unlawful, the judge shall order the alcoholic beverages either sold or destroyed.

(4) If ownership of the alcoholic beverages remains uncertain after trial or after the charges have been dismissed, the judge may order the alcoholic

beverages held, or the alcoholic beverages sold and the proceeds held, for a specified time, until ownership of the alcoholic beverages can be determined.

(d) Holding for Administrative Hearings. - If alcoholic beverages used as evidence in a criminal proceeding are also needed as evidence at an administrative hearing, a judge shall not order any of the dispositions set out in subsection (c), but shall order the alcoholic beverages held for the administrative hearing and for a determination of final disposition by the Commission. The Commission may, before or after an administrative hearing, order any of the dispositions authorized under subsections (b) and (c). If no related criminal proceeding has commenced, the Commission shall not order sale or destruction of alcoholic beverages until notice has been given to the district attorney for the district where the alcoholic beverages were seized or any violation of ABC laws related to the seizure of the alcoholic beverages is likely to be prosecuted.

(e) Sale Procedure. - The sale of unfortified wine or fortified wine shall be by public auction unless those wines would likely become spoiled or lose value in the time required to arrange a public auction. If spoilage or loss of value is likely, the judge ordering the sale or the Commission may authorize sale at the prevailing wholesale price, as determined by the Commission, to one or more persons holding the appropriate retail wine permits in the county in which the wine was seized, or in a neighboring county if there are no such persons in the county in which the wine was seized. Spirituous liquor may be sold only to the local ABC board serving the city or county in which the liquor was seized, or, if there is no local board for that city or county, to the nearest local board. The sale price shall be at least ten percent (10%) less than the price the local board would pay for the same liquor bought through the State warehouse.

(f) Sale Proceeds. - An agency selling alcoholic beverages seized under the provisions of this Chapter shall keep the proceeds in a separate account until some other disposition is ordered by a judge or the Commission. In a criminal proceeding, if the owner or possessor of the alcoholic beverages is found guilty of a violation relating to seizure of the alcoholic beverages, if the owner or possessor is found not guilty or the charge is dismissed or otherwise resolved in favor of the owner or possessor, but the possession of the alcoholic beverages by that owner or possessor would be unlawful, or if the ownership of the alcoholic beverages cannot be determined, the proceeds from the sale of those alcoholic beverages shall be paid to the school fund of the county in which the alcoholic beverages were seized. If the owner or possessor of alcoholic beverages seized for violation of the ABC laws is found not guilty of criminal charges relating to the seizure of those beverages or the charge is dismissed or otherwise resolved in favor of the owner or possessor, and if possession of the alcoholic beverages by that owner or possessor was lawful when the beverages were seized, the proceeds from the sale of those alcoholic beverages shall be paid to the owner or possessor. The agency making the sale may deduct and retain from the amount to be placed in the county school fund the costs of storing the seized alcoholic beverages and of conducting the sale, but may not deduct those costs from the amount to be turned over to an owner or possessor of the alcoholic beverages.

(g)   Court Action by Owner. - Any person who claims any of the following resulting from the seizure of alcoholic beverages may bring an action in the superior court of the county in which the alcoholic beverages were seized:

(1)   To be the owner of alcoholic beverages that are wrongfully held.

(2)   To be the owner of alcoholic beverages that are needed as evidence in another proceeding.

(3)   To be entitled to proceeds from a sale of seized alcoholic beverages.

(4)   To be entitled to restitution for alcoholic beverages wrongfully destroyed. (1923, c. 1, s. 12; C.S., s. 3411(l); 1939, c. 12; 1941, c. 310; 1957, c. 1235, s. 3; 1971, c. 872, s. 1; 1981, c. 412, s. 2; 1993, c. 415, s. 5.)

§ 18B-504. Forfeiture.

(a)   Property Subject to Forfeiture. - The following kinds of property shall be subject to forfeiture:

(1)   Motor vehicles, boats, airplanes, and all other conveyances used to transport nontaxpaid alcoholic beverages in violation of the ABC laws;

(2)   Containers for alcoholic beverages which are manufactured, possessed, sold, or transported in violation of the ABC laws; and

(3)   Equipment or ingredients used in the manufacture of alcoholic beverages in violation of the ABC laws.

(b)   Exemption for Forfeiture. - Property which may be possessed lawfully shall not be subject to forfeiture when it was used unlawfully by someone other than the owner of the property and the owner did not consent to the unlawful use.

(c)   Seizure of Property. - If property subject to forfeiture has not already been seized as part of an arrest or search, a law-enforcement officer may apply to a judge for an order authorizing seizure of that property. An order for seizure may be issued only after criminal process has been issued for an ABC law violation in connection with that property. The order shall describe the property to be seized and shall state the facts establishing probable cause to believe that the property is subject to forfeiture.

(d)   Custody until Trial. - A law-enforcement officer seizing property subject to forfeiture shall provide for its safe storage until trial. The officer may destroy stills and perishable materials seized under subdivision (a)(3), if storage is impractical and if the absence of the property will not be likely to adversely affect the defendant's right to defend against the charge that is the basis for the forfeiture. If the officer having custody of the property is satisfied that it will be returned at the time of trial, he may return the property to the owner upon receiving a bond for the value of the property, signed by sufficient sureties. If the property is not returned at the time of trial, the full amount of the bond shall be forfeited to the court. Property which it is unlawful to possess may not be returned to the owner.

(e)   Disposition after Trial. - The presiding judge in a criminal proceeding for violation of ABC laws may take the following actions after resolution of a charge against the owner or possessor of property subject to forfeiture under this section:

(1)   If the owner or possessor of the property is found guilty of an ABC offense, the judge may order the property forfeited.

(2)   If the owner or possessor of the property is found not guilty, or if the charge is dismissed or otherwise resolved in favor of the owner or possessor, the judge shall order the property returned to the owner or possessor.

(3)   If ownership of the property remains uncertain after trial, the judge may order the property held for a specified time to determine ownership. If the judge finds that ownership cannot be determined with reasonable effort, the judge shall order the property forfeited.

(4) Regardless of the disposition of the charge, if the property is something that may not be possessed lawfully, the judge shall order it forfeited.

(5) If the property is also needed as evidence at an administrative hearing, the judge shall provide that the order does not go into effect until the Commission determines that the property is no longer needed for the administrative proceeding.

(f) Disposition of Forfeited Property. - A judge ordering forfeiture of property may order any one of the following dispositions:

(1) Sale at public auction;

(2) Sale at auction after notice to certain named individuals or groups, if only a limited number of people would have use for that property;

(3) Delivery to a named State or local law-enforcement agency, if the property is not suited for sale, with preference to be given in the following order, to: the agency that seized the property, the ALE Section, the Commission, the local board of the jurisdiction in which the property was seized, and the Department of Justice; or

(4) Destruction, if possession of the property would be unlawful and it could not be used or is not wanted for law enforcement, or if sale or other disposition is not practical.

(g) Proceeds of Sale. - If forfeited property is sold, the proceeds of that sale shall be paid to the school fund of the county in which the property was seized, except as provided in subsection (h). Before placing the proceeds in the school fund the agency making the sale may deduct and retain the costs of storing the property and conducting the sale.

(h) Innocent Parties. - At any time before forfeiture is ordered, an owner of seized property or a holder of a security interest in seized property, other than the defendant, may apply to protect his interest in the property. The application may be made to any judge who has jurisdiction to try the offense with which the property is associated. If the judge finds that the property owner or holder of a security interest did not consent to the unlawful use of the property, and that the property may be possessed lawfully by the owner or holder, the judge may order:

(1) That the property be returned to the owner, if it is not needed as evidence at trial;

(2) That the property be returned to the owner following trial or other resolution of the case; or

(3) That, if the property is sold following trial, a specified sum be paid from the proceeds of that sale to the holder of the security interest.

(i) Defendant Unavailable. - When property is seized for forfeiture, but the owner is unknown, the district attorney may seek forfeiture under this section by an action in rem against the property. If the owner is known and has been charged with an offense, but is unavailable for trial, the district attorney may seek forfeiture either by an action in rem against the property or by motion in the criminal action.

(j) When No Charge is Made. - Any owner of property seized for forfeiture may apply to a judge to have the property returned to him if no criminal charge has been made in connection with that property within a reasonable time after seizure. The judge may not order the return of the property if possession by the owner would be unlawful. (1923, c. 1, s. 6; C.S., s. 3411(f); 1927, c. 18; 1945, c. 635; 1951, c. 850; 1955, c. 560; 1957, c. 1235, s. 1; 1969, c. 789; 1971, c. 872, s. 1; 1977, c. 854, s. 2; 1981, c. 412, s. 2; c. 747, s. 48; 1993, c. 415, s. 6; 2011-145, s. 19.1(q).)

§ 18B-505. Restitution.

When a person is convicted of a violation of the ABC laws, the court may order him to make restitution to any law-enforcement agency for reasonable expenditures made in purchasing alcoholic beverages from him or his agent as part of an investigation leading to his conviction. (1981, c. 412, s. 2.)

§§ 18B-506 through 18B-599. Reserved for future codification purposes.

Article 6.

Elections.

§ 18B-600. Places eligible to hold alcoholic beverage elections.

(a) Kinds of Elections. - The following kinds of alcoholic beverage elections shall be permitted:

(1) Malt beverage;

(2) Unfortified wine;

(3) ABC store; and

(4) Mixed beverage.

(b) County Elections. - Any county may hold a malt beverage, unfortified wine, or ABC store election. A county may hold a mixed beverage election only if the county already operates at least one county ABC store or a county election on ABC stores is to be held at the same time as the mixed beverage election.

(c) City Malt Beverage and Unfortified Wine Elections. - A city may hold a malt beverage or unfortified wine election only if the county in which the city is located has already held such an election, the vote in the last county election was against the sale of that kind of alcoholic beverage, and:

(1) The city has a population of 500 or more; or

(2) The city operates an ABC store.

(d) City ABC Store Elections. - A city may hold an ABC store election only if:

(1) The city has at least 1,000 registered voters; and

(2) The county in which the city is located does not operate ABC stores.

(e) City Mixed Beverage Elections. - A city may hold a mixed beverage election if the city has at least 500 registered voters. Provided, that if a city that qualifies for an election under this subsection approves the sale of mixed beverages, mixed beverages permittees in the city may purchase liquor from the ABC store designated by the local ABC board that has been approved by the Commission for this purpose.

(e1)   Small City Mixed Beverage Elections. - A city may also hold a mixed beverage election if the city has at least 300 registered voters and is located in a county with at least one other city that has approved the sale of mixed beverages. Provided, that if a city that qualifies for an election under this subsection approves the sale of mixed beverages, mixed beverages permittees in the smaller city may purchase liquor from the ABC store designated by any local ABC board in any other city that has approved the sale of mixed beverages.

This subsection shall not apply to Alamance, Avery, Burke, Caldwell, Carteret, Cleveland, Henderson, Onslow, Polk, Robeson, Rowan, Rutherford, and Wilkes Counties.

(e2)   Ski Resorts ABC Elections. - Notwithstanding any other provisions of this section, any city that provides governmental services to as many as 1,000 snow skiers weekly during the normal ski season from December 1 through March 15, may hold an election authorized by subdivision (a)(1), (2), or (4) of this section. If the sale of mixed beverages is approved, purchase-transportation permits shall be issued and the sales of liquor shall be made by any local board designated by the State ABC Commission.

(e3)   Small Town Mixed Beverage Elections. - A town may hold a mixed beverage election if the town has at least 200 registered voters and is located in a county bordering the Neuse River and Pamlico Sound that has not approved the sale of mixed beverages and that county has only one city that has approved the sale of mixed beverages. Provided, that if a town that qualifies for an election under this subsection approves the sale of mixed beverages, mixed beverages permittees in the town may purchase liquor from the ABC store designated by any local ABC board in any other city that has approved the sale of mixed beverages.

(e4)   Multicounty/City ABC Elections. - If a city is located in two or more counties, the following provisions shall apply:

(1)   The city may hold a malt beverage or unfortified wine election if any county in which a portion of the city is located has already held such an election,

the vote in the last election of the particular type was against the sale of that type of alcoholic beverage, and the city has a population of 500 or more.

(2) The city may hold a mixed beverage election if the city has at least 500 registered voters and a county in which a portion of the city is located operates ABC stores, or a municipality in either county in which the city is located operates an ABC store.

(3) If an election is held by a city under this subsection, all of the city voters may vote in the election. If the vote is for approval, alcoholic beverages may be sold on the basis of that approval and under the provisions of this Chapter. If the sale of mixed beverages is approved, the mixed beverage permittees shall purchase their liquor from one or more ABC stores located within the city that have been designated by the local boards for those purchases. The remaining gross receipts shall be distributed in accordance with existing law applicable to those ABC stores, except that after the applicable distributions have been made pursuant to G.S. 18B-805(b), (c), and (d), the local share of the mixed beverages surcharge and the guest room cabinet surcharge required by G.S. 18B-804(b)(8) and (9) shall be distributed one-half to the general fund of the city where the mixed beverage permittees are located and one-half to the local ABC boards from whose stores liquor is purchased.

(e5) Small Resort Town ABC Elections. - A town may hold a mixed beverage election if it:

(1) Was incorporated after 1990 and prior to the effective date of this subsection;

(2) Has at least 100 residents;

(3) Is located in a county that borders another state and that has two other municipalities which have ABC stores; and

(4) At the time of the election, has corporate boundaries that border or include land in three counties.

Provided, that if a town that qualifies for an election under this subsection approves the sale of mixed beverages, mixed beverages permittees in the town may purchase liquor from the ABC store designated by any local ABC board in any other city that has approved the sale of mixed beverages.

(f) Township Elections. - An election may be called on any of the propositions listed in G.S. 18B-602 in any township located within:

(1) A county where ABC stores have heretofore been established by petition pursuant to law.

(2) A county where ABC stores have been established pursuant to law, in which county according to data from the North Carolina Department of Commerce: (i) one-third or more of the employment is travel related, (ii) spending on travel exceeds four hundred million dollars ($400,000,000) per year, and where the entirety of two townships consists of one island (and several smaller islands not making up more than one percent (1%) of the total land area of the two townships) where that island:

a. Has a population of 4,000 or over according to the most recent decennial federal census;

b. Is located with one side facing the ocean and another side facing a coastal sound.

(3) Repealed by Session Laws 2004-203, s. 24, effective August 17, 2004.

An election may be called on any of the propositions listed in G.S. 18B-602(a), (d), and (h) in any township located within a county where the population of all cities in the county that have previously approved the sale of any kind of alcoholic beverages comprises more than twenty percent (20%) of the total county population as of the most recent federal census. In the case of subdivision (2) of this section, an election may be called in the two townships voting together on the proposition contained in G.S. 18B-602(h).

The election shall be held by the county board of elections upon request of the county board of commissioners or upon petition of twenty-five percent (25%) of the registered voters of the township, or in the case of subdivision (2) of this section, of the two townships taken together. The election shall be conducted and the results determined in the same manner as county elections held under this Article. For purposes of this Article, townships holding any election under this subsection shall be treated on the same basis as counties, and municipalities located within those townships shall be treated on the same basis as cities. In the case of an election under subdivision (2) of this subsection, the votes of the two townships counted together shall determine the result of the election.

For purposes of this subsection, the name and boundary of a township is as it is shown on the Redistricting Census 2000 TIGER Files with modifications made by the Legislative Services Office on its computer database as of May 1, 2001.

In any township election held under this subsection, the area within any incorporated municipality is excluded, and no permits may be issued under this subsection in any excluded area.

In order for an establishment to qualify for a permit under this subsection, the establishment's gross receipts from food and nonalcoholic beverages shall be greater than its gross receipts from alcoholic beverages.

(g) Beautification District Elections. - In a county where ABC stores have been approved by an election and a beautification district has been created after May, 1984, and prior to June 30, 1990, an election authorized by subsection (a) of this section may be called in the beautification district. The election shall be called in accordance with G.S. 18B-601(b), conducted, and the results determined in the same manner as county elections held under this Article. For purposes of this Article, beautification districts holding any election shall be treated on the same basis as counties, and municipalities located within those beautification districts shall be treated on the same basis as cities.

(h) Railroad Passenger Terminus Location Elections. - Notwithstanding any other provision of this section, any city or town that is the passenger terminus of a rail line that carries at least 60,000 passengers annually may hold an election authorized by subdivisions (a)(1) and (a)(2) of this section. Any election held under this subsection shall be for the on-premises sale of malt beverages and the on-premises sale of unfortified wine pursuant to G.S. 18B-602(a)(2) and G.S. 18B-602(d)(2). (1937, c. 49, ss. 25, 26; c. 431; 1947, c. 1084, ss. 1, 2, 4; 1951, c. 999, ss. 1, 2; 1957, c. 816; 1963, c. 265, ss. 1-3; 1965, c. 506; 1969, c. 647, s. 1; 1971, c. 872, s. 1; 1973, cc. 32, 33; 1977, c. 149, s. 1; c. 182, s. 2; 1977, 2nd Sess., c. 1138, s. 15; 1979, c. 140, ss. 2, 3; c. 609, s. 1; c. 683, s. 13; 1979, 2nd Sess., c. 1174; 1981, c. 412, s. 2; c. 747, s. 49; 1983, c. 113, s. 1; 1983, c. 457, s. 2; 1985 (Reg. Sess., 1986), c. 919, s. 1; 1987, c. 766; 1989, c. 77; c. 400, s. 6; 1991 (Reg. Sess., 1992), c. 976, s. 1; 1993, c. 193, s. 1; 1995, c. 148, s. 1; 2001-515, s. 4; 2003-218, s. 1; 2004-203, s. 24; 2005-336, s. 1; 2007-386, s. 1; 2010-122, ss. 7(b), 8.)

§ 18B-601. Election procedure.

(a) Generally. - Except as otherwise provided in this section, an alcoholic beverage election shall be conducted in the same manner and under the same rules as a referendum under Chapter 163.

(b) How County Election Called. - A county alcoholic beverage election shall be conducted by the county board of elections. When a county is eligible to hold an election under G.S. 18B-600, the county board of elections shall hold the election upon receiving either:

(1) A written request for an election from the governing body of the county; or

(2) A petition requesting an election signed by at least thirty-five percent (35%) of the voters registered in the county at the time the petition was initiated.

(c) How City Election Called. - A city alcoholic beverage election shall be conducted by the county board of elections or, in the case of a city authorized under Chapter 163 to conduct its own elections, by the city board of elections. When a city is eligible to hold an election under G.S. 18B-600, the board of elections shall hold the election upon receiving either:

(1) A written request for an election from the city governing body; or

(2) A petition requesting an election signed by at least thirty-five percent (35%) of the voters registered in the city at the time the petition was initiated.

(d) Form of Request. - A request or petition for a malt beverage election shall state which of the four propositions in G.S. 18B-602(a) are to be voted upon. A request or petition for an unfortified wine election shall state which of the three propositions in G.S. 18B-602(d) are to be voted upon. More than one kind of alcoholic beverage election may be included in a single request or petition.

(e) Petitions. - A petition for an election shall be on a form provided by the appropriate local board of elections and shall contain the signature, name, address and precinct of each voter who signs. A petition shall be considered initiated at the time the form is delivered by the board of elections to the person who requests it. Within 72 hours after the petition is initiated, the board of elections shall certify the number of registered voters in the city or county at the time it was initiated. The petition shall be returned to the board of elections within 90 days of the time it is initiated. Failure to return the petition within that time shall render it void. The board of elections shall determine the sufficiency of the petition within 30 days after it is returned.

(f)   Election Date. - The board of elections shall conduct and set the date for the alcoholic beverage election in accordance with G.S. 163-287.

(g)   Registration. - No separate registration shall be required to vote in an alcoholic beverage election. Registration shall be closed for an alcoholic beverage election in the same manner and under the same schedule as for any other election.

(h)   Notice. - The board of elections shall give notice of an alcoholic beverage election and notice of the close of registration in the same manner and under the same schedule as for any other election.

(i)   Observers. - The proponents and opponents for an alcoholic beverage election, as determined by the local board of elections, shall have the right to appoint two observers to attend each voting place. The persons authorized to appoint observers shall, three days before the election, submit in writing to the chief judge of each precinct a signed list of the observers appointed for that precinct. The persons appointed as observers shall be registered voters of the precinct for which appointed. The chief judge and judges for the precinct may for good cause reject any appointee and require that another be appointed. Observers shall do no electioneering at the voting place nor in any manner impede the voting process, interfere or communicate with or observe any voter in casting his ballot. Observers shall be permitted in the voting place to make such observation and to take such notes as they may desire. (1937, c. 49, ss. 25, 26; c. 431; 1947, c. 1084, ss. 1, 2, 4; 1951, c. 999, ss. 1, 2; 1957, c. 816; 1963, c. 265, ss. 1-3; 1965, c. 506; 1969, c. 647, s. 1; 1971, c. 872, s. 1; 1973, cc. 32, 33; 1977, c. 149, s. 1; c. 182, s. 2; 1977, 2nd Sess., c. 1138, s. 15; 1979, c. 140, ss. 2, 3; c. 609, s. 1; c. 683, s. 13; 1979, 2nd Sess., c. 1174; 1981, c. 412, s. 2; 1985, c. 705, ss. 1, 2.1; 1987, c. 14; 1993 (Reg. Sess., 1994), c. 762, s. 8; 2013-381, s. 10.3.)

§ 18B-602. Form of ballots.

(a)   Malt Beverage Elections. - Any one or more of the propositions listed below may be placed on the ballot for a malt beverage election. Each voter may vote on each proposition on the ballot. The propositions to be used shall be chosen by the governing body or petitioner requesting the election. The propositions shall read as follows:

(1)   To permit the "on-premises" and "off-premises" sale of malt beverages.

[] FOR

[] AGAINST

(2)   To permit the "on-premises" sale only of malt beverages.

[] FOR

[] AGAINST

(3)   To permit the "off-premises" sale only of malt beverages.

[] FOR

[] AGAINST

(4)   To permit the "on-premises" sale of malt beverages by Class A hotels, motels, and restaurants only; and to permit "off-premises" sales by other permittees.

[] FOR

[] AGAINST

(b)   Determining Results of Malt Beverage Election. - The kind of malt beverage sales described in each proposition that receives a majority of votes "FOR" shall be allowed. If propositions (2) and (4) are both on the ballot and (2) receives a majority of votes "FOR," then sales shall be permitted according to that proposition regardless of the vote on (4). If one of the propositions receiving a majority of votes "FOR" is proposition (1), then the kind of sales described in that proposition shall be allowed regardless of the vote on any other proposition at that election.

(c)   Subsequent Malt Beverage Elections. - A subsequent election in which a majority votes "AGAINST" malt beverage proposition (1) shall not affect the legality of sales that have previously been approved under proposition (2), (3), or (4). A subsequent election in which a majority votes "AGAINST" malt beverage proposition (2) or (3) shall not affect the legality of sales that have previously been approved under proposition (4).

(d)   Unfortified Wine Elections. - Any one or more of the propositions listed below may be placed on the ballot for an unfortified wine election. Each voter may vote on each proposition on the ballot. The propositions to be used shall be chosen by the governing body or petitioner requesting the election. The propositions shall read as follows:

(1)   To permit the "on-premises" and "off-premises" sale of unfortified wine.

[] FOR

[] AGAINST

(2)   To permit the "on-premises" sale only of unfortified wine.

[] FOR

[] AGAINST

(3)   To permit the "off-premises" sale only of unfortified wine.

[] FOR

[] AGAINST

(e)   Determining Results of Unfortified Wine Election. - The kind of unfortified wine sales described in each proposition that receives a majority of votes "FOR" shall be allowed. If one of the propositions receiving a majority of votes "FOR" is proposition (1), then the kind of sales described in that proposition shall be allowed, regardless of the vote on any other proposition at that election.

(f)   Subsequent Unfortified Wine Election. - A subsequent election in which a majority votes "AGAINST" unfortified wine proposition (1) shall not affect the legality of sales previously approved under proposition (2) or (3).

(g)   ABC Store Elections. - The ballot for an ABC store election shall state the proposition as follows:

To permit the operation of ABC stores.

[] FOR

[] AGAINST

(h) Mixed Beverage Elections. - The ballot for a mixed beverage election shall state the proposition as follows:

To permit the sale of mixed beverages in hotels, restaurants, private clubs, community theatres, and convention centers.

[] FOR

[] AGAINST

(1947, c. 1084, ss. 1, 2, 4; 1951, c. 999, ss. 1, 2; 1957, c. 816; 1963, c. 265, ss. 1-3; 1965, c. 506; 1969, c. 647, s. 1; 1971, c. 872, s. 1; 1973, c. 33; 1977, c. 149, s. 1; c. 182, s. 2; 1979, c. 140, s. 3; c. 683, s. 13; 1981, c. 412, s. 2; 1981 (Reg. Sess., 1982), c. 1262, s. 9; 1983, c. 583, s. 6.)

§ 18B-603. Effect of alcoholic beverage elections on issuance of permits.

(a) Malt Beverage Elections. - If a malt beverage election is held under G.S. 18B-602(a) and the sale of malt beverages is approved, the Commission may issue permits to qualified persons and establishments in the jurisdiction that held the election as follows:

(1) If on-premises sales are approved, the Commission may issue on-premises malt beverage permits.

(2) If off-premises sales are approved, the Commission may issue off-premises malt beverage permits.

(3) If both on-premises and off-premises sales are approved, the Commission may issue both on-premises and off-premises malt beverage permits.

(4) If the kinds of sales described in G.S. 18B-602(a)(4) are approved, the Commission may issue on-premises malt beverage permits to restaurants and hotels only and off-premises malt beverage permits to other permittees.

(b) Unfortified Wine Elections. - If an unfortified wine election is held under G.S. 18B-602(d) and the sale of unfortified wine is approved, the Commission may issue permits to qualified persons and establishments in the jurisdiction that held the election as follows:

(1) If on-premises sales are approved, the Commission may issue on-premises unfortified wine permits.

(2) If off-premises sales are approved, the Commission may issue off-premises unfortified wine permits.

(3) If both on-premises and off-premises sales are approved, the Commission may issue both on-premises and off-premises unfortified wine permits.

(c) ABC Store Elections. - If an ABC store election is held under G.S. 18B-602(g) and the establishment of ABC stores is approved, each of the following shall be authorized in the jurisdiction that held the election:

(1) The jurisdiction that held the election may establish and operate ABC stores in the manner described in Articles 7 and 8.

(2) The Commission may issue on-premises and off-premises fortified wine and unfortified wine permits to qualified persons and establishments in that jurisdiction, regardless of any unfortified wine election or any local act, except that neither on-premises nor off-premises unfortified wine permits may be issued in a jurisdiction if:

a. The jurisdiction approved ABC stores before January 1, 1982;

b. The jurisdiction held an unfortified wine election before January 1, 1982; and

c. In that unfortified wine election, the jurisdiction did not approve either on-premises or off-premises sales of unfortified wine.

(3) The Commission may issue brown-bagging permits to restaurants, hotels, and community theatres in the county in which the election was held, whether the election was held by the county or by a city or other jurisdiction within the county. Brown-bagging permits may not be issued, however, for restaurants, hotels, or community theatres in any jurisdiction in which the sale of mixed beverages has been approved.

(d) Mixed Beverage Elections. - If a mixed beverage election is held under G.S. 18B-602(h) and the sale of mixed beverages is approved, the Commission may issue permits to qualified persons and establishments in the jurisdiction that held the election as follows:

(1) The Commission may issue mixed beverage permits.

(2) The Commission may issue on-premises malt beverage, unfortified wine, and fortified wine permits for establishments with mixed beverage permits, regardless of any other election or any local act concerning sales of those kinds of alcoholic beverages.

(3) The Commission may issue off-premises malt beverage permits to any establishment that meets the requirements under G.S. 18B-1001(2) in any township or incorporated municipality which has voted to permit the sale of mixed beverages, regardless of any other local act concerning sales of those kinds of alcoholic beverages. The Commission may also issue off-premises unfortified wine permits to any establishment that meets the requirements under G.S. 18B-1001(4) in any township or incorporated municipality which has voted to permit the sale of mixed beverages, regardless of any other local act concerning sales of those kinds of alcoholic beverages.

(4) The Commission may issue brown-bagging permits for private clubs and congressionally chartered veterans organizations but may no longer issue and may not renew brown-bagging permits for restaurants, hotels, and community theatres. A restaurant, hotel, or community theatre may not be issued a mixed beverage permit under subdivision (1) until it surrenders its brown-bagging permit.

(5) The Commission may continue to issue culinary permits for establishments that do not have mixed beverage permits. An establishment may not be issued a mixed beverage permit under subdivision (1) until it surrenders its culinary permit.

(d1) In any county in which the sale of mixed beverages has been approved in elections in at least three cities that, combined, contain more than two-thirds the total county population as of the most recent federal census, the county board of commissioners may by resolution approve the sale of mixed beverages throughout the county, and the Commission may issue permits as if mixed beverages had been approved in a county election.

(d2) If a county or city holds a mixed beverage election and an ABC store election at the same time and the voters do not approve the establishment of an ABC store, the Commission may issue mixed beverages permits in that county or city. The mixed beverages purchase-transportation permit authorized by G.S. 18B-404(b) shall be issued by a local board operating a store located in the county.

(e) Mixed Beverages at Airports. - When the sale of mixed beverages has been approved in a city election, the Commission may also issue permits under subsection (d) for qualified establishments outside the city but within the same county, if:

(1) The establishment is on the property of an airport;

(2) The airport is operated by the city or by an airport authority in which the city participates; and

(3) The airport services planes which board at least 150,000 passengers annually.

(f) Permits Not Dependent on Elections. - The Commission may issue the following kinds of permits without approval at an election:

(1) Special occasion permits;

(2) Limited special occasion permits;

(3) Brown-bagging permits for private clubs and congressionally chartered veterans organizations;

(4) Culinary permits, except as restricted by subdivision (d)(5);

(5) Special one-time permits issued under G.S. 18B-1002;

(6) All permits listed in G.S. 18B-1100;

(7) The permits authorized by G.S. 18B-1001(1), (3), (5), and (10) for tourism ABC establishments;

(8) The permits authorized by G.S. 18B-1001(1), (3), (5), and (10) for tourism resorts;

(9) The permits authorized by G.S. 18B-1001(1), (3), (5), and (10) for historic ABC establishments.

(f1) Reserved for future codification purposes.

(f2) (See note) Permits for Special ABC Areas. - The Commission may issue the permits provided for in G.S. 18B-1001(1), G.S. 18B-1001(2), G.S. 18B-1001(3), G.S. 18B-1001(4), G.S. 18B-1001(5), G.S. 18B-1001(6), and G.S. 18B-1001(10) to qualified persons and establishments located within a Special ABC area as defined in G.S. 18B-101, provided that: (i) if such area is a municipal corporation, the area shall conduct an election authorized by subdivision (a)(4) of G.S. 18B-600, which election may be held regardless of the number of registered voters located within the municipal corporation; or (ii) if such area is unincorporated but has within such area a private association or club, the board of such private association or club shall call and conduct a special meeting at which meeting a majority of private association members, club members, lot and home owners, votes and approves the sale of mixed beverages, and the board certifies the results of such meeting to the Alcoholic Beverage Control Commission. The mixed beverages purchase-transportation permit authorized by G.S. 18B-404(b) shall be issued by a local board operating a store located in the same county as the Special ABC area.

(g) Miscellaneous. - The definitions in G.S. 18B-1000 shall apply to this section.

(h) Permits Based on Existing Permits. - In any county which borders on the Atlantic Ocean and where (i) the sale of malt beverage on and off premises, the sale of unfortified wine on and off premises, the sale of mixed beverages, and the operation of an ABC system has been allowed in at least six cities in the county, or in any county adjacent to that county in which an ABC system has been allowed, or (ii) the sale of malt beverage on and off premises, the sale of unfortified wine on and off premises, the sale of mixed beverages, and the operation of an ABC system has been allowed in at least eight cities in the county, the Commission may issue permits to sports clubs as defined in G.S. 18B-1000(8) throughout the county.

The Commission may issue the following permits:

(1)   On and Off Premises Malt Beverage;

(2)   On and Off Premises Unfortified Wine;

(3)   On and Off Premises Fortified Wine; or

(4)   Mixed Beverages.

The Commission may also issue on-premises malt beverage, unfortified wine, fortified wine and mixed beverages permits to a sports club located in a county adjacent to any county that has approved the sale of mixed beverages pursuant to G.S. 18B-603(d1), if the county in which the sports club is located borders another state and has at least one city that has approved the sale of mixed beverages. Sports clubs holding mixed beverages permits shall purchase their spirituous liquor at the nearest ABC system store that is located in the county.

The Commission may further issue on-premises malt beverage and on-premises unfortified wine permits to a sports club located in a county bordering on another state that is adjacent to any county in which permits were issued pursuant to this subsection prior to August 1, 1993. The sports clubs must be located in the unincorporated areas of a county, in which the sale of malt beverages and unfortified wine is not permitted, and where there are six or more municipalities in that county where the sale of malt beverages and unfortified wine is permitted. (1947, c. 1084, s. 3; 1969, c. 647, s. 2; 1971, c. 872, s. 1; 1981, c. 412, s. 2; c. 589; 1981 (Reg. Sess., 1982), c. 1240; 1983, c. 113, s. 2; 1985, c. 689, s. 7; 1987, c. 136, ss. 5, 6; c. 307, s. 2; c. 443, s. 2; 1989, c. 629, s. 2; 1991 (Reg. Sess., 1992), c. 920, ss. 11, 13; 1993, c. 415, ss. 7-9; 1995, c. 466, s. 5; 1999-456, s. 10; 1999-461, s. 2; 1999-462, ss. 3, 6, 7, 9; 2000-140, s. 2; 2004-199, s. 9; 2007-402, s. 1.)

§ 18B-604. Timing and effect of subsequent elections.

(a)   Time Limits. - No county alcoholic beverage election may be held within three years of the certification of the results of a previous election on the same kind of alcoholic beverages in that county. No city alcoholic beverage election may be held within three years of the certification of the results of a previous election on the same kind of alcoholic beverage in that city. Otherwise, alcoholic beverage elections may be held at any time, subject to the applicable provisions of this Chapter and Chapter 163.

(b) Effect of Favorable County Vote on City or Township. - If a majority of voters vote in favor of certain alcoholic beverage sales in a county election, sale of that kind of alcoholic beverage shall be lawful throughout the county, regardless of the vote in any city or township at that or any previous or subsequent election, and regardless of any local act making sales unlawful in that city or township, unless the local act was ratified before the effective date of Article II, Section 24(1)(j) of the Constitution of North Carolina. A county malt beverage or unfortified [wine] election in favor of a particular ballot proposition which is more restrictive than the form of sale already allowed in a city or township within that county shall not affect the legality of those previously authorized sales in the city or township.

(c) Effect of Negative County Vote on City or Township. - If a majority of voters vote against certain alcoholic beverage sales in a county election, sale of that kind of alcoholic beverage shall be unlawful throughout the county, except that sale of that alcoholic beverage shall remain lawful in any city or township in which sale is lawful because of a city or township election or a local act.

(d) Effect of City or Township Election on County. - A city or township alcoholic beverage election shall not affect the lawfulness of sale in any part of the county outside that city or township.

(e) Repealed by Session Laws 2003-218, s. 2, effective June 19, 2003.

(f) When Sales Stop. - When the sale of any alcoholic beverage that was previously lawful becomes unlawful because of an election, the sale of that alcoholic beverage shall cease 90 days after certification of the results of the election. (1937, c. 49, ss. 25, 26; c. 431; 1947, c. 1084, ss. 1, 2, 4; 1951, c. 999, ss. 1, 2; 1957, c. 816; 1963, c. 265, ss. 1-3; 1965, c. 506; 1969, c. 647, s. 1; 1971, c. 872, s. 1; 1973, cc. 32, 33; 1977, c. 149, s. 1; c. 182, s. 2; 1977, 2nd Sess., c. 1138, s. 15; 1979, c. 140, ss. 2, 3; c. 609, s. 1; c. 683, s. 13; 1979, 2nd Sess., c. 1174; 1981, c. 412, s. 2; 1993, c. 415, s. 29; 2003-218, s. 2.)

§ 18B-605. Local act elections.

If a jurisdiction has lawfully voted in favor of ABC stores or in favor of the sale of some kind of alcoholic beverage, and the jurisdiction would not be eligible to hold another election under the conditions set by G.S. 18B-600, then that jurisdiction may continue to hold elections as though qualified under G.S. 18B-600. Except for the authority to hold the election, however, the procedures of this Chapter shall apply to any subsequent election. (1981, c. 412, s. 2; 1983, c. 457, s. 4.)

§§ 18B-606 through 18B-699. Reserved for future codification purposes.

Article 7.

Local ABC Boards.

§ 18B-700. Appointment and organization of local ABC boards.

(a) Membership. - A local ABC board shall consist of three or five members appointed for three-year terms unless the board is a board for a merged ABC system under G.S. 18B-703 and a different size membership has been provided for as part of the negotiated merger. If the board is a three-member board, one member of the initial board of a newly created ABC system shall be appointed for a three-year term, one member for a two-year term, and one member for a one-year term. If the board is a five-member board, one member of the initial board of a newly created ABC system shall be appointed for a three-year term, two members for two-year terms, and two members for one-year terms. As the terms of initial board members expire, their successors shall each be appointed for three-year terms. If a board is initially a three-member board and the appointing authority determines a five-member board is preferable, the terms of the two new members shall be for three years. If a local board has five members and the appointing authority determines a three-member board is preferable, the appointing authority shall not reduce the size of the board except upon the expiration of a member's term and only with the approval of the Commission. The appointing authority shall designate one member of the local board as chairman.

(a1) Mission. - The mission of local ABC boards and their employees shall be to serve their localities responsibly by controlling the sale of spirituous liquor and promoting customer-friendly, modern, and efficient stores.

(b) City Boards. - City ABC board members shall be appointed by the city governing body, unless a different method of appointment is provided in a local act enacted before the effective date of this Chapter.

(c) County Boards. - County ABC board members shall be appointed by the board of county commissioners, unless a different method of appointment is provided in a local act enacted before the effective date of this Chapter.

(d) Qualifications. - The appointing authority shall appoint members of a local board on the basis of the appointees' interest in public affairs, good judgment, knowledge, ability, and good moral character.

(e) Vacancy. - A vacancy on a local board shall be filled by the appointing authority for the remainder of the unexpired term. If the chairman's seat becomes vacant, the appointing authority may designate either the new member or an existing member of the local board to complete the chairman's term.

(f) Removal. - A member of a local board may be removed for cause at any time by the appointing authority. Local board members are subject to the removal provisions of G.S. 18B-202.

(g) Compensation of Board Members. - A local board member shall receive compensation in an amount not to exceed one hundred fifty dollars ($150.00) per board meeting unless a different level of monetary compensation is approved by the appointing authority. If a different level is approved by the appointing authority, the appointing authority shall notify the Commission of the approved level of compensation in writing. Any change in compensation approved by the appointing authority shall be reported to the Commission in writing within 30 days of the effective date of the change. No local board member shall receive any nonmonetary compensation or benefits unless specifically authorized by this section.

(g1) Compensation of General Managers of Local Boards. - The salary authorized for the general manager, as defined in G.S. 18B-101, of a local board shall not exceed the salary authorized by the General Assembly for the clerk of superior court of the county in which the appointing authority was originally incorporated unless such compensation is otherwise approved by the appointing authority. The local board shall provide the appointing authority's written confirmation of such approval to the Commission. Any change in compensation approved by the appointing authority shall be reported to the Commission in writing within 30 days of the effective date of the change. The general manager of a local board may receive any other benefits to which all employees of the local board are entitled. The salary authorized for other employees of a local board may not exceed that of the general manager.

(g2) Travel Allowance and Per Diem Rates. - Approved travel on official business by the members and employees of local boards shall be reimbursed pursuant to G.S. 138-6 unless the local board adopts a travel policy that conforms to the travel policy of the appointing authority and such policy is approved by the appointing authority. The local board shall annually provide the appointing authority's written confirmation of such approval to the Commission and a copy of the travel policy authorized by the appointing authority. Any excess expenses not covered by the local board's travel policy shall only be paid with the written authorization of the appointing authority's finance officer. A copy of the written authorization for excess expenses shall be submitted to the Commission by the local board within 30 days of approval.

(h) Conflict of Interest. - The provisions of G.S. 18B-201 shall apply to local board members and employees.

(i) Bond. - Each local board member and the employees designated as the general manager and finance officer of the local board shall be bonded in an amount not less than fifty thousand dollars ($50,000) secured by a corporate surety, for the faithful performance of his duties. A public employees' blanket position bond in the required amount satisfies the requirements of this subsection. The bond shall be payable to the local board and shall be approved by the appointing authority for the local board. The appointing authority may increase the amount of the bond required for any member or employee who handles board funds.

(j) Limited Liability. - A person serving as a member of a local ABC board shall be immune individually from civil liability for monetary damages, except to the extent covered by insurance, for any act or failure to act arising out of this service, except where the person:

(1) Was not acting within the scope of his official duties;

(2) Was not acting in good faith;

(3)   Committed gross negligence or willful or wanton misconduct that resulted in the damage or injury;

(4)   Derived an improper personal financial benefit from the transaction; or

(5)   Incurred the liability from the operation of a motor vehicle.

The immunity in this subsection is personal to the members of local ABC boards, and does not immunize the local ABC board for liability for the acts or omissions of the members of the local ABC board.

(k)   Nepotism. - Members of an immediate family shall not be employed within the local board if such employment will result in one member of the immediate family supervising another member of the immediate family, or if one member of the immediate family will occupy a position which has influence over another member's employment, promotion, salary administration, or other related management or personnel considerations. This subsection applies to local board members and employees.

For the purpose of this subsection, the term "immediate family" includes wife, husband, mother, father, brother, sister, son, daughter, grandmother, grandfather, grandson, and granddaughter. Also included are the step-, half-, and in-law relationships. It also includes other people living in the same household, who share a relationship comparable to immediate family members, if either occupies a position which requires influence over the other's employment, promotion, salary administration, or other related management or personnel considerations.

(l)   Local Acts. - Notwithstanding the provisions of any local act, this section applies to all local boards. (1981, c. 412, s. 2; c. 747, s. 50; 1981 (Reg. Sess., 1982), c. 1262, s. 10; 1989, c. 800, s. 19; 2010-122, ss. 9-16.)

§ 18B-701. Powers and duties of local ABC boards.

(a)   Powers. - A local board shall have authority to:

(1)   Buy, sell, transport, and possess alcoholic beverages as necessary for the operation of its ABC stores;

(2) Adopt rules for its ABC system, subject to the approval of the Commission;

(3) Hire and fire employees for the ABC system;

(4) Designate one employee as manager of the ABC system and determine his responsibilities;

(5) Require bonds of employees as provided in the rules of the Commission;

(6) Operate ABC stores as provided in Article 8;

(7) Issue purchase-transportation permits as provided in Article 4;

(8) Employ local ABC officers or make other provision for enforcement of ABC laws as provided in Article 5;

(9) Borrow money as provided in G.S. 18B-702;

(10) Buy and lease real and personal property, and receive property devised or given, as necessary for the operation of the ABC system;

(11) Invest surplus funds as provided in G.S. 18B-702;

(12) Dispose of property in the same manner as a city council may under Article 12 of Chapter 160A of the General Statutes; and

(13) Perform any other activity authorized or required by the ABC law.

(b) Duties. - A local board shall have the duty to comply with all rules adopted by the Commission pursuant to this Chapter and meet all standards for performance and training established by the Commission pursuant to G.S. 18B-203(a)(20) and (21). Failure to comply with Commission rules shall be cause for removal. (1937, c. 49, ss. 10, 12; cc. 411, 431; 1939, c. 98; 1957, cc. 1006, 1334; 1963, c. 1119, s. 2; 1967, c. 1178; 1969, cc. 118, 902; 1971, c. 872, s. 1; 1973, cc. 85, 185; c. 1000, ss. 1, 2; 1977, c. 618; 1979, c. 467, s. 20; c. 617; 1981, c. 412, s. 2; 2010-122, s. 17; 2011-284, s. 13.)

§ 18B-702. Financial operations of local boards.

(a) Generally. - A local board may transact business as a corporate body, except as limited by this section. A local board shall not be considered a public authority under G.S. 159-7(b)(10).

(b) Budget Officer. - The general manager of the local board shall be the budget officer for the local board. In the absence of a general manager, a local board may impose the duties of budget officer on the chairman or any member of the local board or any other employee of the board.

(c) Annual Balanced Budget. - Each local board shall operate under an annual balanced budget administered in accordance with this section. A budget is balanced when the sum of estimated gross revenues and both restricted and unrestricted funds are equal to appropriations. Expenditures shall not exceed the amount of funds received or in reserve for the purpose to which the funds are appropriated. It is the intent of this section that all monies received and expended by a local board should be included in the budget. Therefore, notwithstanding any other provision of law, no local board may expend any monies, regardless of their source, except in accordance with a budget adopted under this section. The budget of a local board shall cover a fiscal year beginning July 1 and ending June 30.

(d) Preparation and Submission of Budget and Budget Message. - Upon receipt of the budget requests and revenue estimates and the financial information supplied by the finance officer, the budget officer shall prepare a budget for consideration by the local board in such form and detail as may have been prescribed by the budget officer or the local board. The budget, together with a budget message, shall be submitted to the local board, the appointing authority, and the Commission not later than June 1. The budget and budget message should, but need not, be submitted at a formal meeting of the board. The budget message should contain a concise explanation of the goals fixed by the budget for the budget year, explain important features of the activities anticipated in the budget, set forth the reasons for stated changes from the previous year in appropriation levels, and explain any major changes in fiscal policy.

(e) Filing and Publication of the Budget. - On the same day the budget officer submits the budget to the local board, the budget officer shall make a copy for public inspection, and it shall remain available for public inspection until the budget is adopted. The budget officer shall make a copy of the budget available to all news media in the county. The budget officer shall also publish a statement that the budget has been submitted to the local board and is available for public inspection in the office of the general manager of the local board. The statement shall also give notice of the time and place of the budget hearing required by subsection (f) of this section.

(f)   Budget Hearings. - Before adopting the budget, the board shall hold a public hearing at which time any persons who wish to be heard on the budget may appear.

(g)   Adoption of Budget. - Not earlier than 10 days after the day the budget is presented to the board and not later than July 1, the local board shall adopt a budget making appropriations for the budget year in such sums as the board may consider sufficient and proper, whether greater or less than the sums recommended in the budget. The budget shall authorize all financial transactions of the local board. The budget may be in any form that the board considers most efficient in enabling it to make the fiscal policy decisions embodied therein, but it shall make appropriations by department, function, or project and show revenues by major source. The following directions and limitations shall bind the local board in adopting the budget:

(1)   The full amount estimated by the finance officer to be required for debt service during the budget year shall be appropriated.

(2)   The full amount of any deficit in each fund shall be appropriated.

(3)   Working capital funds set aside pursuant to G.S. 18B-805 shall be established by rule of the Commission. "Working capital" means the total of cash, investments, and inventory less all unsecured liabilities. Gross sales means gross receipts from the sale of alcoholic beverages less distributions as defined in G.S. 18B-805(b)(2), (3), (4), and (5). Any expenditure to be charged against working capital funds shall be authorized by resolution of the local board, which resolution shall be deemed an amendment to the budget setting up an appropriation for the object of expenditure authorized. The local board may authorize the budget officer to authorize expenditures from working capital funds subject to such limitations and procedures as it may prescribe. Any such expenditure shall be deemed an amendment and reported to the board at its next regular meeting and recorded in the minutes.

(4)   Estimated revenues shall include only those revenues reasonably expected to be realized in the budget year.

(5) Sufficient funds to meet the amounts to be paid during the fiscal year under continuing contracts previously entered into shall be appropriated unless such contract reserves to the local board the right to limit or not to make such appropriation.

(6) The sum of estimated net revenues and appropriated fund balance in each fund shall be equal to appropriations in that fund. Appropriated fund balance in a fund shall not exceed the sum of cash and investments minus the sum of liabilities, encumbrances, and deferred revenues arising from cash receipts, as those figures stand at the close of the fiscal year next preceding the budget year.

The budget shall be entered in the minutes of the local board and within five days after adoption, and copies thereof shall be filed with the finance officer, the budget officer, the appointing authority, and the Commission.

(h) Amendments to the Budget. - Except as otherwise restricted by law, the local board may amend the budget at any time after adoption, in any manner, so long as the budget, as amended, continues to satisfy the requirements of this section. The local board by appropriate resolution may authorize the budget officer to transfer monies from one appropriation to another within the same fund subject to such limitations and procedures as it may prescribe. Any such transfers shall be reported to the local board at its next regular meeting and shall be entered in the minutes. Amendments to the adopted budget shall also be provided to the appointing authority and the Commission.

(i) Interim Budget. - In case the adoption of the budget is delayed until after July 1, the local board shall make interim appropriations for the purpose of paying salaries, debt service payments, and the usual ordinary expenses of the local board for the interval between the beginning of the budget year and the adoption of the budget. Interim appropriations so made shall be charged to the proper appropriations in the adopted budget.

(j) Finance Officer. - Except as otherwise provided, the local board shall designate (i) a part-time or full-time employee of the board other than the general manager or (ii) the finance officer of the appointing authority with consent of the appointing authority to be the finance officer for the local board. The Commission, for good cause shown, may grant a waiver to allow the general manager of a board also to be the finance officer. Good cause includes, but is not limited to, the fact that the board operates no more than two stores, and any approval for the general manager also to be the finance officer shall apply until the board operates more than two stores; in any event, the approval shall be effective for 36 months. The Commission may grant one or more waivers to a board.

(k) Duties and Powers of the Finance Officer. - The finance officer for a local board shall:

(1) Keep the accounts of the local board in accordance with generally accepted principles of governmental accounting and the rules and regulations of the Commission.

(2) Disburse all funds of the local board in strict compliance with this Chapter, the budget, preaudit obligations, and disbursements as required by this section.

(3) As often as may be requested by the local board or the general manager, prepare and file with the board a statement of the financial condition of the local board.

(4) Receive and deposit all monies accruing to the local board, or supervise the receipt and deposit of money by other duly authorized employees.

(5) Maintain all records concerning the debt and other obligations of the local board, determine the amount of money that will be required for debt service or the payment of other obligations during each fiscal year, and maintain all funds.

(6) Supervise the investment of idle funds of the local board pursuant to subsection (t) of this section.

The finance officer shall perform such other duties as may be assigned by law, by the general manager, budget officer, or local board, or by rules and regulations of the Commission.

(l) Accounting System. - Each local board shall establish and maintain an accounting system designed to show in detail its assets, liabilities, equities, revenues, and expenditures. The system shall also be designed to show appropriations and estimated revenues as established in the budget originally adopted and subsequently amended.

(m) Incurring Obligations. - No obligation may be incurred in a program, function, or activity accounted for in a fund included in the budget unless the budget includes an appropriation authorizing the obligation and an unencumbered balance remains in the appropriation sufficient to pay in the current fiscal year the sums obligated by the transaction for the current fiscal year. No obligation may be incurred for a capital project unless the budget authorizes the obligation and an unencumbered balance remains in the appropriation sufficient to pay the sums obligated by the transaction. If an obligation is evidenced by a contract or agreement requiring the payment of money or by a purchase order for supplies and materials, the contract, agreement, or purchase order shall include on its face a certificate stating that the instrument has been preaudited to assure compliance with this subsection. The certificate, which shall be signed by the finance officer or any deputy finance officer approved for this purpose by the local board, shall take substantially the following form:

"This instrument has been preaudited in the manner required by G.S. 18B-702.

_____

(Signature of finance officer)."

An obligation incurred in violation of this subsection is invalid and may not be enforced. The finance officer shall establish procedures to assure compliance with this subsection.

(n) Disbursements. - When a bill, invoice, or other claim against a local board is presented, the finance officer shall either approve or disapprove the necessary disbursement. If the claim involves a program, function, or activity accounted for in a fund included in the budget or a capital project or a grant project authorized by the budget, the finance officer may approve the claim only if:

(1) The finance officer determines the amount to be payable; and

(2) The budget includes an appropriation authorizing the expenditure and either (i) an encumbrance has been previously created for the transaction or (ii) an unencumbered balance remains in the appropriation sufficient to pay the amount to be disbursed.

A bill, invoice, or other claim may not be paid unless it has been approved by the finance officer or, under subsection (o) of this section, by the local board. The finance officer shall establish procedures to assure compliance with this subsection.

(o) Local Board Approval of Bills, Invoices, or Claims. - The local board may, as permitted by this subsection, approve a bill, invoice, or other claim against the local board that has been disapproved by the finance officer. It may not approve a claim for which no appropriation appears in the budget, or for which the appropriation contains no encumbrance and the unencumbered balance is less than the amount to be paid. The local board shall approve payment by formal resolution stating the board's reasons for allowing the bill, invoice, or other claim. The resolution shall be entered in the minutes together with the names of those voting in the affirmative. The chairman of the board or some other member designated for this purpose shall sign the certificate on the check or draft given in payment of the bill, invoice, or other claim. If payment results in a violation of law, each member of the board voting to allow payment is jointly and severally liable for the full amount of the check or draft given in payment.

(p) Checks or Drafts Signed by Finance Officer. - Except as otherwise provided by law, all checks or drafts on an official depository shall be signed by the finance officer or a properly designated deputy finance officer. The chairman of the local board or general manager of the local board shall countersign these checks and drafts. The Commission may waive the requirements of this subsection if the board determines that the internal control procedures of the unit or authority will be satisfactory in the absence of dual signatures.

(q) Payment of a Bill, Invoice, Salary, or Claim. - A local board may not pay a bill, invoice, salary, or other claim except by a check or draft on an official depository or by a bank wire transfer from an official depository. Except as provided in this subsection, each check or draft on an official depository shall bear on its face a certificate signed by the finance officer or a deputy finance officer approved for this purpose by the local board (or signed by the chairman or some other member of the board pursuant to subsection (o) of this section). The certificate shall take substantially the following form

"This disbursement has been approved in the manner required by G.S. 18B-702.

(Signature of finance officer)."

No certificate is required on payroll checks or drafts on an imprest account in an official depository if the check or draft depositing the funds in the imprest account carried a signed certificate. No certificate is required for expenditures of fifty dollars ($50.00) or less from a petty cash fund, provided the expenditure is accounted for by a receipt for the expended item.

(r)   Borrowing Money. - A local board may borrow money only for the purchase of land, buildings, equipment and stock needed for the operation of its ABC system. A local board may pledge a security interest in any real or personal property it owns other than alcoholic beverages. A city or county whose governing body appoints a local board shall not in any way be held responsible for the debts of that board.

(s)   Audits. - A local board shall submit to the appointing authority and Commission an annual independent audit of its operations, performed in accordance with generally accepted accounting standards and in compliance with a chart of accounts prescribed by the Commission. The audit report shall contain a summary of the requirements of this Chapter, or of any local act applicable to that local board, concerning the distribution of profits of that board and a description of how those distributions have been made, including the names of recipients of the profits and the activities for which the funds were distributed. A local board shall also submit to any other audits and submit any reports demanded by the appointing authority or the Commission.

(t)   Deposits and Investments. - A local board may deposit monies at interest in any bank or trust company in this State in the form of savings accounts or certificates of deposit. Investment deposits shall be secured as provided in G.S. 159-31(b) and the reports required by G.S. 159-33 shall be submitted. A local board may invest all or part of the cash balance of any fund as provided in G.S. 159-30(c) and (d), and may deposit any portion of those funds for investment with the State Treasurer in the same manner as State boards and commissions under G.S. 147-69.3.

(u)   Compliance with Commission Rules. - The Commission shall adopt, and each local board shall comply with, fiscal control rules concerning the borrowing of money, maintenance of working capital, investments, appointment of a budget officer, appointment of a financial officer, daily deposit of funds, bonding of employees, auditing of operations, and the schedule, manner and other procedures for distribution of profits. The Commission may also adopt any other rules concerning the financial operations of local boards which are needed to assure the proper accountability of public funds. The Commission may vary these rules and regulations according to any other criteria reasonably related to the purpose or complexity of the financial operations involved. The Commission has the authority to inquire into and investigate the internal control procedures of a local board and may require any modifications in internal control procedures which, in the opinion of the Commission, are necessary or desirable to prevent embezzlements or mishandling of public monies.

(v)   Penalties. - If a board member or employee of a local board incurs an obligation or pays out or causes to be paid out any funds in violation of this section, the member or employee and the sureties on the official bond are liable for any sums so committed or disbursed. If the finance officer or any properly designated deputy finance officer gives a false certificate to any contract, agreement, purchase order, check, draft, or other document, the finance officer and the sureties on the official bond are liable for any sums illegally committed or disbursed thereby.

(w)   Applicability of Criminal Statutes. - The provisions of G.S. 14-90 and G.S. 14-254 shall apply to any person appointed to or employed by a local board, and any person convicted of a violation of G.S. 14-90 or G.S. 14-254 shall be punished as a Class H felon.

(x)   Local Acts. - Notwithstanding the provisions of any local act, this section applies to all local boards. (1937, c. 49, ss. 10, 12; cc. 411, 431; 1939, c. 98; 1957, cc. 1006, 1335; 1963, c. 1119, s. 2; 1967, c. 1178; 1969, cc. 118, 902; 1971, c. 872, s. 1; 1973, cc. 85, 185; c. 1000, ss. 1, 2; 1977, c. 618; 1979, c. 467, s. 20; c. 617; 1981, c. 412, s. 2; 1981 (Reg. Sess., 1982), c. 1262, s. 11; 1991, c. 459, s. 2; 2010-122, s. 18; 2012-4, s. 2.)

§ 18B-703. Merger of local ABC operations.

(a)   Conditions for Merger. - Any city governing body or board of county commissioners may merge its ABC system with the system of one or more other cities or counties if:

(1)   Stores operated by the systems of those jurisdictions serve the same general area or are in close proximity to each other; and

(2) The merger is approved by the Commission.

(b) Appointment of Board. - Upon merger of ABC systems, the local boards for those systems shall be replaced by one board appointed jointly by the appointing authorities for the previous boards.

(c) Distribution of Profits. - Before merger, the cities or counties involved shall agree upon a formula for distribution of the profits of the new merged ABC system, based as closely as practicable on the distribution previously authorized for the separate systems. This formula for distribution shall be subject to approval by the Commission.

(d) Enforcement. - Local officers hired by the local ABC board for the merged ABC system shall have the same territorial jurisdiction that officers for each of the merged boards would have.

(e) Dissolution. - With the approval of the Commission, the cities or counties that have merged their ABC systems may dissolve the merged operation at any time and resume their prior separate operations.

(f) Other Details Negotiated. - Issues not addressed in this section concerning the merger or dissolution of ABC systems, such as the method of appointment of the merged board, the size of the merged board, or the procedure for dissolution, may be negotiated by the affected cities and counties, subject to the approval of the Commission.

(g) Operation Follows General Law. - Except as otherwise provided in this section, the authority and operation of any local board established under this section shall be the same as for any other local board.

(h) Agreement for Joint Store Operations. - With the approval of the Commission, two or more governing bodies of counties and/or municipalities with ABC systems may enter into a written agreement whereby one or more ABC stores located within the counties and/or municipalities that are parties to the agreement shall be controlled and operated by the local ABC board specified in the agreement, even though said ABC store or stores are located outside the boundaries of the county or municipality of the local ABC board that will be operating the ABC store or stores that are subject to the agreement. The provisions of this section shall be effective as to such agreements insofar as is applicable. Issues not addressed in this section shall be negotiated by the parties, subject to the approval of the Commission. (1981, c. 412, s. 2; c. 747, s. 51; 2001-128, s. 1.)

§ 18B-704. Removal of local board members and employees.

(a) Improper Influence. - Neither the Commission nor its individual members shall attempt to coerce any appointing authority to appoint a particular person as a member of a local board or attempt to coerce a local board to employ any particular applicant.

(b) Purpose. - This section is intended to provide a uniform system of removal for appointing authorities and the Commission.

(c) Cause for Removal. - (i) Disqualification of a local board member or employee under the law, (ii) a violation of the ABC laws, (iii) failure to complete training required by this Chapter or the Commission, or (iv) engaging in any conduct constituting moral turpitude or which brings the local board or the ABC system into disrepute is cause for the Commission to remove any member or employee of a local board. The employment or retention of any employee who is known to be disqualified under the law to hold a position with a local board is cause for the Commission to remove the board members involved.

(d) Removal Process. - The Commission or appointing authority shall provide, in writing, to the local board member or employee the findings of fact upon which the decision for removal is based. The Commission or appointing authority shall also provide the local board member or employee with notice of the availability of a hearing before the Commission to review the removal.

(e) Removal Hearing. - Any local board member or employee removed from office or discharged by the Commission or the appointing authority may request a hearing before the Commission. Such a request operates to stay the action of the Commission or the appointing authority with regard to the matter until after the hearing, unless the Commission finds that the public interest requires immediate action. At the hearing, the employee or the employee's counsel may examine all evidence used against the employee and present evidence in the employee's own behalf. A removal hearing is not subject to the provisions of Chapter 150B of the General Statutes. All hearings shall be conducted informally and in such manner as to preserve the substantial rights of the parties.

(f) Hearing Procedure. - The Commission shall hold the hearing required by subsection (e) of this section within 15 days of the member's or employee's request for a hearing. The standard of review by the Commission is de novo. The Commission or appointing authority shall be represented by a Commission hearing officer. The Commission shall discharge the member or employee if two-thirds of the Commission's members vote for removal. The Commission shall make findings of fact. The Commission may adopt the findings of fact of the Commission or the appointing authority, may add new findings of fact to the original findings of fact, or may substitute new findings of fact for the original findings of fact. The Commission shall make conclusions of law and shall issue a written decision to the member or employee of the local board, and to the appointing authority, within 15 days of the hearing.

(g) Commission Authority. - The Commission shall have the sole power, in its discretion, to determine if cause exists for removal of a local board member or employee who has requested a hearing before the Commission. The Commission's decision in a removal hearing is final.

(h) Appeal. - A local board member or employee may appeal the Commission's final decision to the Court of Appeals. The standard of review for an appeal shall be abuse of discretion. The sole remedy for a local board member or employee shall be the reinstatement of the board member or employee to the local board with back pay. All awards for back pay shall be paid by the local board from which the board member or employee was removed.

(i) Removal Hearing Not a Substitute for Termination of Employee. - Nothing in this section replaces or is intended to replace a local board's policy regarding the termination of an employee for personnel reasons. The removal process under this section is reserved solely for the appointing authority or the Commission to remove a board member or employee for cause.

(j) Local Acts. - Notwithstanding the provisions of any local act, this section applies to all local boards. (2010-122, s. 19.)

§ 18B-705. Compliance with performance standards; remedies.

(a) Local Board Compliance. - The Commission shall establish performance standards pursuant to G.S. 18B-203(a)(20). The Commission shall ensure that all local boards comply with established performance standards by conducting regular or special audits, conducting performance evaluations, or taking other measures, which may include inspections by Commission auditors or alcohol law enforcement agents.

(b) Performance Improvement Plans. - The Commission, upon determining that a local board is failing to meet performance standards established pursuant to G.S. 18B-203(a)(20), shall meet with the chair of the local board and the appointing authority and issue a statement of findings. The appointing authority, in consultation with the Commission and the local board, shall develop and deliver a performance improvement plan to the local board within 60 days of the meeting with the Commission. The performance improvement plan shall include, but not be limited to, recommendations for improved performance based on the performance standards established by the Commission. The plan shall also state a period of time in which the performance improvements are to occur and what action will be taken by the Commission if performance standards are not met within the given time limits. The appointing authority shall allow up to, but no more than, 12 months' time to the local board to implement and show improvement under the performance improvement plan. The local appointing authority, in consultation with the Commission and upon good cause shown, may allow up to an additional six-month period of time for the local board to meet all requirements in the performance improvement plan and to establish that the performance standards established by the Commission are met.

(c) Remedies. - If the Commission determines that the established performance standards identified in the statement of findings cannot be met after a performance improvement plan has been implemented and adequate time has been given, but in no case less than 12 months, the Commission shall take appropriate action to avoid insolvency. This action may include closing the board pursuant to G.S. 18B-801(d), closing a store or multiple stores, or merging the local board with another local board in order to maintain solvency. The Commission may also seize the assets of the local board and liquidate any assets necessary to satisfy any debt in order to maintain the solvency of the local board. Prior to taking action pursuant to this subsection, the Commission shall issue a notice of intent to take such action to the appointing authority and the local board.

(d) Local Acts. - Notwithstanding the provisions of any local act, this section applies to all local boards. (2010-122, s. 20.)

§ 18B-706. Ethics requirements for local boards.

(a) Each local board shall adopt a policy containing a code of ethics, consistent with the provisions of G.S. 18B-201, to guide actions by the local board members and employees of the local board in the performance of their official duties. The policy shall address at least all of the following:

(1) The need to obey all applicable laws regarding official actions taken as a local board member or employee.

(2) The need to uphold the integrity and independence of the local board member or employee's position.

(3) The need to avoid impropriety in the exercise of official duties.

(4) The need to faithfully perform the duties of the position.

(5) The need to conduct the affairs of the board in an open and public manner, including complying with all applicable laws governing open meetings and public records.

(b) Each member of a local board shall receive a minimum of two hours of ethics education within 12 months after initial appointment to the office and again within 12 months after each subsequent appointment to the office. The ethics education shall cover laws and principles that govern conflicts of interest and ethical standards of conduct for local ABC boards. The education may be provided by the Commission or another qualified source approved by the Commission. The local board shall maintain a record verifying receipt of the ethics education by each member of the local board. The local board may require appropriate ethics training and education for employees of the local ABC board.

(c) The Commission shall develop a model ethics policy that local ABC boards may adopt to be in compliance with this section. (2010-122, s. 21.)

§ 18B-707. Reserved for future codification purposes.

§ 18B-708. Reserved for future codification purposes.

§ 18B-709. Reserved for future codification purposes.

Article 8.

Operation of ABC Stores.

§ 18B-800. Sale of alcoholic beverages in ABC stores.

(a) Spirituous Liquor. - Except as provided in Article 10 of this Chapter, spirituous liquor may be sold only in ABC stores operated by local boards.

(b) Fortified Wine. - In addition to spirituous liquor, ABC stores may sell fortified wine. ABC stores may also sell wine products, irrespective of alcohol content by volume, which were classified as fortified wine by the ABC Commission prior to July 7, 2004.

(c) Commission Approval. - No ABC store may sell any alcoholic beverage which has not been approved by the Commission for sale in this State.

(d) Expired.

(e) Each ABC store shall display spirits which are distilled in North Carolina in an area dedicated solely to North Carolina products. (1981, c. 412, s. 2; 1985, c. 59, s. 1; 1989, c. 800, s. 21; 2004-135, s. 4; 2010-31, s. 14.12(a).)

§ 18B-801. Location, opening, and closing of stores.

(a) Number of Stores. - Each local board shall have the authority and duty to operate one ABC store. Additional stores may be operated with the approval of the Commission.

(b) Location of Stores. - A local board may choose the location of the ABC stores within its jurisdiction, subject to the approval of the Commission. In making its decision on a location, the Commission may consider:

(1) Whether the health, safety, or general welfare of the community will be adversely affected.

(2) Whether the citizens of the community or city in which the proposed store is to be located voted for or against ABC stores in the last election on the question.

(3) The proximity of the new location to existing ABC stores operated by the local board or any other board.

(b1) Notwithstanding subsection (b) of this section, no local board may establish an ABC store at any location within the corporate limits of a municipality if the governing body of the municipality has passed a resolution objecting to the location of the proposed ABC store and the resolution is based upon information and evidence presented to the governing body of the municipality at a public hearing. If a municipality objects to the location of a proposed ABC store, the local board may request the Commission to approve the proposed ABC store location notwithstanding the objection of the municipality. The Commission shall have final authority to determine if the operation of an ABC store at the contested proposed location is suitable.

Upon notice given to the Commission by an affected municipality, any statutory and administrative time limits allowed for objections to, or public hearings concerning the location of, an ABC store shall be extended by 45 days to allow a municipality sufficient time to conduct a public hearing and submit its objection and resolution to the Commission.

(c) Closing of Stores. - Subject to the provisions of subsection (a) of this section, a local board may close a store, or the Commission may order a local board to close any store when the local board or the Commission determines that:

(1) Repealed by Session Laws 2010-122, s. 23, effective October 1, 2010.

(2) The store is not operated in accordance with the ABC law; or

(3) The continued operation of that store will adversely affect the health, safety, or general welfare of the community in which the store operates.

(d) Insolvent ABC System. - If an ABC system is insolvent, the local board may apply to the Commission for an order to close the system. Upon receipt of an application, or upon its own motion, the Commission shall investigate the system, and if it finds that further operation of the ABC stores will not be profitable, it may order the system closed. If the Commission orders a local system to close, the Commission may:

(1) After consultation with the local board, its creditors, and other interested parties, schedule a phase out of the system's business activities;

(2) Represent the local board in negotiations with creditors and other interested parties;

(3) Require an accounting or auditing of the local system;

(4) Take possession or arrange for the disposition of any liquor for which the local board has not paid;

(5) Apply to the Superior Court to be appointed as receiver for the local board with all powers and duties of a receiver for a corporation under Article 38 of Chapter 1 of the General Statutes, except that the Commission shall not be required to post the bond required by G.S. 1-504; or

(6) Take any other reasonable steps to promote an orderly closing of the system. (1981, c. 412, s. 2; 1987, c. 135; 1989, c. 770, s. 6; 2009-36, s. 1; 2010-122, ss. 22, 23.)

§ 18B-802. When stores operate.

(a) Time. - No ABC store shall be open, and no ABC store employee shall sell alcoholic beverages, between 9:00 P.M. and 9:00 A.M. The local board shall otherwise determine opening and closing hours of its stores.

(b) Days. - No ABC store shall be open, and no ABC store employee shall sell alcoholic beverages, on any Sunday, New Year's Day, Fourth of July, Labor

Day, Thanksgiving Day, or Christmas Day. A local board may otherwise determine the days on which its stores shall be closed. (1981, c. 412, s. 2.)

§ 18B-803. Store management.

(a) Manager. - A local board shall provide for the management of each store operated by it. The board shall employ at least one manager for each store, who shall operate the store pursuant to the directions of that board.

(b) Bonding of Manager. - Each store manager shall be bonded in an amount not less than fifty thousand dollars ($50,000) secured by a corporate surety, for the honest performance of his duties. A public employees' blanket position bond, honesty form, in the required amount satisfies the requirements of this subsection. The bond shall be payable to the local board and shall be approved by the appointing authority for the local board. The appointing authority may increase the amount of bond required for store managers under this subsection.

(c) Bonding of Other Employees. - A local board or the appointing authority may require any of its other employees who handle funds to obtain bonds. The amount and form of those bonds shall be determined by the local board.

(d) Local Acts. - Notwithstanding the provisions of any local act, this section applies to all local boards. (1981, c. 412, s. 2; 1981 (Reg. Sess., 1982), c. 1262, s. 12; 2010-122, s. 24.)

§ 18B-804. Alcoholic beverage pricing.

(a) Uniform Price of Spirituous Liquor. - The retail price of spirituous liquor sold in ABC stores shall be uniform throughout the State, unless otherwise provided by the ABC law.

(b) Sale Price of Spirituous Liquor. - The sale of spirituous liquor sold at the uniform State price shall consist of the following components:

(1) The distiller's price.

(2) The freight and bailment charges of the State warehouse as determined by the Commission.

(3) A markup for local boards as determined by the Commission.

(4) The tax levied under G.S. 105-113.80(c), which shall be levied on the sum of subdivisions (1), (2), and (3).

(5) An additional markup for local boards equal to three and one-half percent (3 1/2%) of the sum of subdivisions (1), (2), and (3).

(6) A bottle charge of one cent (1¢) on each bottle containing 50 milliliters or less and five cents (5¢) on each bottle containing more than 50 milliliters.

(6a) The bailment surcharge.

(6b) An additional bottle charge for local boards of one cent (1¢) on each bottle containing 50 milliliters or less and five cents (5¢) on each bottle containing more than 50 milliliters.

(7) A rounding adjustment, the formula of which may be determined by the Commission, so that the sale price will be divisible by five.

(8) If the spirituous liquor is sold to a mixed beverage permittee for resale in mixed beverages, a charge of twenty dollars ($20.00) on each four liters and a proportional sum on lesser quantities.

(9) If the spirituous liquor is sold to a guest room cabinet permittee for resale, a charge of twenty dollars ($20.00) on each four liters and a proportional sum on lesser quantities.

(c) Sale Price of Fortified Wine. - The sale price of fortified wine shall include the tax levied by G.S. 105-113.80(b), as well as State and local sales taxes.

(d) Repealed by Session Laws 1985, c. 59, s. 2. (1937, c. 49, s. 4; cc. 237, 411; 1945, c. 954; 1949, c. 974, s. 9; 1961, c. 956; 1963, c. 426, s. 12; c. 916, s. 2; c. 1119, s. 1; 1965, c. 1063; c. 1102, s. 3; 1967, c. 222, s. 2; c. 1240, s. 1; 1971, c. 872, s. 1; 1973, c. 28; c. 473, s. 1; c. 476, s. 133; c. 606; c. 1288, s. 1; cc. 1369, 1396; 1975, cc. 240, 453, 640; 1977, c. 70, ss. 15.1, 15.2, 16; c. 176, ss. 2, 6; 1977, 2nd Sess., c. 1138, ss. 3, 4, 18; 1979, c. 384, s. 1; c. 445, s. 5; c.

482; c. 801, s. 4; 1981, c. 412, s. 2; 1981 (Reg. Sess., 1982), c. 1285, s. 5; 1983, c. 713, ss. 100, 101; 1985, c. 59, s. 2; c. 68, s. 1; c. 114, ss. 7-9; 1991, c. 565, ss. 4, 7; c. 689, ss. 304, 305; 1991 (Reg. Sess., 1992), c. 920, s. 3.)

§ 18B-805. Distribution of revenue.

(a) Gross Receipts. - As used in this section, "gross receipts" means all revenue of a local board, including proceeds from the sale of alcoholic beverages, investments, interest on deposits, and any other source.

(b) Primary Distribution. - Before making any other distribution, a local board shall first pay the following from its gross receipts:

(1) The board shall pay the expenses, including salaries, of operating the local ABC system.

(2) Each month the local board shall pay to the Department of Revenue the taxes due the Department. In addition to the taxes levied under Chapter 105 of the General Statutes, the local board shall pay to the Department one-half of both the mixed beverages surcharge required by G.S. 18B-804(b)(8) and the guest room cabinet surcharge required by G.S. 18B-804(b)(9).

(3) Each month the local board shall pay to the Department of Health and Human Services five percent (5%) of both the mixed beverages surcharge required by G.S. 18B-804(b)(8) and the guest room cabinet surcharge required by G.S. 18B-804(b)(9). The Department of Health and Human Services shall spend those funds for the treatment of alcoholism or substance abuse, or for research or education on alcohol or substance abuse.

(4) Each month the local board shall pay to the county commissioners of the county where the charge is collected the proceeds from the bottle charge required by G.S. 18B-804(b)(6), to be spent by the county commissioners for the purposes stated in subsection (h) of this section.

(c) Other Statutory Distributions. - After making the distributions required by subsection (b), a local board shall make the following quarterly distributions from the remaining gross receipts:

(1) Before making any other distribution under this subsection, the local board shall set aside the clear proceeds of the three and one-half percent (3 1/2%) markup provided for in G.S. 18B-804(b)(5) and the bottle charge provided for in G.S. 18B-804(b)(6b), to be distributed as part of the remaining gross receipts under subsection (e) of this section.

(2) The local board shall spend for law enforcement an amount set by the board which shall be at least five percent (5%) of the gross receipts remaining after the distribution required by subdivision (1). The local board may contract with the ALE Section to provide the law enforcement required by this subdivision. Notwithstanding the provisions of any local act, this provision shall apply to all local boards.

(3) The local board shall spend, or pay to the county commissioners to spend, for the purposes stated in subsection (h), an amount set by the board which shall be at least seven percent (7%) of the gross receipts remaining after the distribution required by subdivision (1). This provision shall not be applicable to a local board which is subject to a local act setting a different distribution.

(d) Working Capital. - After making the distributions provided for in subsections (b) and (c), the local board may set aside a portion of the remaining gross receipts, within the limits set by the rules of the Commission, as cash to operate the ABC system. With the approval of the appointing authority for the board, the local board may also set aside a portion of the remaining gross receipts as a fund for specific capital improvements.

(e) Other Distributions. - After making the distributions provided in subsections (b), (c), and (d), the local board shall pay each quarter the remaining gross receipts to the general fund of the city or county for which the board is established, unless some other distribution or some other schedule is provided for by law. If the governing body of each city and county receiving revenue from an ABC system agrees, those governing bodies may alter at any time the distribution to be made under this subsection or under any local act. Copies of the governing body resolutions agreeing to a new distribution formula and a copy of the approved new distribution formula shall be submitted to the Commission for review and audit purposes. If any one of the governing bodies later withdraws its consent to the change in distribution, profits shall be distributed according to the original formula, beginning with the next quarter.

(f) Surcharge Profit Shared. - When, pursuant to G.S. 18B-603(d1), spirituous liquor is bought at a city ABC store by a mixed beverages permittee for premises located outside the city, the local board operating the store at which the sale is made shall retain seventy-five percent (75%) of the local share of both the mixed beverages surcharge required by G.S. 18B-804(b)(8) and the guest room cabinet surcharge required by G.S. 18B-804(b)(9) and the remaining twenty-five percent (25%) shall be divided equally among the local ABC boards for all other cities in the county that have authorized the sale of mixed beverages.

When, pursuant to G.S. 18B-603(e), spirituous liquor is bought at a city ABC store by a mixed beverages permittee for premises located at an airport outside the city, the local share of both the mixed beverages surcharge required by G.S. 18B-804(b)(8) and the guest room cabinet surcharge required by G.S. 18B-804(b)(9) shall be divided equally among the local ABC boards for all cities in the county that have authorized the sale of mixed beverages.

(g) Quarterly Distributions. - When this section requires a distribution to be made quarterly, at least ninety percent (90%) of the estimated distribution shall be paid to the recipient by the local board within 30 days of the end of that quarter. Adjustments in the amount to be distributed resulting from the closing of the books and from audit shall be made with the next quarterly payment.

(h) Expenditure of Alcoholism Funds. - Funds distributed under subdivisions (b)(4) and (c)(3) of this section shall be spent for the treatment of alcoholism or substance abuse, or for research or education on alcohol or substance abuse. The minutes of the board of county commissioners or local board spending funds allocated under this subsection shall describe the activity for which the funds are to be spent. Any agency or person receiving funds from the county commissioners or local board under this subsection shall submit an annual report to the board of county commissioners or local board from which funds were received, describing how the funds were spent.

(i) Calculation of Statutory Distributions When Liquor Sold at Less Than Uniform Price. - If a local board sells liquor at less than the uniform State price, distributions required by subsections (b) and (c) shall be calculated as though the liquor was sold at the uniform price. (1981, c. 412, s. 2; c. 747, s. 52; 1983, c. 713, ss. 102-104; 1985 (Reg. Sess., 1986), c. 1014, s. 116; 1991, c. 459, s. 3; c. 689, s. 306; 1991 (Reg. Sess., 1992), c. 920, s. 4; 1993, c. 415, s. 27; 1997-443, s. 11A.118(a); 1999-462, s. 8; 2011-145, s. 19.1(q).)

§ 18B-806. Damaged alcoholic beverages.

(a) Owned by Local Board. - All damaged alcoholic beverages owned by a local board shall be destroyed, given to a public or private hospital for medicinal use only, or given to the Commission.

(b) Not Owned by Local Board. - The Commission shall dispose of all damaged alcoholic beverages which are:

(1) Owned by the Commission;

(2) Damaged while in the State warehouse; or

(3) Damaged while in transit between the State warehouse and a local board.

The Commission shall dispose of the alcoholic beverages by giving them to a public or private hospital for medicinal use only, by selling them to a military installation, or by destroying them.

(c) Sale Procedure. - If damaged alcoholic beverages are sold under subsection (b), sale shall be by:

(1) Advertisement for sealed bids;

(2) Negotiated offer, advertisement and upset bids; or

(3) Exchange.

Funds derived from the sale of damaged alcoholic beverages shall be paid to the general fund of the State.

(d) Records. - Local boards and the Commission shall keep detailed records of all disposals of damaged alcoholic beverages, including brand, quantity and disposition. (1981, c. 412, s. 2.)

§ 18B-807. Rules.

The Commission may adopt rules concerning the organization and operation of self-service ABC stores, the size of ABC store signs, the display of alcoholic beverages, solicitation in and around ABC stores, and any other subject relating to the efficient operation of ABC stores. (1981, c. 412, s. 2.)

§ 18B-808. Warning signs regarding dangers of alcohol consumption during pregnancy required; posting.

(a) Each ABC store shall display or cause to be displayed warning signs that meet the requirements of this section on the store's premises to inform the public of the effects of alcohol consumption during pregnancy.

(b) The Commission shall develop the warning signs in accordance with subsection (c) of this section and provide for their distribution and replacements to local ABC boards subject to the requirement of this section. The Commission may charge a reasonable fee, not to exceed twenty-five dollars ($25.00), for each sign, including replacement signs.

(c) The signs required by this section shall:

(1) Be composed of black, capital letters printed on white paper at the minimum weight of one hundred ten pound index. The letters comprising the word "WARNING" shall be highlighted black lettering and shall be larger than all other lettering on the sign.

(2) Contain the message: "WARNING Pregnancy and alcohol do not mix. Drinking alcohol during pregnancy can cause birth defects."

(3) The size of the sign shall be at least eight and one-half inches by 14 inches.

(4) Contain a graphic depiction of the message to assist nonreaders in understanding the message. The depiction of a pregnant female shall be universal and shall not reflect a specific race or culture.

(5) Be in both English and Spanish.

(d) A local ABC board shall ensure that each ABC store manager displays the warning sign in an open and prominent place in the store within 30 days of receipt of the sign from the Commission. (2003-339, s. 2.)

§§ 18B-809 through 18B-899. Reserved for future codification purposes.

Article 9.

Issuance of Permits.

§ 18B-900. Qualifications for permit.

(a) Requirements. - To be eligible to receive and to hold an ABC permit, a person shall:

(1) Be at least 21 years old, unless the person is a manager of a business selling only malt beverages and unfortified wine, in which case the person shall be at least 19 years old;

(2) Be a resident of North Carolina unless:

a. He is an officer, director or stockholder of a corporate applicant or permittee and is not a manager or otherwise responsible for the day-to-day operation of the business; or

b. He has executed a power of attorney designating a qualified resident of this State to serve as attorney in fact for the purposes of receiving service of process and managing the business for which permits are sought; or

c. He is applying for a nonresident malt beverage vendor permit, a nonresident wine vendor permit, or a vendor representative permit;

(3) Not have been convicted of a felony within three years, and, if convicted of a felony before then, shall have had his citizenship restored;

(4) Not have been convicted of an alcoholic beverage offense within two years;

(5) Not have been convicted of a misdemeanor controlled substance offense within two years; and

(6) Not have had an alcoholic beverage permit revoked within three years, except where the revocation was based solely on a permittee's failure to pay the annual registration and inspection fee required in G.S. 18B-903(b1).

(7) Not have, whether as an individual or as an officer, director, shareholder or manager of a corporate permittee, an unsatisfied outstanding final judgment that was entered against him in an action under Article 1A of this Chapter.

To avoid undue hardship, however, the Commission may decline to take action under G.S. 18B-104 against a permittee who is in violation of subdivisions (3), (4), or (5).

(b) Definition of Conviction. - A person has been "convicted" for the purposes of subsection (a) when he has been found guilty, or has entered a plea of guilty or nolo contendere, and judgment has been entered against him. A felony conviction in another jurisdiction shall disqualify a person from being eligible to receive or hold an ABC permit if his conduct would also constitute a felony in North Carolina. A conviction of an alcoholic beverage offense or misdemeanor drug offense in another jurisdiction shall disqualify a person from being eligible to receive or hold an ABC permit if his conduct would constitute an offense in North Carolina, unless the Commission determines that under North Carolina procedure judgment would not have been entered under the same circumstances. Revocation of a permit in another jurisdiction shall disqualify a person if his conduct would be grounds for revocation in North Carolina.

(c) Who Must Qualify; Exceptions. - For an ABC permit to be issued to and held for a business, each of the following persons associated with that business must qualify under subsection (a):

(1) The owner of a sole proprietorship;

(2) Each member of a firm, association or general partnership;

(2a) Each general partner in a limited partnership;

(2b) Each manager and any member with a twenty-five percent (25%) or greater interest in a limited liability company;

(3) Each officer, director and owner of twenty-five percent (25%) or more of the stock of a corporation except that the requirement of subdivision (a)(1) does not apply to such an officer, director, or stockholder unless he is a manager or is otherwise responsible for the day-to-day operation of the business;

(4) The manager of an establishment operated by a corporation other than an establishment with only off-premises malt beverage, off-premises unfortified wine, or off-premises fortified wine permits;

(5) Any manager who has been empowered as attorney-in-fact for a nonresident individual or partnership.

(d) Manager of Off-Premises Establishment. - Although he need not otherwise meet the requirements of this section, the manager of an establishment operated by a corporation and holding off-premises permits for malt beverages, unfortified wine, or fortified wine shall be at least 19 years old and shall meet the requirements of subdivisions (3), (4), (5) and (6) of subsection (a).

(e) Convention Centers. - With the approval of the Commission, the manager of a convention center may contract with another person to provide food and beverages at conventions and banquets at the convention center, and that person may engage in the activities authorized by the convention center's permit, under conditions set by the Commission. The person with whom the convention center contracts must meet the qualifications of this section. (1949, c. 974, ss. 1, 2; 1963, c. 119; c. 426, s. 12; 1965, c. 326; 1971, c. 872, s. 1; 1973, c. 758, s. 2; c. 1012; 1975, c. 19, s. 5; 1977, c. 70, s. 19.1; c. 668, s. 3; c. 977, ss. 1, 2; 1979, c. 286, s. 4; 1981, c. 412, s. 2; c. 747, ss. 53, 54; 1981 (Reg. Sess., 1982), c. 1262, ss. 13, 14; 1983, c. 435, ss. 32, 39; 1987, c. 136, ss. 7, 8; 1993, c. 415, s. 10; 1995, c. 466, s. 6; 2004-203, s. 25(a).)

§ 18B-901. Issuance of permits.

(a) Who Issues. - All ABC permits shall be issued by the Commission. Purchase-transportation permits shall be issued by local boards under G.S. 18B-403.

(b) Notice to Local Government. - Before issuing a retail ABC permit, other than a:

(1) Special occasion permit under G.S. 18B-1001(8);

(2) Limited special occasion permit under G.S. 18B-1001(9);

(3) Temporary permit under G.S. 18B-905; or

(4) Special one-time permit under G.S. 18B-1002

for an establishment, the Commission shall give notice of the permit application to the governing body of the city in which the establishment is located. If the establishment is not inside a city, the Commission shall give notice to the governing body of the county. The Commission shall allow the local governing body 15 days from the time the notice was mailed or delivered to file written objection to the issuance of the permit. To be considered by the Commission, the objection shall state the facts upon which it is based.

(c) Factors in Issuing Permit. - Before issuing a permit, the Commission shall be satisfied that the applicant is a suitable person to hold an ABC permit and that the location is a suitable place to hold the permit for which the applicant has applied. To be a suitable place, the local governing body shall return a Zoning and Compliance Form to the Commission on a form provided by the Commission to show the establishment is in compliance with all applicable building and fire codes and, if applicable, has been notified that it is located in an Urban Redevelopment Area as defined by Article 22 of Chapter 160A of the General Statutes and as required by G.S. 18B-904(e)(2). Other factors the Commission shall consider in determining whether the applicant and the business location are suitable are all of the following:

(1) The reputation, character, and criminal record of the applicant.

(2) The number of places already holding ABC permits within the neighborhood.

(3) Parking facilities and traffic conditions in the neighborhood.

(4) Kinds of businesses already in the neighborhood.

(5)   Whether the establishment is located within 50 feet of a church, public school, or any nonpublic school as defined by Part 1 or Part 2 of Article 39 of Chapter 115C of the General Statutes.

(6)   Zoning laws.

(7)   The recommendations of the local governing body.

(8)   Any other evidence that would tend to show whether the applicant would comply with the ABC laws.

(9)   Whether the operation of the applicant's business at that location would be detrimental to the neighborhood, including evidence admissible under G.S. 150B-29(a) of any of the following:

a.   Past revocations, suspensions, and violations of ABC laws by prior permittees related to or associated with the applicant, or a business with which the applicant is associated, within the immediate preceding 12-month period at this location.

b.   Evidence of illegal drug activity on or about the licensed premises.

c.   Evidence of fighting, disorderly conduct, and other dangerous activities on or about the licensed premises.

(d)   Commission's Authority. - The Commission shall have the sole power, in its discretion, to determine the suitability and qualifications of an applicant for a permit. The Commission shall also have the authority to determine the suitability of the location to which the permit may be issued. (1945, c. 903, s. 1; 1947, c. 1098, ss. 2, 3; 1949, c. 974, s. 1; 1957, cc. 1048, 1448; 1963, c. 426, ss. 10, 12; c. 460, s. 1; 1971, c. 872, s. 1; 1973, c. 476, s. 128; 1975, c. 586, s. 1; c. 654, ss. 1, 2; c. 722, s. 1; 1977, c. 70, s. 19; c. 182, s. 1; c. 669, ss. 1, 2; c. 676, ss. 1, 2; c. 911; 1979, c. 348, ss. 2, 3; c. 683, ss. 5, 6, 11, 12; 1981, c. 412, s. 2; 1993 (Reg. Sess., 1994), c. 749, ss. 1, 2; 2005-392, ss. 2, 3.)

§ 18B-902. Application for permit; fees.

(a)   Form. - An application for an ABC permit shall be on a form prescribed by the Commission and shall be notarized. Each person required to qualify under G.S. 18B-900(c) shall sign and swear to the application and shall submit a full set of fingerprints with the application.

(b) Investigation. - Before issuing a new permit, the Commission, with the assistance of the ALE Section, shall investigate the applicant and the premises for which the permit is requested. The Commission may request the assistance of local ABC officers in investigating applications. An applicant shall cooperate fully with the investigation.

The Department of Justice may provide a criminal record check to the ALE Section for a person who has applied for a permit through the Commission. The ALE Section shall provide to the Department of Justice, along with the request, the fingerprints of the applicant, any additional information required by the Department of Justice, and a form signed by the applicant consenting to the check of the criminal record and to the use of the fingerprints and other identifying information required by the State or national repositories. The applicant's fingerprints shall be forwarded to the State Bureau of Investigation for a search of the State's criminal history record file, and the State Bureau of Investigation shall forward a set of the fingerprints to the Federal Bureau of Investigation for a national criminal history check. The ALE Section and the Commission shall keep all information pursuant to this subsection privileged, in accordance with applicable State law and federal guidelines, and the information shall be confidential and shall not be a public record under Chapter 132 of the General Statutes.

The Department of Justice may charge each applicant a fee for conducting the checks of criminal history records authorized by this subsection.

(c) False Information. - Knowingly making a false statement in an application for an ABC permit shall be grounds for denying, suspending, revoking or taking other action against the permit as provided in G.S. 18B-104 and shall also be unlawful.

(d) Fees. - An application for an ABC permit shall be accompanied by payment of the following application fee:

(1) On-premises malt beverage permit - $400.00.

(2) Off-premises malt beverage permit - $400.00.

(3) On-premises unfortified wine permit - $400.00.

(4) Off-premises unfortified wine permit - $400.00.

(5) On-premises fortified wine permit - $400.00.

(6) Off-premises fortified wine permit - $400.00.

(7) Brown-bagging permit - $400.00, unless the application is for a restaurant seating less than 50, in which case the fee shall be $200.00.

(8) Special occasion permit - $400.00.

(9) Limited special occasion permit - $50.00.

(10) Mixed beverages permit - $1,000.

(11) Culinary permit - $200.00.

(12) Unfortified winery permit - $300.00.

(13) Fortified winery permit - $300.00.

(14) Limited winery permit - $300.00.

(15) Brewery permit - $300.00.

(16) Distillery permit - $300.00.

(17) Fuel alcohol permit - $100.00.

(18) Wine importer permit - $300.00.

(19) Wine wholesaler permit - $300.00.

(20) Malt beverage importer permit - $300.00.

(21) Malt beverage wholesaler permit - $300.00.

(22) Bottler permit - $300.00.

(23) Salesman permit - $100.00.

(24) Vendor representative permit - $50.00.

(25) Nonresident malt beverage vendor permit - $100.00.

(26) Nonresident wine vendor permit - $100.00.

(27) Any special one-time permit under G.S. 18B-1002 - $50.00.

(28) Winery special event permit - $200.00.

(29) Mixed beverages catering permit - $200.00.

(30) Guest room cabinet permit - $1,000.

(31) Liquor importer/bottler permit - $500.00.

(32) Cider and vinegar manufacturer permit - $200.00.

(33) Brew on premises permit - $400.00.

(34) Wine producer permit - $300.00.

(35) Wine tasting permit - $100.00.

(36) Repealed by Session Laws 2005-380, s. 1, effective September 8, 2005, and applicable to wine shipper permit applications submitted on or after that date.

(37) Wine shop permit - $100.00.

(38) Winemaking on premises permit - $400.00.

(39) Wine shipper packager permit - $100.00.

(40) Malt beverage special event permit - $200.00.

(41) Malt beverage tasting permit - $100.00.

(42) Spirituous liquor tasting permit - $100.00.

(e) Repealed by Session Laws 1998-95, s. 29, effective May 1, 1999.

(f) Fee Not Refundable. - The fee required by subsection (d) shall not be refunded.

(g) Fees to Treasurer. - All fees collected by the Commission under this or any other section of this Chapter shall be remitted to the State Treasurer for the General Fund.

(h) Recycling Plan Required. - Each applicant for an on-premises malt beverage permit, on-premises unfortified wine permit, on-premises fortified wine permit, or a mixed beverages permit shall prepare and submit with the application a plan for the collection and recycling of all recyclable beverage containers of all beverages to be sold at retail on the premises. A permittee who is not able to find a recycler for its beverage containers may apply to the Alcoholic Beverage Control Commission for a one-year stay of the requirement to implement a recycling program in compliance with G.S. 18B-1006.1. The application shall be made in a form specified by the Commission, shall detail the efforts made by the permittee to provide for the collection and recycling of beverage containers, and shall specify the impediments to implementation of a recycling plan. The Commission shall submit all such applications to the Division of Environmental Assistance and Outreach of the Department of Environment and Natural Resources for review and certification. The Division of Environmental Assistance and Outreach shall investigate each application and prepare a summary of its investigation and shall submit the summary to the Commission along with a notation indicating certification or denial of the application. A permittee whose application for a stay is certified by the Division of Environmental Assistance and Outreach shall not be required to comply with the recycling requirement of the alcoholic beverage laws and regulations during the one-year stay period so certified. (1949, c. 974, ss. 1, 2; 1963, c. 119; c. 426, s. 12; 1965, c. 326; 1971, c. 872, s. 1; 1973, c. 758, s. 2; c. 1012; 1975, c. 19, s. 5; 1977, c. 70, s. 19.1; c. 668, s. 3; c. 977, ss. 1, 2; 1979, c. 286, s. 4; 1981, c. 412, s. 2; c. 747, ss. 55, 56; 1983, c. 713, s. 105; 1989, c. 737, s. 3; c. 800, s. 7; 1991, c. 267, s. 2; c. 565, ss. 2, 7; c. 669, s. 2; c. 689, ss. 307, 308; 1991 (Reg. Sess., 1992), c. 920, s. 5; 1993, c. 415, s. 11; 1993 (Reg. Sess., 1994), c. 745, s. 28; 1995, c. 404, s. 2; c. 466, s. 7; 1997-134, s. 3; 1997-467, s. 2; 1998-95, s. 29; 2001-262, s. 6; 2001-487, s. 49(f); 2002-147, s. 1; 2003-402, s. 1; 2005-350, s. 2(b); 2005-380, s. 1; 2006-222, s. 2.3; 2006-227, s. 3; 2007-402, s. 2(b); 2008-187, s. 6; 2009-105, s. 1; 2009-377, s. 1; 2010-31, ss. 13.1(b), 14.12(b); 2011-145, s. 19.1(q).)

§ 18B-903. Duration of permit; renewal and transfer.

(a) Duration. - Once issued, ABC permits shall be valid for the following periods, unless earlier surrendered, suspended or revoked:

(1) On-premises and off-premises malt beverage, unfortified wine, and fortified wine permits; culinary permits; and all permits listed in G.S. 18B-1100 shall remain valid indefinitely;

(2) Limited special occasion permits shall be valid for 48 hours before and after the occasion for which the permit was issued;

(3) Special one-time permits issued under G.S. 18B-1002 shall be valid for the period stated on the permit;

(4) Temporary permits issued under G.S. 18B-905 shall be valid for 90 days; and

(5) All other ABC permits shall be valid for one year, from May 1 to April 30.

(b) Renewal. - Application for renewal of an ABC permit shall be on a form provided by the Commission. An application for renewal shall be accompanied by an application fee of twenty-five percent (25%) of the original application fee set in G.S. 18B-902, except that the renewal application fee for each wine shop permit shall be five hundred dollars ($500.00), and the renewal application fee for each mixed beverages permit and each guest room cabinet permit shall be seven hundred fifty dollars ($750.00). A renewal fee shall not be refundable.

(b1) Registration. - Each person holding a malt beverage, fortified wine, or unfortified wine permit issued pursuant to G.S. 18B-902(d)(1) through G.S. 18B-902(d)(6) shall register by May 1 of each year on a form provided by the Commission, in order to provide information needed by the State in enforcing this Chapter and to support the costs of that enforcement. The registration required by this subsection shall be accompanied by an annual registration and inspection fee of two hundred dollars ($200.00) for each permit held. The fee shall be paid by May 1 of each year. A registration fee shall not be refundable. Failure to pay the annual registration and inspection fee shall result in revocation of the permit.

(b2) Recycling Plan Required. - Each person holding an on-premises malt beverage permit, on-premises unfortified wine permit, on-premises fortified wine permit, or a mixed beverages permit shall submit, along with the annual registration or renewal application, either a current plan for the collection and recycling of all recyclable beverage containers of all beverages sold at retail on the premises, or an application for a waiver pursuant to G.S. 18B-902(h).

(c) Change in Ownership. - All permits for an establishment shall automatically expire and shall be surrendered to the Commission if:

(1) Ownership of the establishment changes; or

(2) There is a change in the membership of the firm, association or partnership owning the establishment, involving the acquisition of a twenty-five percent (25%) or greater share in the firm, association or partnership by someone who did not previously own a twenty-five percent (25%) or greater share; or

(3) Twenty-five percent (25%) or more of the stock of the corporate permittee owning the establishment is acquired by someone who did not previously own twenty-five percent (25%) or more of the stock.

(d) Change in Management. - A corporation holding a permit for an establishment for which the manager is required to qualify as an applicant under G.S. 18B-900(c) shall, within 30 days after employing a new manager, submit to the Commission an application for substitution of a manager. The application shall be signed by the new manager, shall be on a form provided by the Commission, and shall be accompanied by a fee of ten dollars ($10.00). The fee shall not be refundable.

(e) Transfer. - An ABC permit may not be transferred from one person to another or from one location to another.

(f) Lost Permits. - The Commission may issue duplicate ABC permits for an establishment when the existing valid permits have been lost or damaged. The request for duplicate permits shall be on a form provided by the Commission, certified by the permittee and the Alcohol Law Enforcement Section, and accompanied by a fee of ten dollars ($10.00).

(g) Name Change. - The Commission may issue new permits to a permittee upon application and payment of a fee of ten dollars ($10.00) for each location when the permittee's name or name of the business is changed. (1971, c. 872, s. 1; 1975, c. 330, s. 1; c. 411, s. 4; 1981, c. 412, s. 2; c. 747, s. 57; 1983, c. 713, s. 106; 1989, c. 800, s. 8; 1991, c. 565, ss. 3, 7; 1991 (Reg. Sess., 1992), c. 920, s. 6; 1998-95, s. 30; 2002-126, s. 29A.13; 2004-203, s. 25(b); 2005-350, s. 2(c); 2007-402, s. 2(c); 2008-187, s. 7; 2009-105, s. 2; 2011-145, s. 19.1(n).)

§ 18B-904. Miscellaneous provisions concerning permits.

(a) Who Receives Permit. - An ABC permit shall authorize the permitted activity only on the premises of the establishment named in the permit. An ABC permit shall be issued to the owner of the business conducted on the premises, or to the management company employed to independently manage and operate the business. The ABC Commission may determine if a management agreement delegates sufficient managerial control and independence to a manager or management company to require an ABC permit to be issued to the manager.

(b) Posting Permit. - Each ABC permit that is held by an establishment shall be posted in a prominent place on the premises.

(c) Business Not Operating. - An ABC permit shall automatically expire and shall be surrendered to the Commission if the person to whom it is issued does not commence the activity authorized by the permit within six months of the date the permit is effective. Before the expiration of the six-month period, the Commission may waive this provision in individual cases for good cause.

(d) Notice of Issuance. - Upon issuing a permit the Commission shall send notice of the issuance, with the name and address of the permittee and the establishment, to:

(1) The Department of Revenue;

(2) The local board, if one exists, for the city or county in which the establishment is located;

(3) The governing body, sheriff, and tax collector of the county in which the establishment is located;

(4) If the establishment is located inside a city, the governing body, chief of police, and tax collector for the city; and

(5) The ALE Section.

(e) Business or Location No Longer Suitable. -

(1) The Commission may suspend or revoke a permit issued by it if, after compliance with the provisions of Chapter 150B of the General Statutes, it finds that the location occupied by the permittee is no longer a suitable place to hold ABC permits or that the operation of the business with an ABC permit at that location is detrimental to the neighborhood.

(2) The Commission shall suspend or revoke a permit issued by it if a permittee is in violation of G.S. 18B-309. Notwithstanding subdivision (e)(1) of this section, the Commission shall, by order and without prior hearing, summarily suspend or revoke a permit issued by it if a permittee is in violation of G.S. 18B-309(c) when, prior to the period of time for which the audit is to be conducted, the city council has filed information designating the location of the Urban Redevelopment Area as required under G.S. 18B-309(a) and has provided actual notice to permittees located in the Urban Redevelopment Area that they are located in such an area and must abide by G.S. 18B-309(c). Upon entry of a summary order under this subdivision, the Commission shall promptly notify all interested parties that the order has been entered and of the reasons therefore. The order will remain in effect until it is modified or vacated by the Commission. The permittee may, within 30 days after receipt of notice of the order, make written request to the Commission for a hearing on the matter. If a hearing is requested, after compliance with the provisions of Chapter 150B of the General Statutes, the Commission shall issue an order to affirm, reverse, or modify its previous action.

(3) Notwithstanding G.S. 18B-906, the Commission shall revoke a permit issued by it if, after complying with the provisions of Chapter 150B of the General Statutes and without a finding of mitigating evidence or circumstances, it finds evidence that the permittee or the permittee's employee has been found responsible by a court of competent jurisdiction or the Commission for two or more violations on separate dates of knowingly allowing a violation of the gambling, disorderly conduct, prostitution, controlled substance, or felony criminal counterfeit trademark laws as those offenses are prohibited pursuant to G.S. 18B-1005(a)(2), (a)(3), or (b), G.S. 18B-1005.1, or G.S. 80-11.1(b)(2) or (3), at a single ABC-licensed premises within a 12-month period. The permittee

and the owner of the property have the responsibility to monitor the conduct on the licensed premises pursuant to G.S. 18B-1005(b) and G.S. 19-1. Revocation of permits pursuant to this subdivision shall only apply to the permits issued to the location where the violations occurred.

(f) Local Government Objections. - The governing body of a city or county may designate an official of the city or county, by name or by position, to make recommendations concerning the suitability of a person or of a location for an ABC permit. The governing body of a city or county shall notify the Commission of an official designated under this subsection. An official designated under this subsection shall be allowed to testify at a contested case hearing in which the suitability of a person or of a location for an ABC permit is an issue without further qualification or authorization.

(g) Nothing in this Chapter shall be deemed to preempt local governments from regulating the location or operation of adult establishments or other sexually oriented businesses to the extent consistent with the constitutional protection afforded free speech, or from requiring any additional fee for licensing as permitted under G.S. 160A-181.1(c). (1939, c. 158, s. 514; 1943, c. 400, s. 6; 1949, c. 974, s. 14; 1953, c. 1207, ss. 2-4; 1957, c. 1440; 1963, c. 426, ss. 4, 5; 1971, c. 872, s. 1; 1981, c. 412, s. 2; c. 747, s. 58; 1989, c. 800, ss. 9, 10; 1991, c. 459, s. 4; 1993, c. 415, s. 12; 1998-46, s. 6; 1999-322, s. 2; 2001-515, s. 3(b); 2005-392, s. 4; 2011-145, s. 19.1(q).)

§ 18B-905. Temporary permits.

When an application has been received in proper form, with the required application fee, the Commission may issue a temporary permit for any of the activities for which permits are authorized under G.S. 18B-1001 and 18B-1100. A temporary permit may be revoked summarily by the Commission without complying with the provisions of Chapter 150B. Revocation of a temporary permit shall be effective upon service of the notice of revocation upon the permittee or upon the expiration of three working days after the notice of the revocation has been mailed to the permittee at either his residence or the address given for the business in the permit application. No further notice shall be required. (1945, c. 903, s. 1; 1947, c. 1098, ss. 2, 3; 1949, c. 974, s. 1; 1957, cc. 1048, 1448; 1963, c. 426, ss. 10, 12; c. 460, s. 1; 1971, c. 872, s. 1; 1973, c. 476, s. 128; 1975, c. 586, s. 1; c. 654, ss. 1, 2; c. 722, s. 1; 1977, c. 70, s. 19; c.

182, s. 1; c. 669, ss. 1, 2; c. 676, ss. 1, 2; c. 911; 1979, c. 348, ss. 2, 3; c. 683, ss. 5, 6, 11, 12; 1981, c. 412, s. 2; 1987, c. 827, s. 1.)

§ 18B-906. Applicability of Administrative Procedure Act.

(a) Act Applies. - An ABC permit is a "license" within the meaning of G.S. 150B-2, and, except for revocation pursuant to G.S. 18B-904(e)(3), a Commission action on issuance, suspension, or revocation of an ABC permit, other than a temporary permit issued under G.S. 18B-905, is a "contested case" subject to the provisions of Chapter 150B except as provided in this section.

(b) Exception on Hearing Location. - Hearings on ABC permits shall be held in Ahoskie, Asheville, Bryson City, Charlotte, Elizabeth City, Fayetteville, Franklin, Goldsboro, Greensboro, Greenville, Hickory, Jacksonville, Kinston, New Bern, Raleigh, Statesville, Wilmington, and Winston-Salem. Hearings shall be held within 100 miles, as best can be determined by the Commission, of the county seat of the county in which the licensed business or proposed business is located. The hearing may be held, however, at any place upon agreement of the Commission and all other parties.

(c) Exception on New Evidence. - In making a final decision in a contested case in which an issue is whether to deny an application for an ABC permit because either the applicant or the location for the proposed ABC permit is unsuitable, the Commission may hear evidence of acts that occurred after the date the contested case hearing was held if the evidence is admissible under G.S. 150B-29(a). New evidence heard under this subsection is not grounds for reversal or remand under G.S. 150B-51(a). (1939, c. 158, s. 514; 1943, c. 400, s. 6; 1945, c. 903, s. 1; 1947, c. 1098, ss. 2, 3; 1949, c. 974, ss. 8, 14; 1953, c. 1207, ss. 2-4; 1957, cc. 1048, 1440; 1963, c. 426, ss. 4, 5, 10-12; c. 460, s. 1; 1971, c. 872, s. 1; 1975, c. 825, s. 1; 1977, c. 176, s. 9; 1981, c. 412, s. 2; 1987, c. 827, s. 1; 1993, c. 415, s. 13; 2005-392, s. 5.)

§§ 18B-907 through 18B-999. Reserved for future codification purposes.

Article 10.

Retail Activity.

§ 18B-1000. Definitions concerning establishments.

The following requirements and definitions shall apply to this Chapter:

(1) Community theatre. - An establishment owned and operated by a bona fide nonprofit organization that is engaged solely in the business of sponsoring or presenting amateur or professional theatrical events to the public. A permit issued for a community theatre is valid only during regularly scheduled theatrical events sponsored by such nonprofit organization.

(1a) Convention center. - An establishment that meets either of the following requirements:

a. A publicly owned or operated establishment that is engaged in the business of sponsoring or hosting conventions and similar large gatherings, including auditoriums, armories, civic centers, convention centers, and coliseums.

b. A privately owned facility located in a city that has a population of at least 200,000 but not more than 250,000 by the 2000 federal census and is located in a county that has previously authorized the issuance of mixed beverage permits by referendum. To qualify as a convention center under this subdivision, the facility shall meet each of the following requirements:

1. The facility shall be certified by the appropriate local official as being consistent with the city's redevelopment plan for the area in which the facility is located.

2. The facility shall contain at least 7,500 square feet of floor space that is available for public use and shall be used exclusively for banquets, receptions, meetings, and similar gatherings.

3. The facility's annual gross receipts from the sale of alcoholic beverages shall be less than fifty percent (50%) of the gross receipts paid to all providers at permitted functions for food, nonalcoholic beverages, alcoholic beverages, service, and facility usage fees (excluding receipts or charges for entertainment and ancillary services not directly related to providing food and beverage service). The person to whom a permit has been issued for a privately owned

facility shall be required to maintain copies of all contracts and invoices for items supplied by providers for a period of three years from the date of the event.

A permit issued for a convention center shall be valid only for those parts of the building used for conventions, banquets, receptions, and other events, and only during scheduled activities.

(1b) Cooking school. - An establishment substantially engaged in the business of operating a school in which cooking techniques are taught for a fee.

(2) Eating establishment. - An establishment engaged in the business of regularly and customarily selling food, primarily to be eaten on the premises. Eating establishments shall include businesses that are referred to as restaurants, cafeterias, or cafes, but that do not qualify under subdivision (6). Eating establishments shall also include lunchstands, grills, snack bars, fast-food businesses, and other establishments, such as drugstores, which have a lunch counter or other section where food is sold to be eaten on the premises.

(3) Food business. - An establishment engaged in the business of regularly and customarily selling food, primarily to be eaten off the premises. Food businesses shall include grocery stores, convenience stores, and other establishments, such as variety stores or drugstores, where food is regularly sold, and shall also include establishments engaged primarily in selling unfortified or fortified wine or both, for consumption off the premises.

(4) Hotel. - An establishment substantially engaged in the business of furnishing lodging. A hotel shall have a restaurant either on or closely associated with the premises. The restaurant and hotel need not be owned or operated by the same person.

(5) Private club. - An establishment that is organized and operated solely for a social, recreational, patriotic, or fraternal purpose and that is not open to the general public, but is open only to the members of the organization and their bona fide guests. This provision does not, however, prohibit such an establishment from being open to the general public for raffles and bingo games as required by G.S. 14-309.11(a) and G.S. 14-309.13. Except for bona fide religious organizations, no organization that discriminates in the selection of its membership on the basis of religion shall be eligible to receive any permit issued under this Chapter.

(5a) Residential private club. - A private club that is located in a privately owned, primarily residential and recreational development.

(6) Restaurant. - An establishment substantially engaged in the business of preparing and serving meals. To qualify as a restaurant, an establishment's gross receipts from food and nonalcoholic beverages shall be not less than thirty percent (30%) of the total gross receipts from food, nonalcoholic beverages, and alcoholic beverages. A restaurant shall also have a kitchen and an inside dining area with seating for at least 36 people.

(7) Retail business. - An establishment engaged in any retail business, regardless of whether food is sold on the premises.

(8) Sports club. - An establishment that meets either of the following requirements:

a. The establishment is substantially engaged in the business of providing equine boarding, training, and coaching services, and the establishment offers on-site dining, lodging, and meeting facilities and hosts horse trials and other events sanctioned or endorsed by the United States Equestrian Federation, Inc.; or

b. The establishment is substantially engaged in the business of providing an 18-hole golf course, two or more tennis courts, or both.

The sports club can either be open to the general public or to members and their guests. To qualify as a sports club, an establishment's gross receipts for club activities shall be greater than its gross receipts for alcoholic beverages. This provision does not prohibit a sports club from operating a restaurant. Receipts for food shall be included in with the club activity fee.

(9) Congressionally chartered veterans organizations. - An establishment that is organized as a federally chartered, nonprofit veterans organization, and is operated solely for patriotic or fraternal purposes.

(10) Wine producer. - A farming establishment of at least five acres committed to the production of grapes, berries, or other fruits for the manufacture of unfortified wine. (1905, c. 498, ss. 6-8; Rev., ss. 3526, 3534; C.S., s. 3371; 1937, c. 49, ss. 12, 16, 22; c. 411; 1955, c. 999; 1967, c. 222, ss. 1, 8; c. 1256, s. 3; 1969, c. 1018; 1971, c. 872, s. 1; 1973, c. 1226; 1977, c. 176, s. 1; 1981, c. 412, s. 2; 1981 (Reg. Sess., 1982), c. 1262, s. 15; 1983, c. 583, s.

1; c. 896, s. 5; 1987, c. 307, s. 1; c. 391, s. 1; 1993, c. 415, ss. 14, 15; 1993 (Reg. Sess., 1994), c. 579, s. 1; 1995, c. 466, s. 8; c. 509, s. 15; 2001-262, s. 7; 2001-487, s. 49(d); 2002-188, s. 1; 2003-135, s. 1; 2009-539, s. 4; 2013-392, s. 2.)

§ 18B-1001. Kinds of ABC permits; places eligible.

When the issuance of the permit is lawful in the jurisdiction in which the premises are located, the Commission may issue the following kinds of permits:

(1) On-Premises Malt Beverage Permit. - An on-premises malt beverage permit authorizes (i) the retail sale of malt beverages for consumption on the premises, (ii) the retail sale of malt beverages in the manufacturer's original container for consumption off the premises, and (iii) the retail sale of malt beverages in a cleaned, sanitized, resealable container as defined in 4 NCAC 2T.0308(a) that is filled or refilled and sealed for consumption off the premises, complies with 4 NCAC 2T.0303, 4 NCAC 2T.0305, and 4 NCAC 2T.0308(d)-(e), and the container identifies the permittee and the date the container was filled or refilled. It also authorizes the holder of the permit to ship malt beverages in closed containers to individual purchasers inside and outside the State. The permit may be issued for any of the following:

a. Restaurants;

b. Hotels;

c. Eating establishments;

d. Food businesses;

e. Retail businesses;

f. Private clubs;

g. Convention centers;

h. Community theatres;

i. Breweries as authorized by G.S. 18B-1104(7).

(2) Off-Premises Malt Beverage Permit. - An off-premises malt beverage permit authorizes (i) the retail sale of malt beverages in the manufacturer's original container for consumption off the premises, (ii) the retail sale of malt beverages in a cleaned, sanitized, resealable container as defined in 4 NCAC 2T.0308(a) that is filled or refilled and sealed for consumption off the premises, complies with 4 NCAC 2T.0303, 4 NCAC 2T.0305, and 4 NCAC 2T.0308(d)-(e), and the container identifies the permittee and the date the container was filled or refilled, and (iii) the holder of the permit to ship malt beverages in closed containers to individual purchasers inside and outside the State. The permit may be issued for any of the following:

a. Restaurants;

b. Hotels;

c. Eating establishments;

d. Food businesses;

e. Retail businesses.

(3) On-Premises Unfortified Wine Permit. - On-Premises Unfortified Wine Permit. - An on-premises unfortified wine permit authorizes the retail sale of unfortified wine for consumption on the premises, either alone or mixed with other beverages, and the retail sale of unfortified wine in the manufacturer's original container for consumption off the premises. The permit also authorizes the permittee to transfer unfortified wine, not more than four times per calendar year, to another on-premises unfortified wine permittee that is under common ownership or control as the transferor. Except as authorized by this subdivision, transfers of wine by on-premises unfortified wine permittees, purchases of wine by a retail permittee from another retail permittee for the purpose of resale, and sale of wine by a retail permittee to another retail permittee for the purpose of resale are unlawful. In addition, a particular brand of wine may be transferred only if both the transferor and transferee are located within the territory designated between the winery and the wholesaler on file with the Commission. Prior to or contemporaneous with any such transfer, the transferor shall notify each wholesaler who distributes the transferred product of the transfer. The notice shall be in writing or verifiable electronic format and shall identify the transferor and transferee, the date of the transfer, quantity, and items transferred. The holder of the permit is authorized to ship unfortified wine in

closed containers to individual purchasers inside and outside the State. Orders received by a winery by telephone, Internet, mail, facsimile, or other off-premises means of communication shall be shipped pursuant to a wine shipper permit and not pursuant to this subdivision. The permit may be issued for any of the following:

a. Restaurants;

b. Hotels;

c. Eating establishments;

d. Private clubs;

e. Convention centers;

f. Cooking schools;

g. Community theatres;

h. Wineries;

i. Wine producers.

(4) Off-Premises Unfortified Wine Permit. - An off-premises unfortified wine permit authorizes the retail sale of unfortified wine in the manufacturer's original container for consumption off the premises and it authorizes the holder of the permit to ship unfortified wine in closed containers to individual purchasers inside and outside the State. The permit may be issued for retail businesses. The permit also authorizes the permittee to transfer unfortified wine, not more than four times per calendar year, to another off-premises unfortified wine permittee that is under common ownership or control as the transferor. Except as authorized by this subdivision, transfers of wine by off-premises unfortified wine permittees, purchases of wine by a retail permittee from another retail permittee for the purpose of resale, and sale of wine by a retail permittee to another retail permittee for the purpose of resale are unlawful. In addition, a particular brand of wine may be transferred only if both the transferor and transferee are located within the territory designated between the winery and the wholesaler on file with the Commission. Prior to or contemporaneous with any such transfer, the transferor shall notify each wholesaler who distributes the transferred product of the transfer. The notice shall be in writing or verifiable

electronic format and shall identify the transferor and transferee, the date of the transfer, quantity, and items transferred. The permit may also be issued to the holder of a viticulture/enology course authorization under G.S. 18B-1114.4. A school obtaining a permit under this subdivision is authorized to sell wines manufactured during its viticulture/enology program at one non-campus location in a county where the permittee holds and offers classes on a regular full-time basis in a facility owned by the permittee. The permit may also be issued for a winery or a wine producer for sale of its own unfortified wine during hours when the winery or wine producer's premises is open to the public, subject to any local ordinance adopted pursuant to G.S. 18B-1004(d) concerning hours for the retail sale of unfortified wine. A winery obtaining a permit under this subdivision is authorized to sell wine manufactured by the winery at one additional location in the county under the same conditions specified in G.S. 18B-1101(5) for the sale of wine at the winery; provided, however, that no other alcohol sales shall be authorized at the additional location. Orders received by a winery by telephone, Internet, mail, facsimile, or other off-premises means of communication shall be shipped pursuant to a wine shipper permit and not pursuant to this subdivision.

(5) On-Premises Fortified Wine Permit. - An on-premises fortified wine permit authorizes the retail sale of fortified wine for consumption on the premises, either alone or mixed with other beverages, and the retail sale of fortified wine in the manufacturer's original container for consumption off the premises. The permit also authorizes the permittee to transfer fortified wine, not more than four times per calendar year, to another on-premises fortified wine permittee that is under common ownership or control as the transferor. Except as authorized by this subdivision, transfers of wine by on-premises fortified wine permittees, purchases of wine by a retail permittee from another retail permittee for the purpose of resale, and sale of wine by a retail permittee to another retail permittee for the purpose of resale are unlawful. In addition, a particular brand of wine may be transferred only if both the transferor and transferee are located within the territory designated between the winery and the wholesaler on file with the Commission. Prior to or contemporaneous with any such transfer, the transferor shall notify each wholesaler who distributes the transferred product of the transfer. The notice shall be in writing or verifiable electronic format and shall identify the transferor and transferee, the date of the transfer, quantity, and items transferred. The holder of the permit is authorized to ship fortified wine in closed containers to individual purchasers inside and outside the State. Orders received by a winery by telephone, Internet, mail, facsimile, or other off-premises means of communication shall be shipped pursuant to a wine shipper permit and not pursuant to this subdivision. The permit may be issued for any of the following:

a. Restaurants;

b. Hotels;

c. Private clubs;

d. Community theatres;

e. Wineries;

f. Convention centers.

(6) Off-Premises Fortified Wine Permit. - An off-premises fortified wine permit authorizes the retail sale of fortified wine in the manufacturer's original container for consumption off the premises and it authorizes the holder of the permit to ship fortified wine in closed containers to individual purchasers inside and outside the State. The permit may be issued for food businesses. The permit may also be issued for a winery for sale of its own fortified wine. Orders received by a winery by telephone, Internet, mail, facsimile, or other off-premises means of communication shall be shipped pursuant to a wine shipper permit and not pursuant to this subdivision. The permit also authorizes the permittee to transfer fortified wine, not more than four times per calendar year, to another off-premises fortified wine permittee that is under common ownership or control as the transferor. Except as authorized by this subdivision, transfers of wine by off-premises fortified wine permittees, purchases of wine by a retail permittee from another retail permittee for the purpose of resale, and sale of wine by a retail permittee to another retail permittee for the purpose of resale are unlawful. In addition, a particular brand of wine may be transferred only if both the transferor and transferee are located within the territory designated between the winery and the wholesaler on file with the Commission. Prior to or contemporaneous with any such transfer, the transferor shall notify each wholesaler who distributes the transferred product of the transfer. The notice shall be in writing or verifiable electronic format and shall identify the transferor and transferee, the date of the transfer, quantity, and items transferred.

(7) Brown-Bagging Permit. - A brown-bagging permit authorizes each individual patron of an establishment, with the permission of the permittee, to bring up to eight liters of fortified wine or spirituous liquor, or eight liters of the two combined, onto the premises and to consume those alcoholic beverages on the premises. The permit may be issued for any of the following:

a. Restaurants;

b. Hotels;

c. Private clubs;

d. Community theatres;

e. Congressionally chartered veterans organizations.

(8) Special Occasion Permit. - A special occasion permit authorizes the host of a reception, party or other special occasion, with the permission of the permittee, to bring fortified wine and spirituous liquor onto the premises of the business and to serve the same to his guests. The permit may be issued for any of the following:

a. Restaurants;

b. Hotels;

c. Eating establishments;

d. Private clubs;

e. Convention centers.

(9) Limited Special Occasion Permit. - A limited special occasion permit authorizes the permittee to bring fortified wine and spirituous liquor onto the premises of a business, with the permission of the owner of that property, and to serve those alcoholic beverages to the permittee's guests at a reception, party, or other special occasion being held there. The permit may be issued to any individual other than the owner or possessor of the premises. An applicant for a limited special occasion permit shall have the written permission of the owner or possessor of the property on which the special occasion is to be held.

(10) Mixed Beverages Permit. - A mixed beverages permit authorizes the retail sale of mixed beverages for consumption on the premises. The permit also authorizes a mixed beverages permittee to obtain a purchase-transportation permit under G.S. 18B-403 and 18B-404, and to use for culinary purposes

spirituous liquor lawfully purchased for use in mixed beverages. The permit may be issued for any of the following:

a. Restaurants;

b. Hotels;

c. Private clubs;

d. Convention centers;

e. Community theatres;

f. Nonprofit organizations; and

g. Political organizations.

(11) Culinary Permit. - A culinary permit authorizes a permittee to possess up to 12 liters of either fortified wine or spirituous liquor, or 12 liters of the two combined, in the kitchen of a business and to use those alcoholic beverages for culinary purposes. The permit may be issued for either of the following:

a. Restaurants;

b. Hotels;

c. Cooking schools.

A culinary permit may also be issued to a catering service to allow the possession of the amount of fortified wine and spirituous liquor stated above at the business location of that service and at the cooking site. The permit shall also authorize the caterer to transport those alcoholic beverages to and from the business location and the cooking site, and use them in cooking.

(12) Mixed Beverages Catering Permit. - A mixed beverages catering permit authorizes a hotel or a restaurant that has a mixed beverages permit to bring spirituous liquor onto the premises where the hotel or restaurant is catering food for an event and to serve the liquor to guests at the event.

(13) Guest Room Cabinet Permit. - A guest room cabinet permit authorizes a hotel having a mixed beverages permit or a private club having a mixed

beverages permit and management contracts for the rental of living units to sell to its room guests, from securely locked cabinets, malt beverages, unfortified wine, fortified wine, and spirituous liquor. A permittee shall designate and maintain at least ten percent (10%) of the permittee's guest rooms as rooms that do not have a guest room cabinet. A permittee may dispense alcoholic beverages from a guest room cabinet only in accordance with written policies and procedures filed with and approved by the Commission. A permittee shall provide a reasonable number of vending machines, coolers, or similar machines on premises for the sale of soft drinks to hotel guests.

A guest room cabinet permit may be issued for any of the following:

a. A hotel located in a county subject to G.S. 18B-600(f).

b. A hotel located in a county that has a population in excess of 150,000 by the last federal census.

c. A qualifying private club located in a county defined in G.S. 18B-101(13a)b.2.

(14) Brew on Premises Permit. - A permit may be issued to a business, located in a jurisdiction where the sale of malt beverages is allowed, where individual customers who are 21 years old or older may purchase ingredients and rent the equipment, time, and space to brew malt beverages for personal use in amounts set forth in 27 C.F.R. § 25.205. The customer must do all of the following:

a. Select a recipe and kettle.

b. Weigh out the proper ingredients and add them to the kettle.

c. Transfer the wort to the fermenter.

d. Add the yeast.

e. Place the ingredients in a fermentation room.

f. Filter, carbonate, and bottle the malt beverage.

A permittee may transfer the ingredients from the fermentation room to the cold room and may assist the customer in all the steps involved in brewing a malt beverage except adding the yeast. A malt beverage produced under this subdivision may not contain more than six percent (6%) alcohol by volume.

(15) Wine-Tasting Permit. - A wine-tasting permit authorizes wine tastings on a premises holding a retail permit, by the retail permit holder or his employee. A wine tasting consists of the offering of a sample of one or more unfortified wine products, in amounts of no more than one ounce for each sample, without charge, to customers of the business. Any person pouring wine at a wine tasting shall be at least 21 years of age.

a. Representatives of the winery, which produced the wine, the wine producer, a wholesaler, or a wholesaler's employee may assist with the tasting. Assisting with a wine tasting includes:

1. Pouring samples for customers.

2. Checking the identification of patrons being served at the wine tasting.

b. When a representative of the winery that produced the wine, the wine producer, a wine wholesaler, or a wine wholesaler's employee assists in a wine tasting conducted by a retail permit holder:

1. The retail permit holder shall designate an employee to actively supervise the wine tasting.

2. A retail permit holder's employee shall not supervise more than three wine-tasting areas.

3. No more than six wines may be tasted at any one tasting area.

4. The wine tasting shall not last longer than four hours from the time designated as the starting time by the retail permit holder.

c. The retail permit holder shall be solely liable for any violations of this Chapter occurring in connection with the wine tasting. The Commission shall adopt rules to assure that the tastings are limited to samplings and not a subterfuge for the unlawful sale or distribution of wine, and that the tastings are not used by industry members for unlawful inducements to retail permit holders. Except for purposes of this subsection, the holder of a wine-tasting permit shall not be construed to hold a permit for the on-premises sale or consumption of alcoholic beverages. Any food business is eligible for a wine-tasting permit.

(16) Wine Shop Permit. - A wine shop permit authorizes (i) the retail sale of malt beverages, unfortified wine, and fortified wine in the manufacturer's original container for consumption off the premises, (ii) the retail sale of malt beverages in a cleaned, sanitized, resealable container as defined in 4 NCAC 2T.0308(a) that is filled or refilled and sealed for consumption off the premises, complies with 4 NCAC 2T.0303, 4 NCAC 2T.0305, and 4 NCAC 2T.0308(d)-(e), and the container identifies the permittee and the date the container was filled or refilled, and (iii) wine tastings on the premises conducted and supervised by the permittee in accordance with subdivision (15) of this section. It also authorizes the holder of the permit to ship malt beverages, unfortified wine, and fortified wine in closed containers to individual purchasers inside and outside the State. The permit may be issued for retail businesses whose primary purpose is selling malt beverages and wine for consumption off the premises and regularly and customarily educating consumers through tastings, classes, and seminars about the selection, serving, and storing of wine. The holder of the permit is authorized to sell unfortified wine for consumption on the premises, provided that the sale of wine for consumption on the premises does not exceed forty percent (40%) of the establishment's total sales for any 30-day period. The holder of a wine-tasting permit not engaged in the preparation or sale of food on the premises is not subject to Part 6 of Article 8 of Chapter 130A of the General Statutes.

(17) Winemaking on Premises Permit. - A permit may be issued to a business, located in a jurisdiction where the sale of unfortified wine is allowed, where individual customers who are 21 years old or older may purchase ingredients and rent the equipment, time, and space to make unfortified wine for personal use in amounts set forth in 27 C.F.R. § 24.75. Except for wine produced for testing equipment or recipes and samples pursuant to this subdivision, the permit holder shall not engage in the actual production or manufacture of wine. Samples may be consumed on the premises only by a person who has a nonrefundable contract to ferment at the premises, and the samples may not exceed one ounce per sample. All wine produced at a winemaking on premises facility shall be removed from the premises by the customer and may only be used for home consumption and the personal use of the customer.

(18) Malt Beverage Tasting Permit. - A malt beverage tasting permit authorizes malt beverage tastings on a premises holding a retail permit by the retail permit holder or his employee. A representative of the brewery whose beverages are being featured at the tasting shall be present at the tasting unless the wholesaler or a wholesaler's employee determines that no

representative of the brewery needs to be present. A malt beverage tasting consists of the offering of a sample of one or more malt beverage products, in amounts of no more than two ounces for each sample, without charge, to customers of the business. Any persons pouring malt beverage at a malt beverage tasting shall be at least 21 years of age.

a. Representatives of the brewery which produced the malt beverage, a wholesaler, or a wholesaler's employee may assist with the tasting. Assisting with a malt beverage tasting includes:

1. Pouring samples for customers.

2. Checking the identification of patrons being served at the malt beverage tasting.

b. When a representative of the brewery that produced the malt beverage, a malt beverage wholesaler, or a malt beverage wholesaler's employee assists in a malt beverage tasting conducted by a retail permit holder:

1. The retail permit holder shall designate an employee to actively supervise the malt beverage tasting.

2. A retail permit holder's employee shall not supervise more than three malt beverage tasting areas.

3. No more than four malt beverages may be tasted at any one tasting area.

4. The malt beverage tasting shall not last longer than four hours from the time designated as the starting time by the retail permit holder.

c. The retail permit holder shall be solely liable for any violations of this Chapter occurring in connection with the malt beverage tasting. The Commission shall adopt rules to assure that the tastings are limited to samplings and not a subterfuge for the unlawful sale or distribution of malt beverages, and that the tastings are not used by industry members for unlawful inducements to retail permit holders. Except for purposes of this subdivision, the holder of a malt beverage tasting permit shall not be construed to hold a permit for the on-premises sale or consumption of alcoholic beverages. Any food business is eligible for a malt beverage tasting permit.

(19) Spirituous liquor tasting permit. - The holder of any distillery permit authorized by G.S. 18B-1105 may conduct a consumer tasting event on the premises of the distillery subject to the following conditions:

a. Any person pouring spirituous liquor at a tasting shall be an employee of the distillery and at least 21 years of age.

b. The person pouring the spirituous liquor shall be responsible for checking the identification of patrons being served at the tasting.

c. Each consumer is limited to tasting samples of 0.25 ounce of each spirituous liquor which total no more than 1.5 ounces of spirituous liquor in any calendar day.

d. The consumer shall not be charged for any spirituous liquor tasting sample.

e. The spirituous liquor used in the consumer tasting event shall be distilled at the distillery where the event is being held by the permit holder conducting the event.

f. A consumer tasting event shall not be allowed when the sale of spirituous liquor is otherwise prohibited.

g. Tasting samples are not to be offered to, or allowed to be consumed by, any person under the legal age for consuming spirituous liquor.

The distillery permit holder shall be solely liable for any violations of this Chapter occurring in connection with the tasting. The Commission shall adopt rules to assure that the tastings are limited to samplings and not a subterfuge for the unlawful sale or distribution of spirituous liquor and that the tastings are not used by industry members for unlawful inducements to retail permit holders. (1945, c. 903, s. 1; 1947, c. 1098, ss. 2, 3; 1949, c. 974, s. 1; 1957, cc. 1048, 1448; 1963, c. 426, ss. 10, 12; c. 460, s. 1; 1971, c. 872, s. 1; 1973, c. 476, s. 128; 1975, c, 586, s. 1; c. 654, ss. 1, 2; c. 722, s. 1; 1977, c. 70, s. 19; c. 182, s. 1; c. 669, ss. 1, 2; c. 676, ss. 1, 2; c. 911; 1979, c. 348, ss. 2, 3; c. 683, ss. 5, 6, 11, 12; 1981, c. 412, s. 2; 1981 (Reg. Sess., 1982), c. 1262, ss. 16, 17, 22; 1983, c. 457, s. 3; c. 583, ss. 2-5; 1985, c. 89, ss. 1-3; c. 596, s. 1; 1987, c. 391, s. 2; c. 434, s. 1; 1989, c. 800, ss. 11, 12; 1991, c. 459, ss. 5, 6; c. 565, ss. 1, 7; c. 669, s. 1; 1991 (Reg. Sess., 1992), c. 920, s. 7; 1993, c. 508, s. 5; 1995, c. 466, s. 10; c. 509, ss. 16-18; 1997-443, s. 16.28; 1997-467, s. 3; 2001-262, s. 1;

2001-487, s. 49(a); 2003-402, s. 5; 2005-350, ss. 1, 2(a); 2006-222, s. 2.1; 2006-227, ss. 1, 9; 2006-264, s. 35.3; 2009-377, s. 2; 2009-539, s. 3; 2010-31, s. 14.12(c); 2011-73, ss. 3, 4; 2011-107, s. 1; 2011-333, ss. 4, 5; 2013-76, s. 1.)

§ 18B-1001.1. Authorization of wine shipper permit.

(a) A winery holding a federal basic wine manufacturing permit located within or outside of the State may apply to the Commission for issuance of a wine shipper permit that shall authorize the shipment of brands of fortified and unfortified wines identified in the application. The applicant shall not be required to pay an application fee for the wine shipper permit. A wine shipper permittee may amend the brands of wines identified in the permit application but shall file any amendment with the Commission. Any winery that applies for a wine shipper permit shall notify in writing any wholesalers that have been authorized to distribute the winery's brands within the State that an application has been filed for a wine shipper permit. A wine shipper permittee may sell and ship not more than two cases of wine per month to any person in North Carolina to whom alcoholic beverages may be lawfully sold. All sales and shipments shall be for personal use only and not for resale. A case of wine shall mean any combination of packages containing not more than nine liters of wine.

(b) A wine shipper permittee that ships to addresses in the State more than 1,000 cases of wine in a calendar year must appoint at least one wholesaler to offer and sell the products of the wine shipper permittee under Article 12 of this Chapter if the wine shipper permittee is contacted by a wholesaler that wishes to sell the products of the wine shipper permittee. This provision shall not be construed to require the wine shipper permittee to appoint the wholesaler that originally contacted the wine shipper permittee. Wine purchased by a resident of the State at the premises of the wine shipper permittee and shipped to an address in the State under G.S. 18B-109(d) shall not be included in calculating the total of 1,000 cases per year.

(c) A wine shipper permittee may contract with the holder of a wine shipper packager permit for the packaging and shipment of wine pursuant to this section. The direct shipment of wine by wine shipper or wine shipper packager permittees pursuant to this section shall be made by approved common carrier only. Each common carrier shall apply to the Commission for approval to provide common carriage of wines shipped by holders of permits issued pursuant to this section.

Each common carrier making deliveries pursuant to this section shall:

(1) Require the recipient, upon delivery, to demonstrate that the recipient is at least 21 years of age by providing a form of identification specified in G.S. 18B-302(d)(1).

(2) Require the recipient to sign an electronic or paper form or other acknowledgment of receipt as approved by the Commission.

(3) Refuse delivery when the proposed recipient appears to be under the age of 21 years and refuses to present valid identification as required by subdivision (1) of this subsection.

(4) Submit any other information that the Commission shall require.

All wine shipper and wine shipper packager permittees shipping wines pursuant to this section shall affix a notice in 26-point type or larger to the outside of each package of wine shipped within or to the State in a conspicuous location stating: "CONTAINS ALCOHOLIC BEVERAGES; SIGNATURE OF PERSON AGED 21 YEARS OR OLDER REQUIRED FOR DELIVERY". Any delivery of wines to a person under 21 years of age by a common carrier shall constitute a violation of G.S. 18B-302(a)(1) by the common carrier. The common carrier and the wine shipper or wine shipper packager permittee shall be liable only for their independent acts.

(d) A wine shipper permittee shall be subject to jurisdiction of the North Carolina courts by virtue of applying for a wine shipper permit and shall comply with any audit or other compliance requirements of the Commission and the Department of Revenue. (2003-402, s. 2; 2004-203, s. 26(a); 2005-380, s. 2; 2006-227, s. 4.)

§ 18B-1001.2. Additional wine shipping requirements.

(a) A wine shipper permittee shall:

(1) Compile and submit to the Commission quarterly a summary indicating all wine products shipped, including brand and price of each product, date of each shipment, quantity of each shipment, and amount of excise and sales tax remitted to the Department of Revenue. The report shall include all wine

products shipped on the permittee's behalf under contract with a wine shipper packager.

(2)   Register with the Department of Revenue as a wine shipper permittee and provide any additional information required by the Department.

(b)   The Commission may adopt rules to carry out the provisions of this section and other related provisions governing the direct shipping of wine. (2003-402, s. 3; 2006-227, s. 5.)

§ 18B-1001.3. Authorization of wine shipper packager permit.

The holder of a wine shipper packager permit may provide services for the warehousing, packaging, and shipment of wine on behalf of a winery holding a wine shipper permit. A wine shipper packager permit authorizes the holder to receive, in closed containers, wine produced by and belonging to a wine shipper permittee and to place the unopened wine in containers or packaging materials as a service to the wine shipper permittee in connection with the marketing and sale of its wine products. A wine shipper packager may package and return wine products to the wine shipper permittee or, on behalf of the wine shipper permittee, may package and ship wine products in closed containers to individual purchasers inside and outside this State in accordance with the provisions of G.S. 18B-1001.1. The permit may be issued to a USDA-approved company specializing in warehousing and contract packaging. (2006-227, s. 6.)

§ 18B-1002. Special one-time permits.

(a)   Kinds of Permits. - In addition to the other permits authorized by this Chapter, the Commission may issue permits for the following activities:

(1)   A permit may be issued to a person who acquires ownership or possession of alcoholic beverages through bankruptcy, inheritance, foreclosure, judicial sale, or other special occurrence, and who does not already have a permit authorizing the sale of that kind of alcoholic beverage. The permit may authorize the sale or other disposition of the alcoholic beverages in a manner prescribed by the Commission.

(2) A permit may be issued to a nonprofit organization to allow the retail sale of malt beverages, unfortified wine, fortified wine, or mixed beverages, or to allow brown-bagging, at a single fund-raising event of that organization. A permit for this purpose shall not be issued for the sale of any kind of alcoholic beverage in a jurisdiction where the sale of that alcoholic beverage is not lawful.

(3) A permit may be issued to a permittee who is going out of business to authorize the sale or other disposition of his alcoholic beverages stock in a manner that would not otherwise be authorized under his permit.

(4) A permit may be issued to a collector of wine or decorative decanters of spirituous liquor authorizing that person to bring into the State, transport, or possess as a collector, a greater amount of those alcoholic beverages than is otherwise authorized by this Chapter, or to sell those alcoholic beverages in a manner prescribed by the Commission.

(5) A permit may be issued to a unit of local government, or to a nonprofit organization or a political organization to serve wine, malt beverages, and spirituous liquor at a ticketed event held to allow the unit of local government or organization to raise funds. For purposes of this subdivision "nonprofit organization" means an organization that is exempt from taxation under Section 501(c)(3), 501(c)(4), 501(c)(6), 501(c)(8), 501(c)(10), 501(c)(19), or 501(d) of the Internal Revenue Code or is exempt under similar provisions of the General Statutes as a bona fide nonprofit charitable, civic, religious, fraternal, patriotic, or veterans' organization or as a nonprofit volunteer fire department, or as a nonprofit volunteer rescue squad or a bona fide homeowners' or property owners' association. For purposes of this subdivision "political organization" means an organization covered by the provisions of G.S. 163-96(a)(1) or (2) or a campaign organization established by or for a person who is a candidate who has filed a notice of candidacy, paid the filing fees or filed the required petition, and been certified as a candidate. The issuance of this permit will also allow the issuance of a purchase-transportation permit under G.S. 18B-403 and 18B-404 and the use for culinary purposes of spirituous liquor lawfully purchased for use in mixed beverages.

(b) Intent. - Permits under this section are to be issued only for the limited circumstances listed in subsection (a) of this section and not as substitutes for other permits required by this Chapter.

(c) Conditions of Permit. - A permit issued under this section shall be valid only for the single transaction or the kind of activity specified in the permit and shall be subject to any conditions the Commission may impose as to the time, place and manner of the authorized activity.

(d) Administrative Procedure. - Denial or revocation of a permit under this section shall not entitle the applicant or permittee to a hearing under Chapter 150B. (1977, c. 854, s. 1; 1981, c. 412, s. 2; 1987, c. 434, s. 2; c. 827, s. 1; 1989, c. 130; c. 800, ss. 13, 14; 2001-262, s. 9; 2008-159, s. 1.)

§ 18B-1003. Responsibilities of permittee.

(a) Premises. - For purposes of this Chapter, a permittee shall be responsible for the entire premises for which the permit is issued. The permittee shall keep the premises clean, well-lighted and orderly.

(b) Employees. - For purposes of this Chapter, a permittee shall be responsible for the actions of all employees of the business for which the permit is issued. Each holder of a salesman's permit shall be responsible for all sales and deliveries made by his helpers.

(c) Certain Employees Prohibited. - A permittee shall not knowingly employ in the sale or distribution of alcoholic beverages any person who has been:

(1) Convicted of a felony within three years;

(2) Convicted of a felony more than three years previously and has not had his citizenship restored;

(3) Convicted of an alcoholic beverage offense within two years; or

(4) Convicted of a misdemeanor controlled substances offense within two years; [or]

(5) A past permit holder under Chapter 18B of the General Statutes whose permit had been revoked within the last 18 months and who had been the permit holder at the location where the person would be employed.

For purposes of this subsection, "conviction" has the same meaning as in G.S. 18B-900(b). To avoid undue hardship, the Commission may, in its discretion, exempt persons on a case-by-case basis from this subsection.

(d) Financial Responsibility. - A permittee shall pay all judgments rendered against him under the provisions of Article 1A of this Chapter. When the Commission is informed, under the provisions of G.S. 18B-127 that there is an outstanding unsatisfied judgment against a permittee, the Commission shall suspend all of the permittee's permits. Notice and hearing are not required for a suspension under this subsection, and the suspension shall become effective immediately upon the Commission's receipt of the report. The suspension shall remain in effect until the permittee demonstrates that he has satisfied the judgment by payment in full. Nothing in this section relieves the permittee of the obligation to pay any applicable fees as a precondition of the reinstatement of his permit. (1981, c. 412, s. 2; 1983, c. 435, s. 40; 2006-253, s. 28.)

§ 18B-1004. Hours for sale and consumption.

(a) Hours. - Except as otherwise provided in this section, it shall be unlawful to sell malt beverages, unfortified wine, fortified wine, or mixed beverages between the hours of 2:00 A.M. and 7:00 A.M., or to consume any of those alcoholic beverages between the hours of 2:30 A.M. and 7:00 A.M., in any place that has been issued a permit under G.S. 18B-1001.

(b) Repealed by Session Laws 1991, c. 689, s. 310.

(c) Sunday Hours. - It shall be unlawful to sell or consume alcoholic beverages on any licensed premises from the time at which sale or consumption must cease on Sunday morning until 12:00 Noon on that day.

(d) Local Option. - A city may adopt an ordinance prohibiting in the city the retail sale of malt beverages, unfortified wine, and fortified wine during any or all of the hours from 12:00 Noon on Sunday until 7:00 A.M. on the following Monday. A county may adopt an ordinance prohibiting, in the parts of the county outside any city, the retail sale of malt beverages, unfortified wine, and fortified wine during any or all of the hours from 12:00 Noon on Sunday until 7:00 A.M. on the following Monday. Neither a city nor a county, however, may prohibit those sales in establishments having brown-bagging or mixed beverages permits.

(e) This section does not prohibit at any time the wholesale delivery and sale of unfortified wine, fortified wine, and malt beverages to retailers issued permits pursuant to G.S. 18B-1001 or G.S. 18B-1002(a)(2) or (5). (1943, c. 339, ss. 1-3; 1949, c. 974, s. 12; 1951, c. 997, s. 1; 1953, c. 675, s. 4; 1963, c. 426, ss. 7-9, 12; 1969, c. 1131; 1971, c. 872, s. 1; 1973, cc. 56, 153; 1979, c. 286, s. 3; 1981, c. 412, s. 2; 1987, c. 35; c. 308; 1991, c. 689, s. 310; 1993, c. 243, ss. 1, 2; c. 415, s. 16.)

§ 18B-1005. Conduct on licensed premises.

(a) Certain Conduct. - It shall be unlawful for a permittee or his agent or employee to knowingly allow any of the following kinds of conduct to occur on his licensed premises:

(1) Any violation of this Chapter;

(2) Any fighting or other disorderly conduct that can be prevented without undue danger to the permittee, his employees or patrons; or

(3) Any violation of the controlled substances, gambling, or prostitution statutes, or any other unlawful acts.

(4) through (6) Repealed by Session Laws 2003-382, s. 1, effective August 1, 2003.

(b) Supervision. - It shall be unlawful for a permittee to fail to superintend in person or through a manager the business for which a permit is issued. (1943, c. 400, s. 6; 1945, c. 708, s. 6; c. 903, s. 1; 1947, c. 1098, ss. 2, 3; 1949, c. 974, ss. 13, 15; c. 1251, s. 3; 1957, c. 1048; 1959, c. 745, s. 2; 1963, c. 426, ss. 6, 10, 12; c. 460, s. 1; 1971, c. 872, s. 1; 1973, c. 30; c. 1295; c. 1452, s. 4; 1977, c. 176, ss. 1-3; 1981, c. 412, s. 2; 1981 (Reg. Sess., 1982), c. 1262, ss. 18, 19; 2003-382, s. 1.)

§ 18B-1005.1. Sexually explicit conduct on licensed premises.

(a) It shall be unlawful for a permittee or his agent or employee to knowingly allow or engage in any of the following kinds of conduct on his licensed premises:

(1) Any conduct or entertainment by any person whose genitals are exposed or who is wearing transparent clothing that reveals the genitals;

(2) Any conduct or entertainment that includes or simulates sexual intercourse, masturbation, sodomy, bestiality, oral copulation, flagellation, or any act that includes or simulates the penetration, however slight, by any object into the genital or anal opening of a person's body; or

(3) Any conduct or entertainment that includes the fondling of the breasts, buttocks, anus, vulva, or genitals.

(b) Supervision. - It shall be unlawful for a permittee to fail to superintend in person or through a manager the business for which a permit is issued.

(c) Exception. - This section does not apply to persons operating theaters, concert halls, art centers, museums, or similar establishments that are primarily devoted to the arts or theatrical performances, when the performances that are presented are expressing matters of serious literary, artistic, scientific, or political value. (2003-382, s. 2.)

§ 18B-1006. Miscellaneous provisions on permits.

(a) School and College Campuses. - No permit for the sale of malt beverages, unfortified wine, or fortified wine shall be issued to a business on the campus or property of a public school or college, other than at a regional facility as defined by G.S. 160A-480.2 operated by a facility authority under Part 4 of Article 20 of Chapter 160A of the General Statutes except for a public school or college function, unless that business is a hotel or a nonprofit alumni organization with a mixed beverages permit or a special occasion permit. This subsection shall not apply on property owned by a local board of education which was leased for 99 years or more to a nonprofit auditorium authority created prior to 1991 whose governing board is appointed by a city board of aldermen, a county board of commissioners, or a local school board. This subsection shall also not apply to the constituent institutions of The University of North Carolina with respect to the sale of beer and wine at (i) performing arts centers located on property owned or leased by the institutions if the seating capacity does not exceed 2,000 seats; (ii) any golf courses owned or leased by the institutions and open to the public for use; or (iii) any stadiums that support a NASCAR-sanctioned one-fourth mile asphalt flat oval short track, that are owned or leased by the institutions, and that only sell malt beverages, unfortified wine, or fortified wine at events that are not sponsored or funded by the institutions. Notwithstanding this subsection, special one-time permits as described in G.S. 18B-1002(a)(5) may be issued to the University of North Carolina at Chapel Hill for the Loudermilk Center for Excellence facility.

(b)   Lockers at Clubs. - A private club or congressionally-chartered veterans organization which has been issued a brown-bagging permit may, but is not required to, provide lockers for its members to store their alcoholic beverages. If lockers are provided, however, they shall not be shared but shall be for individual members. Each locker and each bottle of alcoholic beverages on the premises shall be labelled with the name of the member to whom it belongs. No more than eight liters each of malt beverages or unfortified wine may be stored by a member at one time. No more than eight liters of either fortified wine or spirituous liquor, or eight liters of the two combined, may be stored by a member at one time.

(c)   Wine Sales. - Holders of retail or wholesale permits for the sale of unfortified or fortified wine may buy and sell only wines on the Commission's approved list. The Commission may authorize the importation and purchase of wines not on the approved list by permittees and others. An authorization shall state the kind and amount of wine that may be imported and purchased and the time within which the transaction shall be completed.

(d)   Unlawful Possession or Consumption. - It shall be unlawful for a permittee to possess or consume, or allow any other person to possess or consume, on the licensed premises, any fortified wine or spirituous liquor, the possession or consumption of which is not authorized either by the permits issued to him for the premises or by any other provision of the ABC law.

(e)   Facsimile Permit. - It shall be unlawful for any person to produce or possess any false or facsimile permit, or for a permittee to display any false or facsimile permit on his licensed premises.

(f)   Failure to Surrender Permit. - It shall be unlawful for any person to refuse to surrender any permit to the Commission upon lawful demand of the Commission or its agents.

(g)   Restrictions on Sales at Cooking Schools. - Retail sales of food or alcoholic beverages to be consumed on the premises of a cooking school are restricted to bona fide enrolled students of that school. Violation of this subsection is a ground for administrative action under G.S. 18B-104.

(h)   Purchase Restrictions. - A retail permittee may purchase malt beverages, unfortified wine, or fortified wine only from a wholesaler who maintains a place of business in this State and has the proper permit.

(i)   Tour Boats. - The Commission may issue permits to boats that conduct regularly scheduled tours upon the rivers or waterways of this State under the following conditions:

(1)   A boat shall serve meals on each tour and shall have a dining area with seating for at least 36 people;

(2)   A boat's gross receipts from food and non-alcoholic beverages shall be greater than its gross receipts from alcoholic beverages;

(3)   A boat may hold the permits listed in G.S. 18B-1001(1), (3), (5), (7), and (10), but no off-premises sales may be made pursuant to those permits;

(4)   A boat shall have a home port in an area where issuance of any of the permits listed in subdivision (3) is legal, and all passengers shall enter the boat at the home port or at other ports listed on a preannounced itinerary. The boat's permits are valid during tours that leave and return to the boat's home port, and apply regardless of whether the boat crosses into an area where sales are not legal, if the boat docks only at a port listed on the preannounced itinerary, except in an emergency; and

(5)   A boat conducting tours along the intracoastal waterway and navigable waterways that enters into the intracoastal waterway, pursuant to a preannounced itinerary that includes visits to two or more cities, may serve alcoholic beverages pursuant to ABC permits issued according to the jurisdiction of its home port in the following manner:

a.   While on tour, alcoholic beverages may be served to passengers;

b.   While docked in any other port alcoholic beverages may be served only to tour passengers;

c.   During special city-sponsored events and festivals, in which case the boat may open its galley and bars at dockside to the general public and sell those alcoholic beverages that are lawful in the jurisdiction in which it is docked. Any sales in this manner shall be in accordance with the requirements of any ordinances of the jurisdiction in which the boat is docked.

(6) Liquor purchased for resale in mixed beverages may be purchased only from the local board for the jurisdiction of the boat's home port.

(j) Recreation Districts. - Notwithstanding the provisions of Article 6 of this Chapter, the Commission may issue permits for the sale of malt beverages, unfortified wine, fortified wine, and mixed beverages to qualified businesses in a recreation district.

A "recreation district" is an area that meets any of the following requirements:

(1) An area that is located in a county that has not approved the issuance of permits, has at least two cities that have approved the sale of malt beverages, wine, and the operation of an ABC store, and contains a facility of at least 450 acres where five or more public auto racing events are held each year.

(2) An area that is located in a county that borders a county which has held elections pursuant to G.S. 18B-600(f) and borders on another state and which (i) contains a facility of at least 225 acres where four or more public auto racing events are held each year or (ii) contains a facility of at least 140 acres where 80 or more motor sports events are held each year.

(3) A recreation district includes the area within a half-mile radius of a racing facility that meets the requirements of subdivision (1) or (2) of this subsection.

(4) Repealed by Session Laws 2004-203, s. 27, effective August 17, 2004.

(k) Residential Private Club and Sports Club Permits. - The Commission may issue the permits listed in G.S. 18B-1001, without approval at an election, to a residential private club or a sports club, except if the sale of mixed beverages is not lawful within a jurisdiction and that locality has voted against the sale of mixed beverages in a referendum conducted on or after September 1, 2001. If the issuance of permits is prohibited by the exception in the previous sentence, the Commission may renew existing permits and may continue to issue permits for a business location that had previously held permits under this subsection. No permit may be issued to any residential private club or sports club that practices discrimination on the basis of race, gender or ethnicity.

The mixed beverages purchase-transportation permit authorized by G.S. 18B-404(b) shall be issued by a local board operating a store located in the county.

(l) Repealed by Session Laws 2004-203, s. 65, effective August 17, 2004.

(m) Interstate Interchange Economic Development Zones. -

(1) The Commission may issue permits listed in G.S. 18B-1001(10), without approval at an election, to qualified establishments defined in G.S. 18B-1000(4), (6), and (8) located within one mile of an interstate highway interchange located in a county that:

a. Has approved the sale of malt beverages, unfortified wine, and fortified wine, but not mixed beverages;

b. Operates ABC stores;

c. Borders on another state; and

d. Lies north and east of the Roanoke River.

(2) The Commission may issue permits listed in G.S. 18B-1001(1), (3), (5), and (10) to qualified establishments defined in G.S. 18B-1000(4), (6), and (8) and may issue permits listed in G.S. 18B-1001(2) and (4) to qualified establishments defined in G.S. 18B-1000(3) in any county that qualifies for issuance of permits pursuant to G.S. 18B-1006(k). These permits may be issued without approval at an election and shall be issued only to qualified establishments that meet all of the following requirements:

a. Located within one mile of any interstate highway interchange in that county;

b. Located within one mile of an establishment issued a permit under G.S. 18B-1006(k); and

c. Is, or is located within one-quarter mile of, a hotel with 70 or more rooms.

(3) Repealed by Session Laws 2004-203, s. 28, effective August 17, 2004.

(n) National Historic Landmark District. - The Commission may issue permits listed in G.S. 18B-1001(10), without approval at an election, to qualified establishments defined in G.S. 18B-1000(4) and (6) located within a National Historical Landmark as defined in 16 U.S.C. § 470a(a)(1)(B) located in a county that meets all of the following requirements:

(1) Has approved the sale of malt beverages and unfortified wine but not mixed beverages.

(2) Has at least one city that has approved the operation of an ABC store and the sale of mixed beverages.

(3) Has at least 150,000 population based on the last federal census.

(o) Expired.

(p) The Commission shall issue a special occasion permit under G.S. 18B-1001(8) to a mixed beverage permittee in a sports facility occupied by a major league professional sports team with suites available for sale or lease to patrons of the facility to authorize patrons to make available alcoholic beverages in those suites as if the patron were a host of a reception, party or other special occasion. If the patron occupying the suite so desires, alcoholic beverages by self-service may be made available to any person at least 21 years of age possessing a valid ticket to the event authorizing that person to occupy the suite. At no event may the patron make available a quantity of alcoholic beverages in excess of the amount a person is allowed to buy under G.S. 18B-303(a). A mixed beverage permittee who holds a permit shall provide mixed beverage tax paid spirituous liquor for resale by the container in approved sizes of no larger than 750 milliliters to the host or patron of the suite. This subsection does not authorize any person possessing a valid ticket to an event at the facility to bring alcoholic beverages onto the premises and consume those alcoholic beverages on the premises, or to remove those beverages from the suite.

(q) The hours for sales and consumption of alcoholic beverages on the premises of a permittee who meets the requirements of G.S. 18B-1009 shall be one hour earlier than permitted by G.S. 18B-1004(c). (1981, c. 412, s. 2; 1981 (Reg. Sess., 1982), c. 1262, s. 23; 1985, c. 114, s. 2; c. 301; 1987, c. 515; c. 760; 1989, c. 360; c. 770, s. 49; c. 800, s. 18; 1991, c. 340, s. 1; c. 459, s. 7; 1991 (Reg. Sess., 1992), c. 920, s. 12; 1993, c. 415, ss. 17-19; c. 508, s. 6; 1995, c. 224, s. 1; c. 372, s. 2; c. 458, s. 8; c. 466, ss. 11-12; 1997-182, s. 3;

1997-395, s. 1; 1997-443, s. 16.27(a); 1999-462, ss. 2, 10, 12, 14; 2001-130, ss. 1, 1.4; 2004-199, s. 10; 2004-203, ss. 27, 28, 65; 2005-327, ss. 1, 2, 4; 2006-227, s. 7; 2006-264, s. 100; 2007-323, s. 6.25; 2013-394, s. 5(b); 2013-410, s. 27.9.)

§ 18B-1006.1. Additional requirement for certain permittees to recycle beverage containers.

Holders of on-premises malt beverage permits, on-premises unfortified wine permits, on-premises fortified wine permits, and mixed beverages permits shall separate, store, and provide for the collection for recycling of all recyclable beverage containers of all beverages sold at retail on the premises. A permittee has satisfied the requirements of this section if it implements a recycling program that meets the minimum standards of the model recycling program developed by the Commission pursuant to G.S. 130A-309.14(m). Failure to comply with the requirements of this section shall not be grounds for revocation of a permit. A conviction for violation of this section shall not constitute an alcoholic beverage offense within the meaning of G.S. 18B-900(a)(4). (2005-348, s. 1; 2007-402, s. 2(a); 2008-187, s. 35.5.)

§ 18B-1007. Additional requirements for mixed beverages permittees.

(a) Purchases. - A mixed beverages permittee may purchase spirituous liquor for resale as mixed beverages and a guest room cabinet permittee may purchase spirituous liquor for resale from a guest room cabinet only at an ABC store designated by a local board and only with a purchase-transportation permit issued by that local board under G.S. 18B-403 and 18B-404.

(b) Handling Bottles. - It shall be unlawful for a mixed beverages permittee or the permittee's agent or employee to do any of the following:

(1) Store any other spirituous liquor with liquor possessed for resale in mixed beverages or from a guest room cabinet.

(2) Refill any spirituous liquor container having a mixed beverages tax stamp with any other alcoholic beverage, or add to the contents of such a container any other alcoholic beverage.

(3) Transfer from one container to another a mixed beverages tax stamp.

(4) Possess any container of spirituous liquor not bearing a mixed beverages tax stamp, except for containers being brought onto the premises by the host of a private function under a special occasion permit.

(c) Price List. - Each mixed beverages permittee shall have available for its customers the printed prices of the most common or popular mixed beverages offered for sale by the permittee. Violation of this subsection shall not be a criminal offense, but shall be punishable under G.S. 18B-104.

(d) When a temporary mixed beverages permit has been issued to a new permittee for the continuation of a business at the same location, the permittee going out of business may sell existing mixed beverages inventory to the new permittee, and the Commission may request that the local ABC board restamp the inventory with the mixed beverages tax stamp assigned by the local board to the new mixed beverages permittee. (1981, c. 412, s. 2; c. 746, s. 2; 1981 (Reg. Sess., 1982), c. 1262, s. 20; 1989, c. 800, s. 15; 1991, c. 565, ss. 6, 7; 1991 (Reg. Sess., 1992), c. 920, s. 8; 1995, c. 466, s. 13.)

§ 18B-1008. Rules concerning retail permits.

The Commission is authorized to use broad discretion in further defining the kinds of places eligible for permits under this Article. The rules may state the kind and amount of food that shall be sold to qualify in each category, the relationship between food sales and other receipts, the size of the establishment required for each category, the kinds of facilities needed to qualify, the kinds of activities at which alcoholic beverages may not be sold, and any other matters which are necessary to determine which businesses are bona fide establishments of the kinds listed in G.S. 18B-1000. Rules concerning private clubs may also include requirements that the club have a membership committee to review all applications for membership, that the club charge membership dues substantially greater than what would be paid by a one-time or casual user, that the club restrict use by nonmembers, and that the club provide facilities or activities other than those directly related to the use of alcoholic beverages. (1981, c. 412, s. 2; 2009-381, s. 1.)

§ 18B-1009. In-stand sales.

(a) Nothing in this Chapter shall be construed to prohibit a retail permittee from selling for consumption, malt beverages in the seating areas of stadiums, ballparks, and other similar public places with a seating capacity of 3,000 or more during professional sporting events, provided that:

(1) The seating areas are designated as part of the retail permittee's licensed premises;

(2) The retail permittee has notified the Commission, in writing, of its intent to sell malt beverages in the seating areas at sporting events;

(3) Service of food and nonalcoholic beverages is available in the seating areas;

(4) The retail permittee has certified to the Commission that it has trained its employees:

a. To identify underage persons and intoxicated persons; and

b. To refuse to sell malt beverages to those persons as required by G.S. 18B-305; and

(5) The employees do not verbally shout or hawk the sale of malt beverages.

(b) The North Carolina Alcoholic Beverage Control Commission shall adopt rules for the suspension of alcohol sales in the latter portion of professional sporting events in order to protect public safety at these events. (1997-167, s. 1; 2000-140, s. 93.1(a); 2001-424, s. 12.2(b); 2013-83, ss. 1, 2.)

§§ 18B-1010 through 18B-1099. Reserved for future codification purposes.

Article 11.

Commercial Activity.

§ 18B-1100. Commercial permits.

The Commission may issue the following commercial permits:

(1) Unfortified winery

(2) Fortified winery

(3) Limited winery

(4) Brewery

(5) Distillery

(6) Fuel alcohol

(7) Wine importer

(8) Wine wholesaler

(9) Malt beverages importer

(10) Malt beverages wholesaler

(11) Bottler

(12) Salesman

(13) Vendor representative

(14) Nonresident malt beverage vendor

(15) Nonresident wine vendor

(16) Winery special show

(17) Liquor importer/bottler permit

(18) Cider and vinegar manufacturer

(19) Wine producer permit

(20) Malt beverage special event permit. (1981, c. 412, s. 2; c. 747, s. 59; 1989, c. 737, s. 1; 1995, c. 404, s. 3; 1997-134, s. 1; 2001-262, s. 8; 2001-487, s. 49(g); 2009-377, s. 3.)

§ 18B-1101. Authorization of unfortified winery permit.

The holder of an unfortified winery permit may:

(1) Manufacture unfortified wine;

(2) Sell, deliver and ship unfortified wine in closed containers to wholesalers licensed under this Chapter as authorized by the ABC laws, except that wine may be sold to exporters and nonresident wholesalers only when the purchase is not for resale in this State;

(2a) Receive, in closed containers, unfortified wine produced inside or outside North Carolina under the winery's label from grapes, berries, or other fruits owned by the winery, and sell, deliver, and ship that wine to wholesalers, exporters, and nonresident wholesalers in the same manner as its wine manufactured in North Carolina. This provision may be used only by a winery during its first three years of operation or when there is substantial damage to its grapes, berries, or other fruits from catastrophic crop loss. This provision may be used only three years out of every 10 years and notice must be given to the Commission each time this provision is used;

(3) Ship its wine in closed containers to individual purchasers inside and outside this State in accordance with the provisions of G.S. 18B-1001, 18B-1001.1, and 18B-1001.2, and other applicable provisions of this Chapter;

(4) Furnish or sell "short-filled" packages, on which State taxes have been or will be paid, to its employees for the use of the employees or their families and guests in this State;

(5) Regardless of the results of any local wine election, sell the wine owned by the winery at the winery for on- or off-premise consumption upon obtaining the appropriate permit under G.S. 18B-1001;

(6) Sell the wine manufactured by the winery or produced under the winery's label under subdivision (2a) of this section for on- or off-premise consumption at no more than three other locations in the State, upon obtaining the appropriate permit under G.S. 18B-1001;

(6a) Receive, in closed containers, and sell at the winery, unfortified wine produced inside or outside North Carolina under contract with the winery. Such contract wine must have the winery's name clearly displayed on each bottle. The contract wine may be sold also at affiliated retail outlets of the winery physically located on or adjacent to the winery. Any wine received by a winery under this provision must be made available for sale by the winery to wholesalers for distribution to retailers, without discrimination, in the same manner as if the wine were being imported by the winery;

(7) Obtain a wine wholesaler permit to sell, deliver, and ship at wholesale unfortified wine manufactured at the winery. The authorization of this subdivision applies only to a winery that annually sells, to persons other than exporters and nonresident wholesalers when the purchase is not for resale in this State, no more than 100,000 gallons of unfortified wine manufactured by it at the winery;

(8) Allow winemaking on premises as allowed by a permit issued pursuant to G.S. 18B-1001(17).

A sale under subdivision (4) shall not be considered a retail or wholesale sale under the ABC laws. (1973, c. 511, ss. 1, 2; 1975, c. 411, s. 6; 1979, c. 224; 1981, c. 412, s. 2; c. 747, s. 60; 1985, c. 89, s. 4; 1989, c. 800, s. 2; 2001-262, s. 2; 2001-487, s. 49(b); 2002-102, s. 2; 2003-402, s. 6; 2004-135, s. 2; 2004-199, s. 11; 2007-402, s. 3.)

§ 18B-1102. Authorization of fortified winery permit.

The holder of a fortified winery permit may:

(1) Manufacture, purchase, import and transport brandy and other ingredients and equipment used in the manufacture of fortified wine;

(2) Sell, deliver and ship fortified wine in closed containers to wholesalers licensed under this Chapter as authorized by the ABC laws, except that wine may be sold to exporters and nonresident wholesalers only when the purchase is not for resale in this State;

(3) Ship its wine in closed containers to individual purchasers inside and outside this State in accordance with the provisions of G.S. 18B-1001, 18B-1001.1, and 18B-1001.2, and other applicable provisions of this Chapter;

(4) Furnish or sell "short-filled" packages, on which State taxes have been or will be paid, to its employees for the use of the employees or their families and guests in this State;

(5) Regardless of the results of any local wine election, sell the winery's wine for on-or off-premise consumption upon obtaining the appropriate permit under G.S. 18B-1001.

A sale under subdivision (4) shall not be considered a retail or wholesale sale under the ABC laws. (1945, c. 903, s. 1; 1947, c. 1098, ss. 2, 3; 1949, c. 974, s. 1; 1957, cc. 1048, 1448; 1963, c. 426, ss. 10, 12; c. 460, s. 1; 1971, c. 872, s. 1; 1973, c. 476, s. 128; 1975, c. 411, s. 6; c. 586, s. 1; c. 654, ss. 1, 2; c. 722, s. 1; 1977, c. 70, s. 19; c. 182, s. 1; c. 511, ss. 1, 2; c. 669, ss. 1, 2; c. 676, ss. 1, 2; c. 911; 1979, c. 224; c. 348, ss. 2, 3; c. 683, ss. 5, 6, 11, 12; 1981, c. 412, s. 2; c. 747, s. 60; 1985, c. 89, s. 5; 1989, c. 800, s. 3; 2003-402, s. 7.)

§ 18B-1103. Authorization of limited winery permit.

(a) Special Qualifications. - Any winery which holds an unfortified winery permit and which produces its wine principally from honey, grapes or other fruit or grain grown in this State may obtain a limited winery permit.

(b) Authorized Acts. - The holder of a limited winery permit may give visitors free tasting samples of the wine. The Commission may issue rules regulating these tastings. (1981, c. 412, s. 2; c. 747, s. 61.)

§ 18B-1104. Authorization of brewery permit.

The holder of a brewery permit may:

(1)   Manufacture malt beverages.

(2)   Purchase malt, hops and other ingredients used in the manufacture of malt beverages.

(3)   Sell, deliver and ship malt beverages in closed containers to wholesalers licensed under this Chapter as authorized by the ABC laws, except that malt beverages may be sold to exporters and nonresident wholesalers only when the purchase is not for resale in this State.

(4)   Receive malt beverages manufactured by the permittee in some other state for transshipment to dealers in other states.

(5)   Furnish or sell marketable malt beverage products, or packages which do not conform to the manufacturer's marketing standards, if State taxes have been or will be paid, to its employees for the use of the employees or their families and guests in this State.

(6)   Give its products to its employees and guests for consumption on its premises.

(7)   In an area where the sale of any type of alcoholic beverage is authorized by law, sell the brewery's malt beverages or malt beverages manufactured by the permittee in some other state that have been approved by the Commission for sale in North Carolina only at the brewery upon receiving a permit under G.S. 18B-1001(1).

(8)   Obtain a malt beverage wholesaler permit to sell, deliver, and ship at wholesale only malt beverages manufactured by the brewery. The authorization of this subdivision applies to a brewery that sells, to consumers at the brewery, to wholesalers, to retailers, and to exporters, fewer than 25,000 barrels, as defined in G.S. 81A-9, of malt beverages produced by it per year. A brewery not exceeding the sales quantity limitations in this subdivision may also sell the malt beverages manufactured by the brewery at not more than three other locations in the State, where the sale is legal, upon obtaining the appropriate permits under G.S. 18B-1001. A brewery operating any additional retail location pursuant to this subdivision shall also offer for sale at that location a reasonable selection of competitive malt beverage products.

A sale or gift under subdivision (5) or (6) shall not be considered a retail or wholesale sale under the ABC laws. (1945, c. 903, s. 1; 1947, c. 1098, ss. 2, 3; 1949, c. 974, s. 1; 1957, cc. 1048, 1448; 1963, c. 426, ss. 10, 12; c. 460, s. 1; 1971, c. 872, s. 1; 1973, c. 476, s. 128; 1975, c. 586, s. 1; c. 654, ss. 1, 2; c. 722, s. 1; 1977, c. 70, s. 19; c. 182, s. 1; c. 669, ss. 1, 2; c. 676, ss. 1, 2; c. 911; 1979, c. 348, ss. 2, 3; c. 683, ss. 5, 6, 11, 12; 1981, c. 412, s. 2; 1985, c. 596, s. 2; 1989, c. 800, s. 4; 1991 (Reg. Sess., 1992), c. 920, s. 9; 1993, c. 415, s. 20; 2003-430, s. 1; 2004-203, s. 29; 2011-107, s. 2; 2011-419, s. 1.)

§ 18B-1105. Authorization of distillery permit.

(a) Authorized Acts. - The holder of a distillery permit may:

(1) Manufacture, purchase, import, possess and transport ingredients and equipment used in the distillation of spirituous liquor;

(2) Sell, deliver and ship spirituous liquor in closed containers at wholesale to exporters and local boards within the State, and, subject to the laws of other jurisdictions, at wholesale or retail to private or public agencies or establishments of other states or nations;

(3) Transport into or out of the distillery the maximum amount of liquor allowed under federal law, if the transportation is related to the distilling process.

(b) Distilleries for Fuel Alcohol. - Any person in possession of a Federal Operating Permit pursuant to Title 27, Code of Federal Regulations, Part 19 (April 1, 2010 Edition), shall obtain a fuel alcohol permit before manufacturing any alcohol. The permit shall entitle the permittee to perform only those acts allowed by the Federal Operating Permit, and all conditions of the Federal Operating Permit shall apply to the State permit. (1979, 2nd Sess., c. 1329, s. 1; 1981, c. 412, s. 2; 1989, c. 800, s. 5; 2012-201, s. 10.)

§ 18B-1105.1. Authorization of liquor importer/bottler permit.

The holder of a liquor importer/bottler permit may:

(1) Receive spirituous liquor in closed containers into foreign trade zones at the State Port facilities in Morehead City and Wilmington from ships docked at the State Port facilities for the purpose of bottling, packaging, or labeling.

(2) Bottle, package, or label in this State spirituous liquor imported or received into a foreign trade zone pursuant to this section.

(3) Receive spirituous liquor in closed containers into the foreign trade zones at the State Port facilities in Morehead City and Wilmington from ships docked at the State Port facilities for storage, sale, shipment, and transshipment to the State or a local ABC board warehouse or, subject to the laws of other jurisdictions, to private or public agencies or establishments of other states or nations.

(4) Subject to the record-keeping requirements of G.S. 18B-1115, transport into or out of the foreign trade zones at the State Port facilities in Morehead City and Wilmington, the maximum amount of liquor allowed under federal law, if the transportation is related to the bottling, packaging, labeling, sale, or storage permitted by this section. (1995, c. 404, s. 1.)

§ 18B-1106. Authorization of wine importer permit.

(a) Authorization. - The holder of a wine importer permit may:

(1) Import fortified and unfortified wines from outside the United States in closed containers;

(2) Store those wines;

(3) Sell those wines to wine wholesalers for purposes of resale.

(b) Distribution Agreements. - Wine distribution agreements are governed by Article 12 of this Chapter.

(c) The holder of a wine importer permit may import and sell to wholesalers only wine for which it is a primary American source of supply. To be considered a primary American source of supply, a wine importer must establish that it has lawfully purchased the wine from the winery, or from an agent of the winery, and by written contract or otherwise has been authorized by the winery to distribute the wine to wholesalers in the United States. (1945, c. 903, s. 1; 1947, c. 1098, ss. 2, 3; 1949, c. 974, s. 1; 1957, cc. 1048, 1448; 1963, c. 426, ss. 10, 12; c. 460, s. 1; 1971, c. 872, s. 1; 1973, c. 476, s. 128; 1975, c. 586, s. 1; c. 654, ss. 1, 2; c. 722, s. 1; 1977, c. 70, s. 19; c. 182, s. 1; c. 669, ss. 1, 2; c. 676, ss. 1, 2; c. 911; 1979, c. 348, ss. 2, 3; c. 683, ss. 5, 6, 11, 12; 1981, c. 412, s. 2; 1983, c. 85, s. 1; 1993, c. 415, s. 21; 2006-227, s. 11.)

§ 18B-1107. Authorization of wine wholesaler permit.

(a) Authorization. - The holder of a wine wholesaler permit may:

(1) Receive, possess and transport shipments of fortified and unfortified wine. The wine must be received from one of the following:

a. A primary American source of supply for that wine as recognized by the Commission or as verified by the wholesaler.

b. A licensed North Carolina wholesaler who received the wine from a primary American source of supply and with whom the second wholesaler has a subcontracting agreement for distribution of the wine.

c. Another wholesaler from whom the purchasing wholesaler is purchasing the wholesaler's business or from whom the wholesaler is purchasing the brand or distribution rights for the wine being received.

d. Another wholesaler who also has distribution rights for the wine being received and from whom the wholesaler is acquiring the wine in order to address a temporary inventory shortage.

(2) Sell, deliver and ship wine in closed containers for purposes of resale to wholesalers or retailers licensed under this Chapter as authorized by the ABC laws.

(3) Furnish and sell wine to its employees, subject to the rules of the Commission and the Department of Revenue.

(4) In locations where the sale is legal, furnish wine to guests and any other person who does not hold an ABC permit, for promotional purposes, subject to rules of the Commission.

(5) Sell out-of-date unfortified and fortified wines to holders of cider and vinegar manufacturer permits, provided that each bottle is marked "out-of-date" by the wholesaler.

(b) Distribution Agreements. - Wine distribution agreements are governed by Article 12 of this Chapter. (1945, c. 903, s. 1; 1947, c. 1098, ss. 2, 3; 1949, c. 974, s. 1; 1957, cc. 1048, 1448; 1963, c. 426, ss. 10, 12; c. 460, s. 1; 1971, c. 872, s. 1; 1973, c. 476, s. 128; 1975, c. 586, s. 1; c. 654, ss. 1, 2; c. 722, s. 1; 1977, c. 70, s. 19; c. 182, s. 1; c. 669, ss. 1, 2; c. 676, ss. 1, 2; c. 911; 1979, c. 348, ss. 2, 3; c. 683, ss. 5, 6, 11, 12; 1981, c. 412, s. 2; 1983, c. 85, s. 1; 1997-134, s. 4; 2006-227, s. 12.)

§ 18B-1108. Authorization of malt beverages importer permit.

The holder of a malt beverages importer permit may:

(1) Import malt beverages from outside the United States in closed containers;

(2) Store those malt beverages;

(3) Sell those malt beverages to malt beverage wholesalers for purposes of resale. (1945, c. 903, s. 1; 1947, c. 1098, ss. 2, 3; 1949, c. 974, s. 1; 1957, cc. 1048, 1448; 1963, c. 426, ss. 10, 12; c. 460, s. 1; 1971, c. 872, s. 1; 1973, c. 476, s. 128; 1975, c. 586, s. 1; c. 654, ss. 1, 2; c. 722, s. 1; 1977, c. 70, s. 19; c. 182, s. 1; c. 669, ss. 1, 2; c. 676, ss. 1, 2; c. 911; 1979, c. 348, ss. 2, 3; c. 683, ss. 5, 6, 11, 12; 1981, c. 412, s. 2; 1993, c. 415, s. 22.)

§ 18B-1109. Authorization of malt beverages wholesaler permit.

(a) Authorization. - The holder of a malt beverages wholesaler permit may:

(1) Receive, possess and transport shipments of malt beverages;

(2) Sell, deliver and ship, in closed containers and in quantities of one case or container or more, malt beverages of any brand filed pursuant to G.S. 18B-

1303(a), to wholesalers or retailers licensed under this Chapter, as authorized by the ABC laws;

(3) Furnish and sell malt beverages filed pursuant to G.S. 18B-1303(a) to its employees subject to the rules of the Commission and the Department of Revenue;

(4) In locations where the sale is legal, furnish malt beverages of any brand filed pursuant to G.S. 18B-1303(a) to guests and any other person who does not hold an ABC permit, for promotional purposes, subject to the rules of the Commission.

(b) Repealed by Session Laws 1989, c. 142, s. 3. (1945, c. 903, s. 1; 1947, c. 1098, ss. 2, 3; 1949, c. 974, s. 1; 1957, cc. 1048, 1448; 1963, c. 426, ss. 10, 12; c. 460, s. 1; 1971, c. 872, s. 1; 1973, c. 476, s. 128; 1975, c. 586, s. 1; c. 654, ss. 1, 2; c. 722, s. 1; 1977, c. 70, s. 19; c. 182, s. 1; c. 669, ss. 1, 2; c. 676, ss. 1, 2; c. 911; 1979, c. 348, ss. 2, 3; c. 683, ss. 5, 6, 11, 12; 1981, c. 412, s. 2; c. 747, s. 62; 1989, c. 142, s. 3; 1991, c. 459, s. 8.)

§ 18B-1110. Authorization of bottler permit.

(a) Authorization. - The holder of a bottler permit may:

(1) Receive, possess and transport shipments of malt beverages, unfortified wine and fortified wine;

(2) Bottle, sell, deliver and ship malt beverages, unfortified wine, and fortified wine in closed containers to wholesalers licensed under this Chapter as authorized by the ABC laws;

(3) Furnish or sell packages which do not conform to the manufacturer's marketing standards, if State taxes have been or will be paid, to its employees for the use of the employees or their families and guests in this State.

A sale or gift under subdivision (3) shall not be considered a retail or wholesale sale under the ABC law.

(b) Distribution Agreements. - Wine distribution agreements are governed by Article 12 of this Chapter. (1945, c. 903, s. 1; 1947, c. 1098, ss. 2, 3; 1949, c.

974, s. 1; 1957, cc. 1048, 1448; 1963, c. 426, ss. 10, 12; c. 460, s. 1; 1971, c. 872, s. 1; 1973, c. 476, s. 128; 1975, c. 586, s. 1; c. 654, ss. 1, 2; c. 722, s. 1; 1977, c. 70, s. 19; c. 182, s. 1; c. 669, ss. 1, 2; c. 676, ss. 1, 2; c. 911; 1979, c. 348, ss. 2, 3; c. 683, ss. 5, 6, 11, 12; 1981, c. 412, s. 2; 1983, c. 85, s. 1.)

§ 18B-1111. Authorization of salesman permit.

(a)   Authorized Acts. - The holder of a salesman permit may sell and transport malt beverages for a malt beverage wholesaler or sell and transport unfortified and fortified wine for a wine wholesaler.

(b)   Persons Required to Obtain Permit. - All route salesmen and salesmen working at a wholesaler's warehouse shall obtain the permit described in this section. All salesmen shall be at least 21 years old.

(c)   Validity Period. - A salesman permit shall be valid as provided in G.S. 18B-903(a), except that it shall be valid only so long as the salesman is employed by the same wholesaler. (1951, c. 378, ss. 1, 2, 5-8; 1963, c. 426, s. 13; 1971, c. 872, s. 1; 1975, c. 330, s. 2; c. 411, s. 8; 1981, c. 412, s. 2.)

§ 18B-1112. Authorization of vendor representative permit.

(a)   Authorized Acts. - The holder of a vendor representative permit may represent an unfortified winery, fortified winery, limited winery, brewery, bottler, importer, nonresident malt beverage vendor, or nonresident wine vendor, either as an employee or an agent, to solicit orders for that commercial permittee's product. The vendor representative may sell, deliver, and ship alcoholic beverages in this State only to permittees to whom the commercial permittee he represents may sell, deliver, or ship.

(b)   Number of Permits. - A vendor representative shall secure a separate permit for each commercial permittee he represents. A permit may not be issued without the approval of the commercial permittee. (1981, c. 747, s. 63; 1981 (Reg. Sess., 1982), c. 1262, s. 21.)

§ 18B-1113. Authorization of nonresident malt beverage vendor permit.

The holder of a nonresident malt beverage vendor permit may sell, deliver, and ship malt beverages in this State only to wholesalers, importers, and bottlers licensed under this Chapter, as authorized by the ABC laws. The malt beverages must come to rest at the licensed premises of a malt beverage wholesaler in this State before being resold to a retailer. A nonresident malt beverage vendor permit may be issued to a brewery, an importer, or a bottler outside North Carolina who desires to sell, deliver, and ship malt beverages into this State. (1981, c. 747, s. 63; 1993, c. 415, s. 23.)

§ 18B-1114. Authorization of nonresident wine vendor permit.

The holder of a nonresident wine vendor permit may sell, deliver, and ship unfortified and fortified wine in this State only to wholesalers, importers, and bottlers licensed under this Chapter, as authorized by the ABC laws. The unfortified and fortified wine must come to rest at the licensed premises of a wine wholesaler in this State before being resold to a retailer. A nonresident wine vendor permit may be issued to a winery, a wholesaler, an importer, or a bottler outside North Carolina who desires to sell, deliver, and ship unfortified and fortified wine into this State. The holder of a nonresident wine vendor permit may sell, deliver, and ship into this State only wine for which it is a primary American source of supply. To be considered a primary American source of supply, a nonresident wine vendor must establish that it has lawfully purchased the wine from the winery, or from an agent of the winery, and by written contract or otherwise has been authorized by the winery to distribute the wine to wholesalers in the United States. (1981, c. 747, s. 63; 1993, c. 415, s. 24; 2006-227, s. 13.)

§ 18B-1114.1. Authorization of winery special event permit.

(a) Authorization. - The holder of an unfortified winery permit, a limited winery permit, a viticulture/enology course authorization, or a wine producer permit may obtain a winery special permit allowing the winery or wine producer to give free tastings of its wine, and to sell its wine by the glass or in closed containers, at trade shows, conventions, shopping malls, wine festivals, street festivals, holiday festivals, agricultural festivals, balloon races, local fund-raisers, and other similar events approved by the Commission.

(b)   Limitation. - A winery special event permit is valid only in a jurisdiction that has approved the establishment of ABC stores or has approved the sale of unfortified wine. (1989, c. 737, s. 2; 1991, c. 267, s. 1; 1991 (Reg. Sess., 1992), c. 1007, s. 24; 1993, c. 553, s. 71; 2001-262, s. 3; 2001-487, s. 49(e); 2005-350, s. 3(b).)

§ 18B-1114.2. Effect of cider and vinegar manufacturer permit.

The holder of a cider and vinegar manufacturer permit may purchase and transport unlimited quantities of out-of-date unfortified or fortified wines from wine wholesalers for the sole purpose of manufacturing a food product item. Any manufacturer of cider or vinegar may apply for this permit. (1997-134, s. 2.)

§ 18B-1114.3. Authorization of wine producer permit.

(a)   Authorization. - The holder of a wine producer permit may:

(1)   Ship crops grown on land owned by it in North Carolina to a winery, inside or outside the State, for the manufacture and bottling of unfortified wine from those crops and may receive that wine back in closed containers.

(2)   Sell, deliver, and ship the unfortified wine manufactured from its crops in closed containers to wholesalers and retailers licensed under this Chapter as authorized by the ABC laws and also sell to exporters and nonresident wholesalers when the purchase is not for resale in this State.

(3)   Regardless of the results of any local wine election, sell the wine manufactured from its crops for on-or off-premise consumption upon obtaining the appropriate permit under G.S. 18B-1001.

(b)   Limitation on Sales. - The holder of a wine producer permit may not sell, in total, annually, more than 20,000 gallons of wine manufactured off its premises from crops it has grown. (2001-262, s. 4; 2001-487, s. 49(c).)

§ 18B-1114.4. Viticulture/Enology course authorization.

(a) Authorization. - The holder of a viticulture/enology course authorization may:

(1) Manufacture wine from grapes grown on the school's campus or the school's contracted or leased property for the purpose of providing instruction and education on the making of unfortified wines.

(2) Possess wines manufactured during the viticulture/enology program for the purpose of conducting wine-tasting seminars and classes for students who are 21 years of age or older.

(3) Sell wines produced during the course to wholesalers or to retailers upon obtaining a wine wholesaler permit under G.S. 18B-1107, except that the permittee may not receive shipments of wines from other producers.

(4) Sell wines produced during the course, upon obtaining a permit under G.S. 18B-1001(4).

(b) Limitation. - Authorization for a viticulture/enology course shall be granted by the Commission only for a community college or college that offers a viticulture/enology program as a part of its curriculum offerings for students of the school. Wines may be manufactured only from grapes grown in a viticulture/enology course vineyard that is located on the school's campus or the school's contracted or leased property.

(c) The holder of a viticulture/enology course authorization who obtains a wine wholesaler permit under G.S. 18B-1107 subject to the limitation in subsection (a) of this section may obtain a winery special event permit under G.S. 18B-1114.1, and where the permit is valid may participate in approved events and sell at retail at those events any wine produced incident to the operation of the viticulture/enology program. The holder of a viticulture/enology course authorization may participate in not more than six winery special events within a 12-month period and may sell up to 25 cases of wine at each event. Net proceeds from the program's retail sale of wine pursuant to this subsection shall be retained by the school and used for support of the viticulture/enology program.

(d) The holder of a viticulture/enology course authorization shall not be considered a winery for the purposes of this Chapter or Chapter 105 of the General Statutes. (2002-102, s. 1; 2005-350, s. 3(a); 2009-539, s. 2.)

§ 18B-1114.5. Authorization of malt beverage special event permit.

(a) Authorization. - The holder of a brewery, malt beverage importer, or nonresident malt beverage vendor permit may obtain a malt beverage special event permit allowing the permittee to give free tastings of its malt beverages and to sell its malt beverages by the glass or in closed containers at trade shows, conventions, shopping malls, malt beverage festivals, street festivals, holiday festivals, agricultural festivals, balloon races, local fund-raisers, and other similar events approved by the Commission. Except for a brewery operating under the provisions of G.S. 18B-1104(7), all malt beverages sampled or sold pursuant to this section must be purchased from a licensed malt beverages wholesaler.

(b) Limitation. - A malt beverage special event permit is valid only in a jurisdiction that has approved the establishment of ABC stores or has approved the sale of malt beverages. A malt beverage special event shall not be used as subterfuge for malt beverages suppliers to ship directly to retail permittees unless otherwise authorized by law. (2009-377, s. 4.)

§ 18B-1115. Commercial transportation.

(a) Permit Required. - Unless a person holds a permit which otherwise allows him to transport more than 80 liters of malt beverages other than draft malt beverages in kegs, 50 liters of unfortified wine, or eight liters of fortified wine or spirituous liquor, or is a retailer authorized to transport alcoholic beverages under G.S. 18B-405, each person transporting alcoholic beverages in excess of those quantities shall have the permit described in this section.

(b) When Transportation Legal. - No person may obtain a permit under this section to transport spirituous liquor unless the transportation is for delivery to a federal reservation over which North Carolina has ceded jurisdiction to the United States, for delivery to an ABC store, or for transport through this State to another state.

(c) Common Carriers. - Railroad companies and other common carriers having regularly established schedules of service in this State may transport alcoholic beverages into, out of, and between points in this State without a permit. Those companies shall keep accurate records of the character, volume and number of containers transported and shall allow the Commission and alcohol law-enforcement agents to inspect those records at any time. The Commission may require common carriers to make reports of shipments.

(d) Motor Vehicle Carriers. - Alcoholic beverages may be transported over the public highways of this State by motor vehicle carriers under the following conditions:

(1) The carrier shall notify the Commission of the character of the alcoholic beverages it will transport and of its authorization from the appropriate regulatory authority.

(2) The carrier shall obtain, at no charge, a fleet permit from the Commission authorizing the transportation.

(3) The driver or person in charge of each vehicle transporting alcoholic beverages shall possess a copy of the carrier's fleet permit certified by the carrier to be an exact copy of the original.

(4) The driver or person in charge of each vehicle transporting alcoholic beverages shall possess a bill of lading, invoice or other memorandum of shipment showing the name and address of the person from whom the alcoholic beverages were received, the character and contents of the shipment, the quantity and volume of the shipment, and the name and address of the person to whom the alcoholic beverages are being shipped.

(5) The driver or person in charge of each vehicle transporting the alcoholic beverages shall display all documents required by this section upon request of any law-enforcement officer. Failure to produce these documents or failure of the documents to disclose clearly and accurately the information required by this section shall be prima facie evidence of a violation of this section.

(6) Each carrier shall keep accurate records of character, volume and number of containers transported and shall allow the Commission and alcohol law-enforcement agents to inspect those records at any time. The Commission may require carriers to make reports of shipments.

(e) Transportation of Spirituous Liquor. - In addition to the requirements of subsection (d), motor vehicle carriers engaged in transporting spirituous liquor shall:

(1) Deposit with the Commission a surety bond for one thousand dollars ($1,000) conditioned that the carrier will not unlawfully transport spirituous liquor into or through this State. The bond, which shall be approved by the Commission, shall be payable to the State of North Carolina. If the bonded carrier is convicted of a violation covered by the bond, the proceeds of the forfeited bond shall be paid to the school fund of the county in which the liquor was seized.

(2) Include in its bill of lading, invoice or other memorandum of shipment the North Carolina code numbers of the spirituous liquor being transported.

(3) Include in its bill of lading, invoice or other memorandum of shipment the route which the vehicle will follow, and the vehicle shall not vary substantially from that stated route.

(f) Malt Beverages and Wine Transported by Boats. - The owner or operator of any boat may transport malt beverages, unfortified wine and fortified wine over the waters of this State if he satisfies all requirements of subsection (d).

(g) State Warehouse Carrier. - The Commission may exempt a carrier for the State or a local board warehouse from any of the requirements of this section provided that it determines that the requirements of this section are otherwise satisfied. (1923, c. 1, s. 15; C.S., s. 3411(o); 1939, c. 158, s. 503; 1971, c. 872, s. 1; 1975, c. 411, s. 7; 1977, c. 70, s. 20; c. 176, s. 7; 1979, c. 286, s. 5; 1981, c. 412, s. 2; c. 747, s. 63; 1987, c. 136, s. 9; 1989, c. 553, s. 4; 1993, c. 508, s. 7; 2005-335, s. 1.)
§ 18B-1116. Exclusive outlets prohibited.

(a) Prohibitions. - It shall be unlawful for any manufacturer, bottler, or wholesaler of any alcoholic beverages, or for any officer, director, or affiliate thereof, either directly or indirectly to:

(1) Require that an alcoholic beverage retailer purchase any alcoholic beverages from that person to the full or partial exclusion of any other alcoholic beverages offered for sale by other persons in this State; or

(2) Have any direct or indirect financial interest in the business of any alcoholic beverage retailer in this State or in the premises where the business of any alcoholic beverage retailer in this State is conducted; or

(3) Lend or give to any alcoholic beverage retailer in this State or his employee or to the owner of the premises where the business of any alcoholic beverage retailer in this State is conducted, any money, service, equipment, furniture, fixtures or any other thing of value.

A brewery qualifying under G.S. 18B-1104(7) to act as a wholesaler or retailer of its own malt beverages is not subject to the provisions of this subsection concerning financial interests in, and lending or giving things of value to, a wholesaler or retailer with respect to the brewery's transactions with the retail business on its premises. The brewery is subject to the provisions of this subsection, however, with respect to its transactions with all other wholesalers and retailers.

(b) Exemptions. - The Commission may grant exemptions from the provisions of this section. In determining whether to grant an exemption, the Commission shall consider the public welfare, the quantity and value of articles involved, established trade customs not contrary to the public interest, and the purposes of this section.

(c) As used in this section, the phrase "giving things of value" shall not include the dividing or removing of individual containers of alcohol from larger packages of alcohol or the delivery of such to the retail permittee. (1945, c. 708, s. 6; 1953, c. 1207, s. 1; 1971, c. 872, s. 1; 1981, c. 412, s. 2; c. 747, s. 63; 1993, c. 415, s. 25; 2005-380, s. 3.)

§ 18B-1117. Repealed by Session Laws 1989, c. 142, s. 3.

§ 18B-1118. Purchase restrictions.

The holder of a malt beverage wholesaler, wine wholesaler, malt beverage importer, wine importer, or bottler permit may not purchase malt beverages or wine for resale in this State from a nonresident who does not have the proper nonresident vendor permit. (1985, c. 114, s. 3.)

§ 18B-1119. Supplier's financial interest in wholesaler.

(a) A supplier or an officer, director, employee or affiliate of a supplier may financially assist a proposed purchaser in acquiring ownership of a wholesaler's business by participation in a limited partnership arrangement in which the supplier, officer, director, employee, or affiliate is a limited partner and the proposed purchaser seeking to acquire ownership of the wholesaler's business is a general partner. Such limited partnership arrangement may exist for no longer than eight years. If the general partner defaults in the agreement with the limited partner, and the limited partner acquires title to the general partner's interest, the limited partner must divest itself of the general partner's interest within 180 days.

(b) A supplier or an officer, director, employee or affiliate of a supplier may financially assist a proposed purchaser in acquiring ownership of a wholesaler's business by making a business loan and taking as security the assets of the wholesaler's business. The business loan may exist for no longer than eight years. If the wholesaler defaults on the loan and it is necessary for the supplier to take title to the assets of the business, the supplier may operate the business for a period not to exceed 180 days, by which time the supplier must divest itself of the business. The supplier may make the subsequent purchaser a business loan, taking as security the assets of the wholesaler's business. It shall also be permissible for the wholesaler and supplier to agree on the sale of the wholesaler's business to the supplier, provided that the supplier shall divest itself of the wholesaler's business within 180 days.

(c) A supplier or an officer, director, employee or affiliate of a supplier may have a security interest in the inventory or property of its wholesaler to secure payment for such inventory or other loans for other purposes. (1989, c. 142, s. 2.)

§§ 18B-1120 through 18B-1199. Reserved for future codification purposes.

Article 12.

Wine Distribution Agreements.

§ 18B-1200. Construction; findings and purpose; exceptions.

(a)   This Article shall be liberally construed and applied to promote its underlying purposes and policies.

(b)   The underlying purposes and policies of the Article are:

(1)   To promote the compelling interest of the public in fair business relations between wine wholesalers and wineries, and in the continuation of wine wholesalerships on a fair basis;

(2)   To protect wine wholesalers against unfair treatment by wineries;

(3)   To provide wine wholesalers with rights and remedies in addition to those existing by contract or common law; and

(4)   To govern all wine wholesalerships, including any renewals or amendments, to the full extent consistent with the Constitution of this State and the United States.

(c)   The effect of this Article may not be waived or varied by contract or agreement. Any contract or agreement purporting to do so is void and unenforceable to the extent of that waiver or variance.

(d)   A North Carolina winery holding a valid wine wholesaler permit issued pursuant to G.S. 18B-1101(7) and G.S. 18B-1107, when acting as its own master wholesaler, shall not be subject to the provisions of G.S. 18B-1204, 18B-1205, and 18B-1207. (1983, c. 85, s. 2; 2005-340, s. 1; 2005-350, s. 4; 2006-264, s. 98; 2007-484, s. 37.)

§ 18B-1201. Definitions.

As used in this Article, unless the context requires otherwise:

(1) "Agreement" means a commercial relationship between a wine wholesaler and a winery. The agreement may be of a definite or indefinite duration and is not required to be in writing. Any of the following constitutes prima facie evidence of an "agreement" within the meaning of this definition:

a. A relationship whereby the wine wholesaler is granted the right to offer and sell a brand offered by a winery;

b. A relationship whereby the wine wholesaler, as an independent business, constitutes a component of a winery's distribution system;

c. A relationship whereby the wine wholesaler's business is substantially associated with a brand offered by a winery;

d. A relationship whereby the wine wholesaler's business is substantially reliant on a winery for the continued supply of wine;

e. The shipment, preparation for shipment, or acceptance of any order by any winery or its agent for any wine or beverages to a wine wholesaler within this State;

f. The payment by a wine wholesaler and the acceptance of payment by any winery or its agent for the shipment of any order of wine or beverages intended for sale within this State.

(2) "Territory" or "sales territory" means the area of primary sales responsibility expressly or implicitly designated by any agreement between any wine wholesaler and winery for a brand offered by any winery.

(3) "Wine wholesaler" means any holder of a wine wholesaler permit, wine importer permit, or bottler permit issued under the authority of this Chapter.

(4) "Winery" means any holder of an unfortified winery permit, fortified winery permit, limited winery permit, or nonresident wine vendor permit issued under the authority of this Chapter who sells at least 1,250 cases of wine in North Carolina per year. (1983, c. 85, s. 2; 2010-122, s. 26; 2011-73, s. 1.)

§ 18B-1202. No inducement, coercion, or discrimination.

No winery may:

(1) Induce, coerce, or attempt to induce or coerce any wine wholesaler to accept delivery of any alcoholic beverage or any other commodity which has not been ordered by the wine wholesaler;

(2) Induce, coerce, or attempt to induce or coerce any wine wholesaler to do any illegal act by any means, including threatening to amend, cancel, terminate, or refuse to renew any agreement existing between a winery and a wine wholesaler;

(3) Require a wine wholesaler to assent to any condition, stipulation, or provision limiting the wholesaler in his privilege to sell a product offered by any other winery;

(4) Unlawfully discriminate on the basis of race, color, creed, sex, religion, or national origin in awarding or maintaining agreements covered by this Article. Wineries who contract with wholesalers in this State shall make reasonable efforts to establish and maintain agreements with wholesalers who are females and members of minority groups. (1983, c. 85, s. 2.)

§ 18B-1203. Primary area of responsibility; no discrimination.

(a) Each agreement shall designate the sales territory of the wholesaler. No winery may enter into more than one agreement for each brand of wine or beverage it offers in any territory. A wholesaler shall not distribute any brand of wine to a retailer whose premises are located outside the territory designated in the wholesaler's agreement for that brand. With the approval of the Commission, a wholesaler may distribute wine outside the wholesaler's designated territory during periods of temporary service interruption when requested to do so by the winery and the wholesaler whose service is interrupted. Unless the winery and wine wholesaler agree otherwise in writing, the territory designated as the wholesaler's "area of primary sales responsibility" as of the effective date of this section shall be the wholesaler's designated sales territory. Redesignations of sales territories occurring after July 1, 2011, shall be reported to the Commission within 30 days. No provisions of this Article, however, may prohibit the continuation of a multi-wholesaler agreement entered into before March 21, 1983, as between the winery and the original wine wholesalers thereto, provided that upon termination of any such agreement, the affected territory shall be designated for a single wholesaler.

(b) A wholesaler shall service retail permit holders within its designated territory without discrimination. Upon request from a retail permit holder, each wholesaler shall make a good faith effort to make available any brand of wine the wholesaler is authorized to distribute in the territory. The provisions of this subsection shall not apply to retail permit holder private label brands. (1983, c. 85, s. 2; 2011-73, s. 2.)

§ 18B-1204. Cancellation.

Notwithstanding the terms, provisions, or conditions of any agreement, no winery may amend, cancel, terminate, or refuse to continue to renew any agreement, or cause a wholesaler to resign from an agreement, unless good cause exists for amendment, termination, cancellation, nonrenewal, noncontinuation, or resignation. "Good cause" does not include a change in ownership of a winery. "Good cause" does include:

(1) Revocation of the wholesaler's permit or license to do business in this State;

(2) Bankruptcy or receivership of the wholesaler;

(3) Assignment for the benefit of creditors or similar disposition of the assets of the wholesaler; or

(4) Failure of the wholesaler to comply substantially, without reasonable excuse or justification, with any reasonable and material requirement imposed upon him by the winery, including a substantial failure by a wine wholesaler to:

a. Maintain a sales volume of the brands offered by the winery, or

b. Render services comparable in quality, quantity, or volume to the sales volumes maintained and services rendered by other wholesalers of the same brands within the State.

In any determination as to whether a wholesaler has failed to comply substantially, without reasonable excuse or justification, with any reasonable and material requirement imposed upon him by the winery, consideration shall be given to the relative size, population, geographical location, number of retail outlets, demand for the products applicable to the territory of the wholesaler in question and to comparable territories, and any reasonable sales quota set by the agreement. The burden of proving good cause for amendment, termination, cancellation, nonrenewal, noncontinuation, or resignation is on the winery. (1983, c. 85, s. 2.)

§ 18B-1205. Notice of intent to terminate.

(a) Except as provided in subsection (c), a winery shall provide a wholesaler at least 90 days prior written notice of any intention to amend, terminate, cancel, or not renew any agreement. The notice, a copy of which shall be mailed at the same time to the Commission, shall state all the reasons for the intended amendment, termination, cancellation, or nonrenewal.

(b) When the reasons relate to conditions that can be rectified by the wholesaler, he has 60 days in which to do so. If the wholesaler rectifies the conditions within the 60-day period, he shall give written notice thereof to the winery and to the Commission. If the wholesaler has rectified the conditions, the proposed amendment, termination, cancellation, or nonrenewal is void, except that when the winery contends that the wholesaler has not completely rectified the conditions, the winery may, within 15 days after the expiration of the 60-day period, request a hearing before the Commission to determine if the wholesaler has rectified all the conditions.

(c) When the reasons relate to conditions that cannot be rectified by the wholesaler within the 60-day period, the wholesaler may request a hearing before the Commission to determine if the winery has good cause for the amendment, termination, cancellation, or nonrenewal of the agreement. The burden of proving good cause for the amendment, termination, cancellation, or nonrenewal is on the winery.

(d) Upon receiving a written request from the winery or wholesaler for a hearing, the Commission shall, after notice and hearing, determine if the wholesaler has rectified the conditions or if good cause exists for the amendment, termination, cancellation, or nonrenewal of the agreement, as appropriate. In any case in which a petition is made to the Commission for such a determination, the agreement in question shall continue in effect, pending the Commission's decision and any judicial review thereof.

(e) In all proceedings before the Commission, the Commission shall ensure that no agreements covered by this Article result in unlawful discrimination on the basis of race, color, creed, sex, religion, or national origin.

(f) No notice is required and an agreement may be immediately terminated, amended, canceled, or allowed to expire if the reason for the amendment, termination, cancellation, or nonrenewal is:

(1) The bankruptcy or receivership of the wholesaler;

(2) An assignment for the benefit of creditors or similar disposition of the assets of the business; or

(3) Revocation of the wholesaler's permit or license. (1983, c. 85, s. 2.)

§ 18B-1206. Transfer of business.

(a) No winery may unreasonably withhold or delay consent to any transfer of the wholesaler's business or transfer of the stock or other interest in the wholesaleship whenever the wholesaler to be substituted meets the material and reasonable qualifications and standards required of the winery's wholesalers.

(b) Notwithstanding subsection (a), no winery may withhold consent to, or in any manner retain a right of prior approval of, the transfer of the wholesaler's business to a member or members of the family of the wholesaler. Subsequent to such a transfer, the rights and obligations of the wholesaleship and its owners are in all respects governed by the provisions of this Chapter. As used in this subsection, "family" means the spouse, parents, siblings, and lineal descendants, including those by adoption, of the wholesaler. (1983, c. 85, s. 2.)

§ 18B-1207. Judicial remedies.

(a) If a winery violates any provision of this Article, a wholesaler may maintain a suit against the winery. The court may grant injunctive and other appropriate relief, including damages to compensate the wholesaler for the value of the agreement and any good will, to remedy violations of this Article.

(b) Any winery that amends, cancels, terminates, or refuses to renew any wine agreement, or causes a wholesaler to resign from an agreement shall compensate the wine wholesaler for the wine wholesaler's wine inventory. The amount of compensation shall include the F.O.B. costs of the wine inventory and any freight charges incurred by the wine wholesaler in receiving them.

(c) For any violation of the provisions of this Article, the Commission may take any of the following actions against the winery:

(1) Suspend the winery's permit for a specific period of time no longer than three years;

(2) Revoke the winery's permit;

(3) Issue an order suspending the shipment of the winery's products to one or more designated sales territories previously served by the wholesaler who has been terminated or who is the successor in interest to a wholesaler who sold the winery's products in the designated territory.

(4) Impose a monetary penalty up to fifteen thousand dollars ($15,000) for a first offense and up to thirty-five thousand ($35,000) for the second offense. The clear proceeds of monetary penalties imposed pursuant to this subdivision shall be remitted to the Civil Penalty and Forfeiture Fund in accordance with G.S. 115C-457.2.

In any case in which the Commission is entitled to suspend or revoke a permit, the Commission may accept from the winery an offer in compromise to pay a monetary penalty. The Commission may either accept a compromise or revoke a permit, but not both. The Commission may accept a compromise and suspend the permit in the same case.

(d) Notwithstanding the choice of forum agreed to by the parties, venue for all actions under this Article shall be determined by the trial judge based upon the convenience of witnesses and the promotion of the ends of justice. (1983, c. 85, s. 2; 1989, c. 800, ss. 16, 17; 1998-215, s. 28.)

§ 18B-1208. Price of product.

No winery, whether by means of a term or condition of an agreement or otherwise, may directly or indirectly fix or maintain the prices at which the wholesaler may sell any wine or beverage. (1983, c. 85, s. 2.)

§ 18B-1209. Retaliatory action prohibited.

No winery may take retaliatory action against a wholesaler who files or manifests an intention to file a complaint alleging that the winery violated a State or federal law or rule. Retaliatory action includes refusal without good cause to continue the agreement or a material reduction in the quality of service or quantity of products available to the wholesaler under the agreement. (1983, c. 85, s. 2.)

§ 18B-1210. Management.

No winery may require or prohibit any change in management or personnel of any wholesaler unless the current or potential management or personnel fails to meet reasonable qualifications and standards required by the winery. (1983, c. 85, s. 2.)

§ 18B-1211. No discrimination.

No winery may discriminate among its wholesalers in any business dealings, including the price of wine sold to the wholesaler, unless the classification among its wholesalers is based upon reasonable grounds. (1983, c. 85, s. 2.)

§ 18B-1212. No waiver.

No winery may require any wholesaler to waive compliance with any provision of this Chapter. Nothing in this Chapter, however, may be construed to limit or prohibit good faith settlements of disputes voluntarily entered into between the parties. (1983, c. 85, s. 2.)

§ 18B-1213. Obligations of purchaser.

The purchaser of a winery, and any successor to the import rights of a winery, is obligated to all the terms and conditions of an agreement in effect on the date of the purchase or other acquisition of the right to distribute a brand, except for good cause, which includes,

(1) Revocation of the wholesaler's permit or license to do business in this State,

(2) Bankruptcy or insolvency of the wholesaler,

(3) Assignment for the benefit of creditors or similar disposition of the assets of the wholesaler, or

(4) Failure by the wholesaler to comply substantially, without reasonable excuse or justification, with any reasonable and material requirement imposed upon the wholesaler by the winery.

As used in this Article, "purchase" includes the sale of stock, sale of assets, merger, lease, transfer, or consolidation. (1983, c. 85, s. 2; 2010-122, s. 25.)

§ 18B-1214. Prohibited practices enumerated.

It is a violation of this Article for any winery, directly or indirectly, to engage in any of the following practices:

(1) To restrict the sale of any equity or indebtedness or the transfer of any securities of any wholesaler or in any way prevent or attempt to prevent the transfer, sale, or issuance of shares of stock or indebtedness to employees, personnel of the wholesaler, or heirs of the principal owner, as long as basic

financial requirements of the winery are complied with and the sale, transfer, or issuance does not have the effect of accomplishing a sale of the wholesaler;

(2) To impose unreasonable standards of performance upon a wholesaler;

(3) To prohibit directly or indirectly the right of free association among wholesalers for any lawful purpose. (1983, c. 85, s. 2.)

§ 18B-1215. Intent of nondiscrimination.

It is the intent of this Article that there shall be no unlawful discrimination based on race, color, creed, sex, religion, or national origin in any aspect of the awarding or maintaining of agreements covered by this Article. (1983, c. 85, s. 2.)

§ 18B-1216. Relation of Article to other laws.

Nothing in this Article relieves a winery or wholesaler of any obligation, duty, or prohibition imposed by any other provision of this Chapter or by G.S. 75-1.1 or by any other provision of State law, and the remedies provided in this Article are nonexclusive. (1983, c. 85, s. 2.)

§§ 18B-1217 through 18B-1299. Reserved for future codification purposes.

Article 13.

Beer Franchise Law.

§ 18B-1300. Purpose.

Pursuant to the authority of the State under the Twenty-First Amendment to the United States Constitution, the General Assembly finds that regulation of the business relations between malt beverage manufacturers and importers and the wholesalers of such products is necessary to:

(1) Maintain stability and healthy competition in the malt beverage industry in this State.

(2) Promote and maintain a sound, stable and viable three-tier system of distribution of malt beverages to the public.

(3) Promote the compelling interest of the public in fair business relations between malt beverage suppliers and wholesalers, and in the continuation of beer franchise agreements on a fair basis.

(4) Maintain a uniform system of control over the sale, purchase and distribution of malt beverages in the State. (1989, c. 142, s. 1.)

§ 18B-1301. Definitions.

(1) "Supplier" means a brewer, bottler, or importer of malt beverages, including anyone who holds a brewery, malt beverages importer or nonresident malt beverages vendor permit.

(2) "Wholesaler" means the holder of a malt beverages wholesaler permit. (1989, c. 142, s. 1; 1995, c. 466, s. 14.)

§ 18B-1302. Franchise agreement.

(a) Nature of Agreement. - A franchise agreement is a commercial relationship between a wholesaler and supplier of a definite or indefinite duration, whether written or oral, including:

(1) A relationship whereby a wholesaler is granted the right to offer and sell the brands of malt beverages offered by the supplier; or

(2) An agreement whereby a supplier grants to a wholesaler a license to use a trade name, trademark, service mark or related characteristic and in

which there is a community of interest in the marking of the products of the supplier by lease or otherwise.

(b) Existence of Agreement. - A franchise agreement as described in subsection (a) exists when:

(1) The supplier has shipped malt beverages to a wholesaler or accepted an order for malt beverages from the wholesaler;

(2) A wholesaler has paid or the supplier has accepted payment for an order of malt beverages intended for sale within this State;

(3) The supplier and wholesaler have filed with the Commission a distribution agreement as required by G.S. 18B-1303; or

(4) A supplier acquires the right to manufacture a malt beverage product, or the trade name for such product, or the right to distribute a product, for which a wholesaler has a franchise agreement. (1989, c. 142, s. 1; 2005-350, s. 5.)

§ 18B-1303. Filing of distribution agreement; no discrimination.

(a) Filing. - It is unlawful for a supplier to provide malt beverages to a wholesaler unless the Commission has received notification from the supplier designating the brands of the supplier which the wholesaler is authorized to sell and the territory in which such sales may take place. If the supplier sells several brands, the agreement need not apply to all brands. A franchise agreement applies to all supplier products under the same brand name, and different categories of products manufactured under a common identifying trade name are considered to be the same brand. No supplier may provide by a distribution agreement for the distribution of a brand to more than one wholesaler for the same territory. A wholesaler shall not distribute any brand of malt beverage to a retailer whose premises are located outside the territory specified in the wholesaler's distribution agreement for that brand. A wholesaler may, however, with the approval of the Commission distribute malt beverages outside its designated territory during periods of temporary service interruption when requested to do so by the supplier and the wholesaler whose service is interrupted.

(b) No Discrimination. - A wholesaler shall service all retail permit holders within his designated territory without discrimination and shall make a good faith effort to make available to each retail permit holder in the territory each brand of malt beverage which the wholesaler has been authorized to distribute in that area.

(c) No Price Maintenance. - A franchise agreement shall not, either expressly or by implication or in its operation, establish or maintain the resale price of any brand of malt beverages by a wholesaler. (1989, c. 142, s. 1; 1991, c. 459, s. 9; 1993, c. 415, s. 28; 1995, c. 466, s. 15; 2012-4, s. 1.)

§ 18B-1304. Prohibitions.

It is unlawful for a supplier, or an officer, agent or representative of a supplier, to:

(1) Coerce or attempt to coerce or persuade a wholesaler to violate any provision of the ABC laws or rules of the Department of Revenue.

(2) Except as authorized by G.S. 18B-1305(a1), alter in a material way, terminate, fail to renew, or cause a wholesaler to resign from, a franchise agreement with a wholesaler except for good cause and with the notice required by G.S. 18B-1305.

(3) Withdraw money from or otherwise access a wholesaler's bank accounts without the wholesaler's consent.

(4) Present a franchise agreement, amendment, or renewal to a wholesaler that attempts to waive compliance with any provision of this Article or that requires a wholesaler to waive compliance with any provision of this Article. A wholesaler entering into a franchise agreement containing provisions in conflict with this Article shall not be deemed to waive rights protected by, or in compliance with, any provision of this Article.

(5) Induce or coerce, or attempt to induce or coerce, any wholesaler to assent to any franchise agreement, amendment, or renewal that does not comply with this Article and the laws of this State.

(6) Coerce or attempt to coerce a wholesaler, or its designated or anticipated successor, to sign a franchise agreement, amendment, or renewal to a franchise agreement by threatening to refuse to approve or delay issuing an approval for the sale, transfer, or merger of a wholesaler's business.

(7) Terminate, cancel, or nonrenew or attempt to terminate, cancel, or nonrenew a franchise agreement on the basis that the wholesaler fails to agree or consent to an amendment to the franchise agreement.

(8) Prohibit a wholesaler from distributing the product of any other supplier, except that a supplier may prohibit a wholesaler from distributing the product of another supplier if reasonable grounds exist for prohibiting the wholesaler's acquisition of the product and the acquisition would result in the wholesaler acquiring eighty percent (80%) or more by volume of all malt beverage products sold in the territory being acquired at the time of the acquisition.

(9) Refuse to approve or require a wholesaler to terminate a brand manager or successor manager without good cause. A supplier has good cause only if the person designated for approval by the wholesaler fails to meet reasonable standards and qualifications.

(10) Discriminate in price, allowance, rebate, refund, payment term, commission, discount, or service between wholesalers licensed in North Carolina. As used in this subsection, "discriminate" means the granting of a more favorable price, allowance, rebate, refund, payment term, commission, discount, or service to one North Carolina wholesaler than to another North Carolina wholesaler based on the quantity of malt beverages purchased or for any other reason, but "discriminate" shall exclude the granting of more favorable freight and transportation costs, price promotions on malt beverage products for special events in a particular market not to exceed 14 consecutive days, point-of-sale advertising materials, sponsorships, consumer specialty items, consumer sweepstakes, and novelties. A supplier may, however, offer a lower price or discount in order to match that of a competing supplier on a similar category of malt beverage products in the entire State or in a particular market. (1989, c. 142, s. 1; 2012-4, s. 1.)

§ 18B-1305. Cause for termination of franchise agreement.

(a) Meaning of Good Cause. - Good cause for altering or terminating a franchise agreement, or failing to renew or causing a wholesaler to resign from such an agreement, exists when the wholesaler fails to comply with provisions of the agreement which are reasonable, material, not unconscionable, and which are not discriminatory when compared with the provisions imposed, by their terms or in the manner of enforcement, on other similarly situated wholesaler by the supplier. The meaning of good cause set out in this section may not be modified or superseded by provisions in a written franchise agreement prepared by a supplier if those provisions purport to define good cause in a manner different than specified in this section. In any dispute over alteration, termination, failure to renew or causing a wholesaler to resign from a franchise agreement, the burden is on the supplier to establish that good cause exists for the action.

(a1) Termination by a Small Brewery. - A brewery's authorization to distribute its own malt beverage products pursuant to G.S. 18B-1104(8) shall revert back to the brewery, in the absence of good cause, following the fifth business day after confirmed receipt of written notice of such reversion by the brewery to the wholesaler. The brewery shall pay the wholesaler fair market value for the distribution rights for the affected brand. For purposes of this subsection, "fair market value" means the highest dollar amount at which a seller would be willing to sell and a buyer willing to buy at the time the self-distribution rights revert back to the brewery, after each party has been provided all information relevant to the transaction.

(b) Notice of Cause. - At least 90 days before altering, terminating or failing to renew a franchise agreement for good cause, the supplier must give the wholesaler written notice of the intended action and the specific reasons for it. If the cause for the alteration, termination or failure to renew is subject to correction by the wholesaler, and the wholesaler makes such correction within 45 days of receipt of the notice, the notice shall be void.

(c) Termination for Cause without Advance Notice. - A supplier may terminate or fail to renew a franchise agreement for any of the following reasons, and the termination shall be complete upon receipt by the wholesaler of a written notice of the termination and the reason:

(1) Insolvency of the wholesaler, the dissolution or liquidation of the wholesaler, or the filing of any petition by or against the wholesaler under any bankruptcy or receivership law which materially affects the wholesaler's ability to remain in business.

(2) Revocation of the wholesaler's State or federal permit or license for more than 30 days.

(3) Conviction of the wholesaler, or of a partner or individual who owns ten percent (10%) or more of the partnership or stock of the wholesaler, of a felony which might reasonably be expected to adversely affect the goodwill or interest of the wholesaler or supplier. The provisions of this subdivision shall not apply, however, if the wholesaler or its existing partners or stockholders shall have the right to purchase the interest of the offending partner or stockholder, and such purchase is completed within 30 days of the conviction.

(4) Fraudulent conduct by the wholesaler in its dealings with the supplier or its products.

(5) Failure of the wholesaler to pay for the supplier's products according to the established terms of the supplier.

(6) Assignment, sale or transfer of the wholesaler's business or control of the wholesaler without the written consent of the supplier, except as provided in G.S. 18B-1307.

(d) Absence of Good Cause. - Good cause for alteration, termination or failure to renew a franchise agreement does not include:

(1) The failure or refusal of the wholesaler to engage in any trade practice, conduct or activity which would violate federal or State law.

(2) The failure or refusal of the wholesaler to take any action which would be contrary to the provisions of this Article.

(3) A change in the ownership of the supplier or the acquisition by another supplier of the brewery, brand or trade name or trademark, or acquisition of the right to distribute a product, from the original supplier.

(4) Sale or transfer of the rights to manufacture, distribute, or use the trade name of the brand to a successor supplier.

(5) Failure of the wholesaler to meet standards of operation or performance that have been imposed or revised unilaterally by the supplier without a fair opportunity for the individual wholesaler to bargain as to the terms, unless the

supplier has implemented the standards on a national basis and those standards are consistently applied to all similarly situated North Carolina wholesalers in a nondiscriminatory manner.

(6) The establishment of a franchise agreement between a wholesaler and another supplier, or similar acquisition by a wholesaler of the right to distribute a brand of another supplier.

(7) The desire of a supplier to consolidate its franchises. (1989, c. 142, s. 1; 2012-4, s. 1; 2012-194, s. 45.5.)

§ 18B-1306. Remedies for wrongful termination.

(a) Injunctive Relief. - A wholesaler whose franchise agreement is altered, terminated or not renewed in violation of this Article may bring an action to enjoin such unlawful alteration, termination or failure to renew. The action may be brought in the county in which the wholesaler has its principal place of business or in any county in which the wholesaler receives or distributes the products in issue. Any injunction issued pursuant to this subsection shall require the wholesaler to supply the customers in its territory with their reasonable retail requirements and to otherwise serve the territory.

(b) Monetary Damages. - In lieu of injunctive relief, a wholesaler whose franchise agreement is altered, terminated or not renewed in violation of this Article shall be entitled to recover monetary damages from the supplier. The amount to which the wholesaler is entitled shall be the value of the wholesaler's business distributing the supplier's products, including:

(1) The laid-in costs to the wholesaler of the inventory of the supplier's products, including any State and local taxes paid on the inventory by the wholesaler, plus a reasonable charge for handling of the products upon surrender of the inventory to the supplier.

(2) The fair market value of all assets, including ancillary businesses of the wholesaler used in distributing the supplier's products. The total compensation to be paid to the wholesaler shall be reduced, however, by any amount received by the wholesaler from sale of assets of the business used in distributing the supplier's products as well as by the value such assets have to the wholesaler unrelated to the supplier's products. "Fair market value" means the highest

dollar amount at which a seller would be willing to sell and a buyer willing to buy at a time prior to the alteration, termination or failure to renew, when each possesses all information relevant to the transaction. (1989, c. 142, s. 1; 2012-4, s. 1.)

§ 18B-1307. Transfer or merger of wholesaler's business.

(a) Right of Transfer to Designated Family Member upon Death. - Upon the death of a wholesaler, that individual's interest in the wholesaler business, including the rights under the franchise agreement with the supplier, may be transferred or assigned to a designated family member. The transfer or assignment shall not be effective until written notice is given to the supplier, but the supplier's consent is not required for the transfer or assignment. "Designated family member" means the deceased wholesaler's spouse, child, grandchild, parent, brother or sister, who is entitled to inherit the deceased wholesaler's ownership interest under the terms of the deceased wholesaler's will or other testamentary device or under the laws of intestate succession. With respect to an incapacitated individual having an ownership interest in a wholesaler, the term "designated family member" also means the person appointed by the court as the conservator of such individual's property. The term also includes the appointed and qualified personal representative and the testamentary trustee of a deceased wholesaler.

(b) Approval of Certain Transfers and Mergers. - Upon notice to and approval by the supplier, an individual owning an interest in a wholesaler may sell, assign or transfer that interest, including the wholesaler's rights under its franchise agreement with the supplier, to any qualified person. Likewise, a wholesaler may merge with another wholesaler in the State, transferring to the new wholesaler entity the merging wholesaler's existing franchise rights. Within 30 days of receipt of notice of the intended sale, assignment, transfer, or merger, the supplier shall request any additional relevant, material information reasonably necessary for deciding whether to approve the transaction. The supplier shall have 30 days from receipt of that information to object to the sale, assignment, transfer, or merger. The supplier may object only if the proposed transferee, or the wholesalership resulting from the merger, fails to meet qualifications and standards that are nondiscriminatory, material, reasonable and consistently applied to North Carolina wholesalers by the supplier. The burden shall be upon the supplier to prove that the proposed transferee or merged wholesaler is not qualified. In determining whether the proposed transferee or merged wholesaler is a qualified person, the supplier shall consider, but is not limited to, the following factors:

(1) Whether the proposed transferee has the financial capacity to purchase the wholesaler or the specified interest upon terms that will not jeopardize the future operation of the business, or whether the new entity resulting from a merger will have such financial capacity to operate successfully, and whether under such ownership the wholesaler will be able to provide financial support necessary to the successful operation of the business, including market spending, capital expenditures, and any equity capitalization or refinancing requirements.

(2) Whether the proposed transferee, or the new entity resulting from a merger, has the proven business experience to hire and maintain a management team to successfully operate the business.

(3) If the proposed transferee does not have experience in the beer business, whether the transferee has other experience to enable it to operate a distributorship successfully and whether the transferee is willing to participate in training provided by the supplier.

(4) Whether the proposed transferee, or a party to the merger, already is a wholesaler for the supplier in a different territory and, if so, whether sufficient time and attention can be devoted to an additional market area.

In determining whether a proposed transferee, or the entity resulting from a merger, is a qualified person, a supplier must consider the business on its own merits and may not designate a specifically identified person as the only purchaser who will be approved. Nothing in this subsection is intended to or should be construed to interfere with a supplier's right to match and reassign to a designee the right to purchase the ownership interest, subject to the designee purchasing the ownership interest at the price and on the conditions applicable to the purchase proposed by the transferee.

(c) Damages. - A supplier who disapproves or prevents a proposed assignment or change of ownership or merger in violation of this section shall be liable to the wholesaler who proposed to make the sale, assignment, transfer, or merger for the difference between the disapproved sale price and a subsequent actual price of a sale of the same assets completed within a reasonable period. If, however, the proposed transfer or sale was to a business associate at a bargain price, the amount of compensation shall be at least the fair market value of the interest proposed to be sold or transferred, minus the proceeds of an actual sale of the interest completed within a reasonable time. (1989, c. 142, s. 1; 2012-4, s. 1.)

§ 18B-1308. Article part of all franchise agreements.

The provisions of this Article shall be part of all franchise agreements as defined in G.S. 18B-1302 and may not be altered by the parties. A wholesaler's rights under this Article may not be waived or superseded by the provisions of a written franchise agreement prepared by a supplier that are in any way inconsistent with or contrary to any part of this Article. The rights of a wholesaler under this Article shall remain in effect regardless of a provision in a written franchise agreement prepared by a supplier that purports to require arbitration of a franchise dispute or that purports to require legal remedies to be sought in a different jurisdiction. (1989, c. 142, s. 1; 2012-4, s. 1.)

§ 18B-1309. Mediation at direction of Alcoholic Beverage Control Commission.

If a dispute arises between a wholesaler and supplier under this Article, and such dispute appears likely to lead to litigation, the Commission, upon request of any party or on its own initiative, may require the parties to participate in mediation in an effort to resolve the dispute. This authority shall be in addition to the Commission's authority to issue declaratory rulings pursuant to G.S. 150B-4. The Commission may designate the mediator, in which case the Commission shall pay the mediator's fee, or the Commission may direct the parties to agree upon and share the costs of a mediator. If the parties then cannot agree upon a mediator, the Commission shall designate the mediator, and the fees shall be divided evenly by the parties. The Commission shall direct that the mediation be completed within a specified period of time. Except for injunctive relief, no lawsuit or other legal action concerning the dispute may be filed until the mediation is completed and is unsuccessful, unless necessary to avoid expiration of a statute of limitation. (2012-4, s. 1.)

Chapter 18C.

North Carolina State Lottery.

Article 1.

General Provisions and Definitions.

§ 18C-101. Citation.

This Chapter shall be known and may be cited as the North Carolina State Lottery Act. (2005-344, s. 1.)

§ 18C-102. Purpose and intent.

The General Assembly declares that the purpose of this Chapter is to establish a State-operated lottery to generate funds for the public purposes described in this Chapter. (2005-344, s. 1; 2005-276, s. 31.1(b).)

§ 18C-103. Definitions.

As used in this Chapter, unless the context requires otherwise:

(1)   "Commission" means the North Carolina State Lottery Commission.

(2)   "Commissioner" means a member of the Commission.

(3)   "Director" means the person selected by the Commission to be the chief administrator of the North Carolina State Lottery.

(4)   "Game" or "lottery game" means any procedure or amusement authorized by the Commission where prizes are distributed among persons who have paid, or unconditionally agreed to pay, for tickets or shares that provide the opportunity to win those prizes and does not utilize a video gaming machine as defined in G.S. 14-306.1(c).

(5)   "Lottery" means any lottery game or series of games established and operated pursuant to this Chapter.

(6) "Lottery contractor" means a person other than a lottery retailer with whom the Commission has contracted for the purpose of providing goods or services to the Commission on an ongoing basis.

(6a) "Lottery supplier" means a person, other than a lottery retailer, with whom the Commission has contracted for the purpose of providing goods or services to the Commission for an individual purchase which may include a maintenance program.

(7) "Person" means any natural person or corporation, limited liability company, trust, association, partnership, joint venture, subsidiary, or other business entity.

(7a) "Potential contractor" or "lottery potential contractor" means any person other than a lottery retailer who submits a bid, proposal, or offer to procure a contract for goods or services for the Commission on an ongoing basis.

(8) "Retailer", "lottery retailer", or "lottery game retailer" means a person with whom the Commission has contracted to sell tickets or shares in lottery games.

(9) "Share" means any method of participation in a lottery game, other than by a ticket purchased on an equivalent basis with a ticket.

(10) "Ticket" means any tangible evidence authorized by the Commission to demonstrate participation in a lottery game.

(11) Repealed by Session Laws 2009-357, s. 5, effective July 27, 2009. (2005-344, s. 1; 2005-276, s. 31.1(c); 2009-357, s. 5; 2009-570, s. 32(a).)

§§ 18C-104 through 18C-109: Reserved for future codification purposes.

Article 2.

North Carolina State Lottery Commission.

§ 18C-110. Establishment of the North Carolina State Lottery Commission to be a self-supporting agency of the State.

There is created the North Carolina State Lottery Commission to establish and oversee the operation of a Lottery. The Commission shall be located in the Department of Commerce for budgetary purposes only; otherwise, the Commission shall be an independent, self-supporting, and revenue-raising agency of the State. The Commission shall reimburse other governmental entities that provide services to the Commission. (2005-344, s. 1.)

§ 18C-111. Commission membership; appointment; selection of chair; vacancies; removal; meetings; compensation.

(a) The Commission shall consist of nine members, five of whom shall be appointed by the Governor, two of whom shall be appointed by the General Assembly upon the recommendation of the President Pro Tempore of the Senate, and two of whom shall be appointed by the General Assembly upon the recommendation of the Speaker of the House of Representatives. Commissioners may be removed by the appointing authority for cause. The Governor shall select the chair of the Commission from among its membership, who shall serve at the pleasure of the Governor.

(b) Of the initial appointees of the Governor, three members shall serve a term of one year, one member shall serve a term of two years, and one member shall serve a term of three years. Of the initial appointees of the General Assembly upon the recommendation of the President Pro Tempore of the Senate, one member shall serve a term of two years, and one member shall serve a term of three years. Of the initial appointees of the General Assembly upon the recommendation of the Speaker of the House of Representatives, one member shall serve a term of two years, and one member shall serve a term of three years. All succeeding appointments shall be for terms of five years. Members shall not serve for more than two successive terms.

(c) Vacancies shall be filled by the appointing authority for the unexpired portion of the term in which they occur.

(d) The Commission shall meet at least quarterly upon the call of the chair. A majority of the total membership of the Commission shall constitute a quorum.

(e)   Members of the Commission shall receive per diem, subsistence, and travel as provided in G.S. 138-5 and G.S. 138-6. (2005-344, s. 1; 2005-276, s. 31.1(d); 2006-259, s. 8(c).)

§ 18C-112. Qualifications of Commissioners.

(a)   Of the members of the Commission appointed by the Governor, at least one member shall have a minimum of five years' experience in law enforcement.

(b)   Of the members appointed by the General Assembly upon the recommendation of the President Pro Tempore of the Senate, one member shall be a certified public accountant.

(c)   Of the members of the Commission appointed by the General Assembly upon the recommendation of the Speaker of the House of Representatives, one member shall have retail sales experience as an owner or manager.

(d)   In making appointments to the Commission, the appointing authorities shall consider the composition of the State with regard to geographic representation and gender, ethnic, racial, and age composition.

(e)   If any member takes any of the following actions, the member vacates office as a member of the Commission and the vacancy shall be filled as provided by G.S. 18C-111(c):

(1)   Files a notice of candidacy under G.S. 163-106 or G.S. 163-323 or a petition under G.S. 163-107.1 or G.S. 163-325.

(2)   Is nominated to fill a vacancy among party nominees under G.S. 163-114 or G.S. 163-115.

(3)   Files a petition as an unaffiliated candidate under G.S. 163-122.

(4)   Files a declaration of intent as a write-in candidate under G.S. 163-123.

(5)   Is nominated by party convention under G.S. 163-98. (2005-344, s. 1; 2005-276, s. 31.1(e); 2011-145, s. 6.18; 2011-391, s. 10.)

§ 18C-113. Meetings; records.

(a)   Meetings of the Commission shall be subject to Article 33C of Chapter 143 of the General Statutes.

(b)   Except as provided in this Article, records of the Commission shall be open and available to the public in accordance with Chapter 132 of the General Statutes.

(c)   Personnel records of the Commission are subject to Article 7 of Chapter 126 of the General Statutes.

(d)   Only the following information concerning a lottery winner is a public record: (i) name, (ii) city and state of residence, (iii) game played, (iv) amount won, and (v) date won. For purposes of this subsection, amount won means the nominal prize amount, the cash payment if different from the nominal prize amount, and the cash payment after taxes are withheld. (2005-344, s. 1; 2009-357, s. 6.)

§ 18C-114. Powers and duties of the Commission.

(a)   The Commission shall have the following powers and duties:

(1)   To specify the types of lottery games and gaming technology to be used in the Lottery.

(2)   To prescribe the nature of lottery advertising which shall comply with the following:

a.   All advertising shall include resources for responsible gaming information.

b.   No advertising may intentionally target specific groups or economic classes.

c.   No advertising may be misleading, deceptive, or present any lottery game as a means of relieving any person's financial or personal difficulties.

d. No advertising may have the primary purpose of inducing persons to participate in the Lottery.

(3) To specify the number and value of prizes for winning tickets or shares in lottery games, including cash prizes, merchandise prizes, prizes consisting of deferred payments or annuities, and prizes of tickets or shares in the same lottery game or other lottery games.

(4) To specify the rules of lottery games and the method for determining winners of lottery games.

(5) To specify the retail sales price for tickets or shares for lottery games.

(6) To establish a system to claim prizes, including determining the time periods within which prizes must be claimed, to verify the validity of tickets or shares claimed to win prizes, and to effect payment of those prizes.

(7) To conduct a background investigation, including a criminal history record check, of applicants for the position of Director, which may include a search of the State and National Repositories of Criminal Histories based on the fingerprints of applicants.

(8) To charge a fee of potential contractors and lottery contractors to not exceed the cost of the criminal record check of the potential contractors and lottery contractors.

(9) To specify the manner of distribution, dissemination, or sale of lottery tickets or shares to lottery game retailers or directly to the public.

(10) To determine the incentives, if any, for any lottery employees, lottery retailers, lottery contractors, or electronic computer terminal operators.

(11) To specify the authority, compensation, and role of the Director, and to specify the authority, selection, and role of the other employees of the Commission. All of the following apply to all employees of the Commission:

a. No employee of the Commission may have a financial interest in any lottery potential contractor or lottery contractor, other than an interest as part of a mutual fund.

b. No employee of the Commission with decision-making authority shall participate in any decision involving the retailer or potential contractor with whom the employee has a financial interest.

c. No employee of the Commission who leaves the employment of the Commission may represent any lottery contractor, potential contractor, or retailer before the Commission for a period of one year following termination of employment with the Commission.

d. A background investigation shall be conducted on each applicant for employment with the Commission.

e. The Commission shall bond all employees with access to lottery funds or revenue or security.

(12) To approve and authorize the Director to enter into agreements with other states to operate and promote multistate lotteries consistent with the purposes set forth in this Chapter.

(13) Any other powers necessary for the Commission to carry out its responsibilities under this Chapter.

(b) Article 3D of Chapter 147 of the General Statutes shall not apply to the Commission. (2005-344, s. 1; 2005-276, s. 31.1(f); 2009-357, s. 1; 2009-570, s. 32(b), (c).)

§ 18C-115. Reports.

The Commission shall send quarterly and annual reports on the operations of the Commission to the Governor, State Treasurer, the Lottery Oversight Committee, and to the General Assembly. The reports shall include complete statements of lottery revenues, prize disbursements, expenses, net revenues, and all other financial transactions involving lottery funds, including the occurrence of any audit. (2005-344, s. 1; 2006-225, s. 2.)

§ 18C-116. Audits.

The State Auditor shall conduct annual audits of all accounts and transactions of the Commission and any other special postaudits the State Auditor considers to be necessary. (2005-344, s. 1.)

§§ 18C-117 through 18C-119: Reserved for future codification purposes.

Article 3.

North Carolina State Lottery Director.

§ 18C-120. Selection of the Director; powers and duties.

(a) The Commission shall select a Director to operate and administer the Lottery and to serve as the Secretary of the Commission. Except as to the provisions of Articles 6 and 7 of Chapter 126 of the General Statutes, the Director shall be exempt from the North Carolina Human Resources Act.

(b) The Director shall have the following powers and duties, under the supervision of the Commission:

(1) To provide for the reporting of payment of lottery game prizes to State and federal tax authorities and for the withholding of State and federal income taxes from lottery game prizes as provided in State and federal law.

(2) To conduct a background investigation, including a criminal history record check, of applicants for employment with the Commission, lottery retailers, and lottery potential contractors, which may include a search of the State and National Repositories of Criminal Histories based on the fingerprints of applicants.

(3) To set the salaries of all Commission employees, subject to the approval of the Commission. Except for the provisions of Articles 6 and 7 of Chapter 126 of the General Statutes, all employees of the Commission shall be exempt from the North Carolina Human Resources Act.

(4) To enter into contracts with lottery retailers, lottery contractors, or lottery suppliers upon approval by the Commission.

(5) To provide for the security and accuracy in the operation and administration of the Commission and the Lottery, including examining the background of all prospective employees, lottery potential contractors, lottery contractors, and lottery retailers.

(6) To coordinate and collaborate with the appropriate law enforcement authorities regarding investigations of violations of the laws relating to the operation of the Lottery and make reports to the Commission regarding those investigations.

(7) To confer with the Commission on the operation and administration of the Lottery and make available for inspection by the Commission all books, records, files, documents, and other information of the Lottery.

(8) To study the operation and administration of other lotteries and to collect demographic and other information concerning the Lottery and make recommendations to improve the operation and administration of the Lottery to the Commission, to the Governor, and to the General Assembly.

(9) To provide monthly financial reports to the Commission of all lottery revenues, prize disbursements, expenses, net revenues, and all other financial transactions involving lottery funds.

(10) To enter into agreements with other states to operate and promote multistate lotteries consistent with the purposes set forth in this Chapter and upon the approval of the Commission. (2005-344, s. 1; 2005-276, s. 31.1(g); 2009-357, s. 7; 2013-382, s. 9.1(c).)

§ 18C-121. Accountability; books and records.

The Director shall have made and kept books and records that accurately and completely reflect each day's transactions, including the distribution of tickets or shares to lottery game retailers, receipt of funds, prize claims, prizes paid directly by the Commission, expenses, and all other financial transactions involving lottery funds necessary to permit preparation of financial statements that conform with generally accepted accounting principles. (2005-344, s. 1; 2005-276, s. 31.1(h).)

§ 18C-122. Independent audits.

(a) Biennially, at the beginning of the calendar year, the Commission shall engage an independent firm experienced in security procedures, including computer security and systems security, to conduct a comprehensive study and evaluation of all aspects of security in the operation of the Commission and of the Lottery. At a minimum, such a security assessment should include a review of network vulnerability, application vulnerability, application code review, wireless security, security policy and processes, security/privacy program management, technology infrastructure and security controls, security organization and governance, and operational effectiveness.

(b) The portion of the security audit report containing the overall evaluation of the Commission and of lottery games in terms of each aspect of security shall be presented to the Commission, to the Governor, and to the General Assembly.

(c) The portion of the security audit report containing specific recommendations shall be confidential, shall be presented only to the Director and to the Commission, and shall be exempt from Chapter 132 of the General Statutes. The Commission may hear the report of such an audit, discuss, and take action on any recommendations to address that audit under G.S. 143-318.11(a)(1).

(d) Biennially at the end of the fiscal year, in addition to the audits required by G.S. 18C-116 and by subsection (a) of this section, beginning in 2010, the Commission shall engage an independent auditing firm that has experience in evaluating the operation of lotteries to perform an audit of the Lottery. The results of this audit shall be presented to the Commission, to the Governor, and to the General Assembly. (2005-344, s. 1; 2005-276, s. 31.1(i); 2009-357, s. 15.)

§§ 18C-123 through 18C-129: Reserved for future codification purposes.

Article 4.

Operation of Lottery.

§ 18C-130. Types of lottery games; lottery games and lottery advertising; certain disclosures and information to be provided.

(a) The Commission shall determine the types of lottery games that may be used in the Lottery. Games may include instant lotteries, online games, games played on computer terminals or other devices, and other games traditional to a lottery or that have been conducted by any other state government-operated lottery.

(b) In lottery games using tickets, each ticket in a particular game shall have printed on it a unique number distinguishing it from every other ticket in that lottery game and an abbreviated form of the game-play rules, including resources for responsible gaming information. In lottery games using tickets, each ticket may have printed on it a depiction of one or more cartoon characters, whose primary appeal is not to minors. In lottery games using tickets with preprinted winners, the overall estimated odds of winning prizes shall be printed on each ticket. No name or photograph of a current or former elected official shall appear on the tickets of any lottery game.

(c) In games using electronic computer terminals or other devices to play lottery games, no coins or currency shall be dispensed to players from those electronic computer terminals or devices.

(d) No games shall be based on the outcome of a particular sporting event or on the results of a series of sporting events.

(e) Lottery advertising shall be tastefully designed and presented in a manner to minimize the appeal of lottery games to minors. The use of cartoon characters or of false, misleading, or deceptive information in lottery advertising is prohibited. All advertising promoting the sale of lottery tickets or shares for a particular game shall include the actual or estimated overall odds of winning the game.

(f) The Commission shall make available a detailed tabulation of the estimated number of prizes of each particular prize denomination that are expected to be awarded in each lottery game or the estimated odds of winning these prizes at the time that lottery game is offered for sale to the public.

(g) The Commission shall, in consultation with the Department of Health and Human Services, develop and provide information to the public about gambling addiction and treatment. (2005-344, s. 1; 2005-276, ss. 31.1(j), 31.1(j1); 2006-259, s. 8(a).)

§ 18C-131. Sales and sale price of tickets and shares; sales to minors prohibited.

(a) The Commission may sell tickets and shares directly to the public, contract with lottery game retailers to sell tickets and shares, or distribute tickets or shares through any other method authorized by the Commission.

(b) No ticket or share in a lottery game shall be sold or resold for more than the retail sales price established by the Commission.

(c) The minimum retail price of each ticket or share in any lottery game shall be fifty cents (50¢). The minimum retail price shall not apply to any discounts or promotions authorized by the Commission for a particular lottery game.

(d) It shall be unlawful for a person to sell a lottery ticket or share to a person under the age of 18 years. No person under the age of 18 years shall purchase a lottery ticket or share. A person who violates this subsection shall be guilty of a Class 1 misdemeanor.

(e) It shall be a defense for the person who sold a ticket or share in violation of subsection (d) of this section if the person does either of the following:

(1) Shows that the purchaser produced a valid drivers license, a special identification card issued under G.S. 20-37.7, a military identification card, or a passport, showing the purchaser to be at least 18 years old and bearing a physical description of the person named on the card that reasonably describes the purchaser.

(2) Produces evidence of other facts that reasonably indicated at the time of sale that the purchaser was at least 18 years old. (2005-344, s. 1; 2006-259, s. 8(b).)

§ 18C-132. Procedures for drawings and claiming prizes; payment of prizes; protection of information concerning certain prize winners.

(a) If a lottery game uses a daily or less frequent drawing of winning numbers, a drawing among entries including second chance drawings where the value of the prize is five thousand dollars ($5,000) or more, or a drawing among finalists, all of the following conditions shall be met:

(1) The drawings shall be open to the public.

(2) The drawings shall be witnessed by an independent certified public accountant or by an auditor employed by a certified public accounting firm.

(3) Any equipment used in the drawings shall be inspected by the independent certified public accountant or auditor employed by a certified public accounting firm and an employee of the Commission both before and after the drawings.

(4) Audio and visual records of the drawings and inspections shall be made.

If a lottery game uses a drawing among entries for (i) a second chance drawing or (ii) any other promotion conducted by the lottery, where the value of the prize is less than five thousand dollars ($5,000) in value, the requirements of subdivisions (2) and (3) of this subsection do not apply.

(b) Prizes that remain unclaimed after the period set by the Commission for claiming the prizes shall not be considered abandoned property. If a valid claim is not made for a prize within the applicable period, the unclaimed prize money shall be handled in accordance with this Chapter.

(c) After the expiration of the claim period for prizes for each lottery game, the Commission shall make available a detailed tabulation of the total number of prizes of each prize denomination that was actually claimed and paid directly by the Commission.

(d) No prize shall be paid for a lottery ticket or share that is stolen, counterfeit, altered, fraudulent, unissued, produced or issued in error, unreadable, not received or recorded by the Commission by the applicable deadlines, lacking in captions that conform and agree with the play symbols as appropriate to the lottery game involved, or not in compliance with any additional specific rules and public or confidential validation and security tests appropriate to the particular game involved.

(e)   No valid claim for a prize in any lottery game shall be paid more than once. The Director, Commission, and the State shall be discharged of all liability upon payment of a prize.

(f)   Winners of less than six hundred dollars ($600.00) shall be permitted to claim prizes from any of the following:

(1)   The same lottery game retailer who sold the winning ticket or share.

(2)   Any other lottery retailer.

(3)   The Commission.

(g)   Winners of six hundred dollars ($600.00) or more shall claim prizes directly from the Commission.

(h)   The right of any person to a prize shall not be assignable. Payment of any prize may be paid to a person designated pursuant to a court order. Any prize or portion of a prize remaining unpaid at the death of a prize winner shall be paid to the estate of the deceased prize winner or to the trustee of a trust established by the prize winner or as designated in the deceased prize winner's will, living trust, or other prepared legal instrument if a copy of the trust document or instrument has been filed with the Director, and no written notice of revocation has been received by the Director prior to the prize winner's death.

(i)   No ticket or share in a lottery game shall be purchased by, and no prize shall be paid to, a member of the Commission, the Director, or employee of the Commission, or to any spouse, parent, or child living in the same household as a person disqualified by this subsection.

(j)   No prize shall be paid to a person under the age of 18.

(k)   If a prize winner submits to the Commission a copy of a protective order without attachments, if any, issued to that person under G.S. 50B-3 or a lawful order of any court of competent jurisdiction restricting the access or contact of one or more persons with that prize winner or a current and valid Address

Confidentiality Program authorization card issued pursuant to the provisions of Chapter 15C of the General Statutes, that prize winner's identifying information shall be treated as confidential information under G.S. 132-1.2 as long as the protective order remains in effect or the prize winner remains a certified program participant in the Address Confidentiality Program. That prize winner's identifying information shall be available for inspection by a law enforcement agency or by a person identified in a court order if inspection of the address by that person is directed by that court order.

(l)   All prizes are subject to the State income tax. (2005-344, s. 1; 2005-276, s. 31.1(k); 2006-225, s. 4; 2009-357, ss. 8, 14.)

§ 18C-133. Lottery game-play rules and winner validation procedures.

(a)   By purchasing a ticket or share in a lottery game, a player agrees to abide by, and be bound by, the game-play rules adopted by the Commission that apply to any particular lottery game involved.

(b)   All players acknowledge that the determination of whether the player is a winner is subject to the game-play rules and the winner validation procedures and confidential validation tests established by the Commission for the particular lottery game involved. (2005-344, s. 1.)

§ 18C-134. Setoff for debt collection against lottery prizes.

(a)   Purpose. - The Commission must establish a debt set-off program by which lottery prize payments may be used to satisfy a debt owed or collected by a claimant agency that is at least fifty dollars ($50.00). The collection remedy under this section is in addition to and not in substitution for any other remedy available by law.

(b)   Notification. - A claimant agency is automatically enrolled in the Commission's debt set-off program if it is enrolled in the Department of Revenue debt set-off program. To provide for more efficient operations, the Department of Revenue shall provide to the Commission on a periodic basis all updates to its debt set-off program as soon as practicable.

(c) Setoff. - The Commission must match the information submitted by the claimant agency with persons who are entitled to a State lottery prize payment in an amount of six hundred dollars ($600.00) or more. If there is a match, the Commission must set off the debt against the lottery winnings to which the debtor would otherwise be entitled. When there are multiple claims to be set off, the priority in claims to set off is the same as provided in G.S. 105A-12. The winnings that exceed the amount of the debt, if any, must be paid to that person. The Commission must mail the debtor written notice that the setoff has occurred and must transfer the net proceeds collected to the claimant agency. If the claimant agency is a State agency, that agency must credit the amount received to a nonreverting trust account and must follow the procedure set in G.S. 105A-8.

(d) Collection Assistance Fee. - To recover the costs incurred by the Commission in collecting debts under this section, a collection assistance fee of five dollars ($5.00) may be imposed on each debt collected through setoff. The Commission must collect this fee as part of the debt and retain it. To recover the costs incurred by local agencies in submitting debts for collection under this section, a collection assistance fee of fifteen dollars ($15.00) may be imposed on each local agency debt collected through setoff. The Commission must collect this fee as part of the debt and remit it to the clearinghouse that submitted the debt. The collection assistance fees do not apply to child support debts. If the Commission is able to collect only part of a debt through setoff, the Commission's collection assistance fee has priority over the local collection assistance fee and over the remainder of the debt. The local collection assistance fee has priority over the remainder of the debt.

(e) Confidentiality. - Notwithstanding any confidentiality statute of a claimant agency, the exchange of information among the Commission, the Department of Revenue, the claimant agency, the organization submitting debts on behalf of a local agency, and the debtor necessary to implement this section is lawful. The information an agency or organization obtains from the Commission in accordance with the exemption in this subsection may be used by the agency or organization only in the pursuit of its debt collection duties and practices.

(f) Definitions. - The definitions in G.S. 105A-2 apply in this section. (2005-344, s. 1; 2005-276, s. 31.1(k1); 2009-357, ss. 9, 10.)

§§ 18C-135 through 18C-139: Reserved for future codification purposes.

Article 5.

Lottery Game Retailers.

§ 18C-140. Contracting with lottery game retailers.

The Commission may contract with lottery game retailers to sell tickets or shares for lottery games upon such terms and conditions as it considers appropriate. The contract entered into between the Commission and the lottery game retailer shall be considered a permit for purposes of Chapter 18B of the General Statutes. No contract to act as a lottery game retailer is assignable or transferable. All contracts with lottery game retailers shall provide that the Director may terminate the contract if the lottery game retailer violates a provision of this Chapter. (2005-344, s. 1; 2005-276, s. 31.1(l).)

§ 18C-141. Selection of lottery game retailers.

(a) The Director shall recommend to the Commission those persons with whom to contract as lottery game retailers. To the extent practicable, the Director shall meet the minority participation goals under Article 8 of Chapter 143 of the General Statutes.

(b) The Director may not recommend contracting with any of the following:

(1) A natural person under 21 years of age. This minimum age shall not prohibit employees of a lottery game retailer who are under 21 years of age from selling lottery tickets or shares during their employment.

(2) A person who would be engaged exclusively in the business of selling lottery tickets or shares or operating electronic computer terminals or other devices solely for entertainment.

(3) A person who is not current in filing all applicable tax returns to the State and in payment of all taxes, interest, and penalties owed to the State, excluding items under formal appeal under applicable statutes. Upon request of the

Director, the Department of Revenue shall provide this information about a specific person to the Commission.

(4)   A person who resides in the same household as a member of the Commission, the Director, or any other employee of the Commission.

(c)   Upon approval of the Commission, the Director shall enter into a contract with the person to sell tickets or shares upon such terms and conditions as the Commission directs. (2005-344, s. 1; 2005-276, s. 31.1(m).)

§ 18C-142. Compensation for lottery game retailers.

The amount of compensation paid to lottery game retailers for their sales of lottery tickets or shares shall be seven percent (7%) of the face value of the tickets or shares sold for each lottery game. The Commission shall require submission of reports and remission of lottery revenues to the Commission on a timely basis. (2005-344, s. 1; 2005-276, s. 31.1(n); 2009-357, s. 11.)

§ 18C-143. Responsibilities of lottery game retailers.

(a)   A lottery game retailer shall comply with all provisions of this Article and the contract with the Commission.

(b)   A lottery game retailer shall sell no lottery tickets or shares unless the retailer conspicuously displays a certificate of authority, signed by the Director, to sell lottery tickets or shares. The Commission shall issue a certificate of authority to each lottery game retailer for purposes of display for each retail outlet owned or operated by the lottery game retailer. No certificate is assignable or transferable.

(c)   A lottery game retailer shall furnish an appropriate bond or letter of credit, if so requested by the Director. The Commission may authorize the Director to purchase blanket bonds covering the activities of any or all lottery game retailers.

(d)   The Commission shall adopt rules to establish procedures governing how the lottery game retailers:

(1)   Account for all tickets or shares in their custody, including tickets and shares sold.

(2)   Account for the money collected from the sale of tickets and shares.

(3)   Remit funds to the Commission, provided that all payments shall be in the form of electronic fund transfers or other recorded financial instruments as authorized by the Commission and approved by the Director.

(e)   No lottery retailer or applicant to be a lottery retailer shall pay, give, or make any economic opportunity, gift, loan, gratuity, special discount, favor, hospitality, or service, excluding food and beverages having an aggregate value not exceeding one hundred dollars ($100.00) in any calendar year, to the Director, to any member or employee of the Commission, or to any member of the immediate family residing in the same household as one of these individuals.

(f)   All lottery proceeds minus applicable retailer commissions are held in trust by lottery retailers until such time as they are received by the Commission. A lottery retailer shall have a fiduciary duty to preserve and account for lottery proceeds including any unsold tickets. (2005-344, s. 1; 2005-276, s. 31.1(o); 2009-357, s. 13.)

§§ 18C-144 through 18C-149: Reserved for future codification purposes.

Article 6.

Lottery Potential Contractors and Lottery Contractors.

§ 18C-150. Procurements.

The Commission shall be exempt from Article 3 of Chapter 143 of the General Statutes but may use the services of the Department of Administration in procuring goods and services for the Commission. However, the Commission shall include in all contracts to be awarded by the Commission under this section a standard clause which provides that the State Auditor and internal auditors of the Commission may audit the records of the contractor during and after the term of the contract to verify accounts and data affecting fees and performance. The Commission shall not award a cost plus percentage of cost contract for any purpose. For purposes of this provision, "cost plus percentage of cost contract" is defined as a contract under which the contractor receives payment for indeterminate costs plus a stated percentage or amount of profit based upon such costs. This provision shall not apply to Commission contracts that require costs to be predetermined and approved by the Commission and a total not to exceed the amount specified in each contract to be paid to the contractor. (2005-344, s. 1; 2010-194, s. 1; 2011-326, s. 15(a).)

§ 18C-151. Contracts.

(a) Except as otherwise specifically provided in this subsection for contracts for the purchase of services, apparatus, supplies, materials, or equipment, Article 8 of Chapter 143 of the General Statutes, including the provisions relating to minority participation goals, shall apply to contracts entered into by the Commission. If this subsection and Article 8 of Chapter 143 are in conflict, the provisions of this subsection shall control. In recognition of the particularly sensitive nature of the Lottery and the competence, quality of product, experience, and timeliness, fairness, and integrity in the operation and administration of the Lottery and maximization of the objective of raising revenues, a contract for the purchase of services, apparatus, supplies, materials, or equipment requiring an estimated aggregate expenditure of three hundred thousand dollars ($300,000) or more may be awarded by the Commission only after the following have occurred:

(1) The Commission has invited proposals to be submitted by advertisement by electronic means or advertisement in a newspaper having general circulation in the State of North Carolina and containing the following information:

a. The time and place where a complete description of the services, apparatus, supplies, materials, or equipment may be had.

b. The time and place for opening of the proposals.

c. A statement reserving to the Commission the right to reject any or all proposals.

(2) Proposals may be rejected for any reason determined by the Commission to be in the best interest of the Lottery.

(3) All proposals shall be accompanied by a bond or letter of credit in an amount equal to not less than five percent (5%) of the proposal and the fee to cover the cost of the criminal record check conducted under G.S. 114-19.6.

(4) The Commission has complied with the minority participation goals of G.S. 143-128.2 and G.S. 143-128.3.

(5) The Commission may not award a contract to a lottery potential contractor who has been convicted of a felony or any gambling offense in any state or federal court of the United States within 10 years of entering into the contract, or employs officers and directors who have been convicted of a felony or any gambling offense in any state or federal court of the United States within 10 years of entering into the contract.

(6) The Commission shall investigate and compare the overall business practices, ethical reputation, criminal record, civil litigation, competence, integrity, background, and regulatory compliance record of lottery potential contractors.

(7) The Commission may engage an independent firm experienced in evaluating government procurement proposals to aid in evaluating proposals for a major procurement.

(8) The Commission shall award the contract to the responsible lottery potential contractor or lottery supplier who submits the best proposal that maximizes the benefits to the State.

(b) Upon the completion of the bidding process, a contract may be awarded to a lottery contractor or lottery supplier with whom the Commission has previously contracted for the same purposes.

(c) Before a contract is awarded, the Director shall conduct a thorough background investigation of all of the following:

(1) The potential contractor to whom the contract is to be awarded.

(2) Any parent or subsidiary corporation of the potential contractor to whom the contract is to be awarded.

(3) All shareholders with a five percent (5%) or more interest in the potential contractor or parent or subsidiary corporation of the potential contractor to whom the contract is to be awarded. For purposes of this subdivision, "shareholders" means any natural person or those individuals with capabilities to make operating decisions for the potential contractor or parent or subsidiary corporation of the potential contractor to whom the contract is to be awarded.

(4) All officers and directors of the potential contractor or parent or subsidiary corporation of the potential contractor to whom the contract is to be awarded.

(d) The Commission may terminate the contract, without penalty, of a lottery contractor that fails to comply with the Commission's instruction to implement the recommendations of the State Auditor or an independent auditor in an audit conducted of Lottery security or operations.

(e) After entering into a contract with a lottery contractor, the Commission shall require the lottery contractor to periodically update the information required to be disclosed under G.S. 18C-152(c). Any contract with a lottery contractor who does not periodically update the required disclosures may be terminated by the Commission.

(f) No lottery contractor, potential contractor, or lottery supplier may pay, give, or make any economic opportunity, gift, loan, gratuity, special discount, favor, hospitality, or service, excluding food and beverages having an aggregate value not exceeding one hundred dollars ($100.00) in any calendar year, to the Director, any member or employee of the corporation, or a member of the immediate family residing in the same household as any of these individuals. (2005-344, s. 1; 2005-276, s. 31.1(p); 2006-259, s. 8(d); 2009-357, s. 3; 2009-570, s. 32(d); 2012-194, s. 64; 2013-360, s. 6.8.)

§ 18C-152. Investigation of lottery potential contractors.

(a) Lottery potential contractors shall cooperate with the Director in completing any investigation required under G.S. 18C-151(c), including any appropriate investigation authorizations needed to facilitate these investigations.

(b) The Commission shall adopt rules that provide for disclosures of information required to be disclosed under subsection (c) of this section by lottery potential contractors to ensure that the potential contractors provide all the information necessary to allow for a full and complete evaluation by the Director and Commission of the competence, integrity, background, and character of the lottery potential contractors. Information shall be disclosed for the following:

(1) If the potential contractor is a corporation, the officers, directors, and each stockholder in that corporation; however, in the case of owners of equity securities of a publicly traded corporation, only the names and addresses of those known to the corporation to own beneficially five percent (5%) or more of the securities need be disclosed.

(2) If the potential contractor is a trust, the trustee and all persons entitled to receive income or benefits from the trust.

(3) If the potential contractor is an association, the members, officers, and directors.

(4) If the potential contractor is a partnership or joint venture, all of the general partners, limited partners, or joint venturers.

(5) For any potential contractor, any person who can exercise control or authority, or both, on behalf of the potential contractor. For any potential contractor, any person who can exercise control or authority, or both, on behalf of the potential contractor.

(c) For purposes of this subsection, the term "potential contractor" shall include the potential contractor and each of the persons applicable under subsection (b) of this section. At a minimum, the potential contractor required to disclose information for a thorough background investigation under G.S. 18C-151 shall do all of the following:

(1) Disclose the potential contractor's name, phone number, and address.

(2) Disclose all the states and jurisdictions in which the potential contractor does business and the nature of the business for each state or jurisdiction.

(3) Disclose all the states and jurisdictions in which the potential contractor has contracts to supply gaming goods or services, including lottery goods and services, and the nature of the goods or services involved for each state or jurisdiction.

(4) Disclose all the states and jurisdictions in which the potential contractor has applied for, has sought renewal of, has received, has been denied, has pending, or has had revoked a lottery or gaming license or permit of any kind or had fines or penalties assessed on a license, permit, contract, or operation and the disposition of such in each such state or jurisdiction. If any lottery or gaming license, permit, or contract has been revoked or has not been renewed or any lottery or gaming license, permit, or application has been either denied or is pending and has remained pending for more than six months, all of the facts and circumstances underlying the failure to receive that license shall be disclosed.

(5) Disclose the details of any finding or plea, conviction, or adjudication of guilt in a state or federal court of the potential contractor for any felony or any other criminal offense other than a minor traffic violation.

(6) Disclose the details of any bankruptcy, insolvency, reorganization, or corporate or individual purchase or takeover of another corporation, including bonded indebtedness, or any pending litigation of the potential contractor.

(7) If at least twenty-five percent (25%) of the cost of a potential contractor's contract is subcontracted, the potential contractor shall disclose all of the information required by this section for the subcontractor as if the subcontractor were itself a potential contractor.

(8) Make any additional disclosures and information the Commission determines to be appropriate for the contract involved.

(d) All documents compiled by the Director in conducting the investigation of the lottery potential contractors shall be held as confidential information under Chapter 132 of the General Statutes. (2005-344, s. 1; 2005-276, s. 31.1(q); 2009-357, s. 4.)

§§ 18C-153 through 18C-159: Reserved for future codification purposes.

Article 7.

North Carolina State Lottery Fund.

§ 18C-160. North Carolina State Lottery Fund.

An enterprise fund, to be known as the North Carolina State Lottery Fund, is created within the State treasury. The North Carolina State Lottery Fund is appropriated to the Commission and may be expended without further action of the General Assembly for the purposes of operating the Commission and the lottery games. (2005-344, s. 1.)

§ 18C-161. Types of income to the North Carolina State Lottery Fund.

The following revenues shall be deposited in the North Carolina State Lottery Fund:

(1)   All proceeds from the sale of lottery tickets or shares.

(2)   The funds for initial start-up costs provided by the State.

(3)   All other funds credited or appropriated to the Commission from any source.

(4)   Interest earned by the North Carolina State Lottery Fund. (2005-344, s. 1.)

§ 18C-162. Allocation of revenues.

(a)   The Commission shall allocate revenues to the North Carolina State Lottery Fund in order to increase and maximize the available revenues for education purposes, and to the extent practicable, shall adhere to the following guidelines:

(1)   At least fifty percent (50%) of the total annual revenues, as described in this Chapter, shall be returned to the public in the form of prizes.

(2) At least thirty-five percent (35%) of the total annual revenues, as described in this Chapter, shall be transferred as provided in G.S. 18C-164.

(3) No more than eight percent (8%) of the total annual revenues, as described in this Chapter, shall be allocated for payment of expenses of the Lottery. Advertising expenses shall not exceed one percent (1%) of the total annual revenues.

(4) No more than seven percent (7%) of the face value of tickets or shares, as described in this Chapter, shall be allocated for compensation paid to lottery game retailers.

(b) To the extent that the expenses of the Commission are less than eight percent (8%) of total annual revenues, the Commission may allocate any surplus funds:

(1) To increase prize payments; or

(2) To the benefit of the public purposes as described in this Chapter.

(c) Unclaimed prize money shall be held separate and apart from the other revenues and allocated as follows:

(1) Fifty percent (50%) to enhance prizes under subdivision (a)(1) of this section.

(2) Fifty percent (50%) to the Education Lottery Fund to be allocated in accordance with G.S. 18C-164(c). (2005-344, s. 1; 2005-276, s. 31.1(r); 2007-323, s. 5.2(c); 2009-357, s. 12.)

§ 18C-163. Expenses of the Lottery.

Expenses of the Lottery may include any of the following:

(1) The costs incurred in operating and administering the Commission, including initial start-up costs.

(2) The costs resulting from any contracts entered into for the purchase or lease of goods or services required by the Commission.

(3)   A transfer of one million dollars ($1,000,000) annually to the Department of Health and Human Services for gambling addiction education and treatment programs.

(4)   The costs of supplies, materials, tickets, independent studies and audits, data transmission, advertising, promotion, incentives, public relations, communications, bonding for lottery game retailers, printing, and distribution of tickets and shares.

(5)   The costs of reimbursing other governmental entities for services provided to the Commission.

(6)   The costs for any other goods and services needed to accomplish the purposes of this Chapter. (2005-344, s. 1; 2005-276, s. 31.1(s).)

§ 18C-164. Transfer of net revenues.

(a)   The funds remaining in the North Carolina State Lottery Fund after receipt of all revenues to the Lottery Fund and after accrual of all obligations of the Commission for prizes and expenses shall be considered to be the net revenues of the North Carolina State Lottery Fund. The net revenues of the North Carolina State Lottery Fund shall be transferred four times a year to the Education Lottery Fund, which shall be created in the State treasury.

(b)   From the Education Lottery Fund, the Office of State Budget and Management shall transfer a sum equal to five percent (5%) of the net revenue of the prior year to the Education Lottery Reserve Fund. A special revenue fund for this purpose shall be established in the State treasury to be known as the Education Lottery Reserve Fund, and that fund shall be capped at fifty million dollars ($50,000,000). Monies in the Education Lottery Reserve Fund may be appropriated only as provided in subsection (e) of this section.

(c)   The General Assembly shall appropriate the remaining net revenue of the Education Lottery Fund annually in the Current Operations Appropriations Act for education-related purposes, based upon estimates of lottery net revenue to the Education Lottery Fund provided by the Office of State Budget and Management and the Fiscal Research Division of the Legislative Services Commission.

(d)   Repealed by Session Laws 2013-360, s. 6.11(c), effective June 30, 2013.

(e)   If the actual net revenues are less than the appropriation for that given year, then the Governor may transfer from the Education Lottery Reserve Fund an amount sufficient to equal the appropriation by the General Assembly.

(f)   Actual net revenues in excess of the amounts appropriated in a fiscal year shall remain in the Education Lottery Fund. (2005-344, s. 1; 2005-276, s. 31.1(t); 2006-259, s. 8(e); 2013-360, s. 6.11(c).)

§§ 18C-165 through 18C-169: Reserved for future codification purposes.

Article 8.

Miscellaneous.

§ 18C-170. Preemption of local regulation.

A county or municipality shall not enact any ordinance or regulation relating to the Lottery, and this Chapter preempts all existing county or municipal ordinances or regulations that would impose additional restrictions or requirements in the operation of the Lottery. To the extent that this Chapter conflicts with any local act, this Chapter prevails to the extent of the conflict. (2005-344, s. 1; 2005-276, s. 31.1(t1).)

§ 18C-171. Lawful activity.

Other than this Chapter, any other public or local law, ordinance, or regulation providing any penalty, restriction, regulation, or prohibition for the manufacture, transportation, storage, distribution, advertising, possession, or sale of any lottery tickets or shares, or for the operation of any lottery game shall not apply to the operation of the Commission or lottery games established by this Chapter where the penalty, restriction, regulation, or prohibition applies only to the Lottery as operated by the North Carolina State Lottery Commission. (2005-344, s. 1; 2005-276, s. 31.1(u).)

§ 18C-172. Lottery Oversight Committee.

(a) Creation and Membership. - The Lottery Oversight Committee is established. The Committee shall be located administratively in the General Assembly. The Committee shall consist of nine members appointed as provided below. In making appointments, each appointing officer shall select members who have appropriate experience and knowledge of the issues to be examined by the Committee and shall strive to ensure racial, gender, and geographical diversity among the membership.

(1) Three members shall be appointed by the Speaker of the House of Representatives, at least one being an educator and at least one being a person trained or experienced in financial management.

(2) Three members shall be appointed by the President Pro Tempore of the Senate, at least one being an educator and at least one being a person trained or experienced in financial management.

(3) Three members shall be appointed by the Governor, at least one being an educator and at least one being a person trained or experienced in financial management.

(b) Terms. - Terms on the Committee are for three years and begin on January 1, except the terms of the initial members, which begin on appointment. A member continues to serve until a successor is appointed. A vacancy shall be filled within 30 days by the officer who made the original appointment.

(c) Purpose and Powers. - The Committee shall:

(1) Review whether expenditures of the net revenues of the Lottery have been in accordance with Article 7 of this Chapter, and study ways to ensure that net proceeds from the Lottery will not be used to supplant education funding but to provide additional funding for education.

(2) Receive and review reports submitted to the General Assembly pursuant to Chapter 18C of the General Statutes.

(3) Study other Lottery matters as the Committee considers necessary to fulfill its mandate.

(d) Reports. - The Committee shall report its analysis and any findings and recommendations to the General Assembly by September 15 of each year. The Committee may make interim reports to the General Assembly regarding the expenditure of net Lottery revenues.

(e) Organization. - The President Pro Tempore of the Senate and the Speaker of the House of Representatives shall each designate a cochair of the Committee. The Committee shall meet at least once a quarter upon the joint call of the cochairs. A quorum of the Committee is six members. No action may be taken except by a majority vote at a meeting at which a quorum is present.

(f) Funding. - From funds available to the General Assembly, the Legislative Services Commission shall allocate monies to fund the work of the Committee. Members of the Committee receive subsistence and travel expenses as provided in G.S. 120-3.1 and G.S. 138-5.

(g) Staff. - The Legislative Services Commission, through the Legislative Services Officer, shall assign professional staff to assist the Committee in its work. Upon the direction of the Legislative Services Commission, the Director of Legislative Assistants of the Senate and of the House of Representatives shall assign clerical staff to the Committee. The expenses for clerical employees shall be borne by the Committee. (2006-225, s. 1.)

§ 18C-173. Limits on compensation increases.

Notwithstanding G.S. 18C-114(a)(11) and G.S. 18C-120(b)(3), the Lottery Commission, during any fiscal year, may not expend funds for merit and performance-based salary increases in excess of the funds that would have been expended had the Lottery Commission employees received the same across-the-board salary increases granted by the General Assembly to State employees subject to the North Carolina Human Resources Act. These merit and performance-based salary increases may be awarded on an aggregated average basis according to rules adopted by the Lottery Commission. (2008-107, s. 26.12A; 2013-382, s. 9.1(c).)

Chapter 19.

Offenses Against Public Morals.

Article 1.

Abatement of Nuisances.

§ 19-1. What are nuisances under this Chapter.

(a) The erection, establishment, continuance, maintenance, use, ownership or leasing of any building or place for the purpose of assignation, prostitution, gambling, illegal possession or sale of alcoholic beverages, illegal possession or sale of controlled substances as defined in the North Carolina Controlled Substances Act, or illegal possession or sale of obscene or lewd matter, as defined in this Chapter, shall constitute a nuisance. The activity sought to be abated need not be the sole purpose of the building or place in order for it to constitute a nuisance under this Chapter.

(b) The erection, establishment, continuance, maintenance, use, ownership or leasing of any building or place wherein or whereon are carried on, conducted, or permitted repeated acts which create and constitute a breach of the peace shall constitute a nuisance.

(b1) The erection, establishment, continuance, maintenance, use, ownership or leasing of any building or place wherein or whereon are carried on, conducted, or permitted repeated activities or conditions which violate a local ordinance regulating sexually oriented businesses so as to contribute to adverse secondary impacts shall constitute a nuisance.

(b2) The erection, establishment, continuance, maintenance, use, ownership, or leasing of any building or place for the purpose of carrying on, conducting, or engaging in any activities in violation of G.S. 14-72.7.

(c) The building, place, vehicle, or the ground itself, in or upon which a nuisance as defined in subsection (a), (b), or (b1) of this section is carried on, and the furniture, fixtures, and contents, are also declared a nuisance, and shall be enjoined and abated as hereinafter provided.

(d) No nuisance action under this Article may be brought against a place or business which is subject to regulation under Chapter 18B of the General Statutes when the basis for the action constitutes a violation of laws or regulations under that Chapter pertaining to the possession or sale of alcoholic beverages. (Pub. Loc. 1913, c. 761, s. 25; 1919, c. 288; C.S., s. 3180; 1949, c. 1164; 1967, c. 142; 1971, c. 655; 1977, c. 819, ss. 1, 2; 1981, c. 412, s. 4; c. 747, s. 66; 1998-46, s. 7; 1999-371, s. 1; 2007-178, s. 3; 2013-229, s. 1.)

§ 19-1.1. Definitions.

As used in this Chapter relating to illegal possession or sale of obscene matter or to the other conduct prohibited in G.S. 19-1(a), the following definitions shall apply:

(1) "Breach of the peace" means repeated acts that disturb the public order including, but not limited to, homicide, assault, affray, communicating threats, unlawful possession of dangerous or deadly weapons, and discharging firearms.

(1a) "Knowledge" or "knowledge of such nuisance" means having knowledge of the contents and character of the patently offensive sexual conduct which appears in the lewd matter, or knowledge of the acts of lewdness. With regard to nuisances involving assignation, prostitution, gambling, the illegal possession or sale of alcoholic beverages, the illegal possession or sale of controlled substances as defined in the North Carolina Controlled Substances Act, or repeated acts which create and constitute a breach of the peace, evidence that the defendant knew or by the exercise of due diligence should have known of the acts or conduct constitutes proof of knowledge.

(2) "Lewd matter" is synonymous with "obscene matter" and means any matter:

a. Which the average person, applying contemporary community standards, would find, when considered as a whole, appeals to the prurient interest; and

b. Which depicts patently offensive representations of:

1. Ultimate sexual acts, normal or perverted, actual or simulated;

2. Masturbation, excretory functions, or lewd exhibition of the genitals or genital area;

3. Masochism or sadism; or

4. Sexual acts with a child or animal.

Nothing herein contained is intended to include or proscribe any writing or written material, nor to include or proscribe any matter which, when considered as a whole, and in the context in which it is used, possesses serious literary, artistic, political, educational, or scientific value.

(3) "Lewdness" is synonymous with obscenity and shall mean the act of selling, exhibiting or possessing for sale or exhibition lewd matter.

(4) "Matter" means a motion picture film or a publication or both.

(5) "Motion picture film" shall include any:

a. Film or plate negative;

b. Film or plate positive;

c. Film designed to be projected on a screen for exhibition;

d. Films, glass slides or transparencies, either in negative or positive form, designed for exhibition by projection on a screen;

e. Video tape, compact disc, digital video disc, or any other medium used to electronically reproduce images on a screen.

(6) "Person" means any individual, partnership, firm, association, corporation, or other legal entity.

(7) "Place" includes, but is not limited to, any building, structure or places, or any separate part or portion thereof, whether permanent or not, or the ground itself.

(7a) "Preserving the status quo" as used in G.S. 19-2.3 means returning conditions to the last actual, peaceable, lawful, and noncontested status which preceded the pending controversy and not allow the nuisance to continue.

(7b) "Prostitution" means offering in any manner or receiving of the body in return for a fee, for acts of vaginal intercourse, anal intercourse, fellatio, cunnilingus, masturbation, or physical contact with a person's genitals, pubic area, buttocks, or breasts, or other acts of sexual conduct offered or received for pay and sexual gratification.

(8) "Publication" shall include any book, magazine, pamphlet, illustration, photograph, picture, sound recording, or a motion picture film which is offered for sale or exhibited in a coin-operated machine.

(9) "Sale of obscene or lewd matter" means a passing of title or right of possession from a seller to a buyer for valuable consideration, and shall include, but is not limited to, any lease or rental arrangement or other transaction wherein or whereby any valuable consideration is received for the use of, or transfer or possession of, lewd matter.

(10) "Sale" as the term relates to proscribed acts other than sale of obscene or lewd matter shall have the same meaning as the term is defined in Chapter 18B and Chapter 90 of the General Statutes prohibiting the illegal sale of alcoholic beverages and controlled substances respectively.

(11) "Used for profit" shall mean any use of real or personal property to produce income in any manner, including, but not limited to, any commercial or business activities, or selling, leasing, or otherwise providing goods and services for profit. (1977, c. 819, s. 3; 1981, c. 412, s. 4; c. 747, s. 66; 1999-371, s. 2.)

§ 19-1.2. Types of nuisances.

The following are declared to be nuisances wherein obscene or lewd matter or other conduct prohibited in G.S. 19-1(a) is involved:

(1) Any and every place in the State where lewd films are publicly exhibited as a predominant and regular course of business, or possessed for the purpose of such exhibition;

(2) Any and every place in the State where a lewd film is publicly and repeatedly exhibited, or possessed for the purpose of such exhibition;

(3) Any and every lewd film which is publicly exhibited, or possessed for such purpose at a place which is a nuisance under this Article;

(4) Any and every place of business in the State in which lewd publications constitute a principal or substantial part of the stock in trade;

(5) Any and every lewd publication possessed at a place which is a nuisance under this Article;

(6) Every place which, as a regular course of business, is used for the purposes of lewdness, assignation, gambling, the illegal possession or sale of alcoholic beverages, the illegal possession or sale of controlled substances as defined in the North Carolina Controlled Substances Act, or prostitution, and every such place in or upon which acts of lewdness, assignation, gambling, the illegal possession or sale of alcoholic beverages, the illegal possession or sale of controlled substances as defined in the North Carolina Controlled Substances Act, or prostitution, are held or occur. (1977, c. 819, s. 3; 1981, c. 412, s. 4; c. 747, s. 66; 1999-371, s. 3.)

§ 19-1.3. Personal property as a nuisance; knowledge of nuisance.

The following are also declared to be nuisances, as personal property used in conducting and maintaining a nuisance under this Chapter:

(1) All moneys paid as admission price to the exhibition of any lewd film found to be a nuisance;

(2) All valuable consideration received for the sale of any lewd publication which is found to be a nuisance;

(3) All money or other valuable consideration, vehicles, conveyances, or other property received or used in gambling, prostitution, the illegal sale of alcoholic beverages or the illegal sale of substances proscribed under the North Carolina Controlled Substances Act, as well as the furniture and movable contents of a place used in connection with such prohibited conduct.

From and after service of a copy of the notice of hearing of the application for a preliminary injunction, provided for in G.S. 19-2.4 upon the place, or its manager, or acting manager, or person then in charge, all such parties are deemed to have knowledge of the contents of the restraining order and the use of the place occurring thereafter. Where the circumstantial proof warrants a determination that a person had knowledge of the nuisance prior to such service of process, the court may make such finding. (1977, c. 819, s. 3; 1981, c. 412, s. 4; c. 747, s. 66; 1999-371, s. 4.)

§ 19-1.4. Liability of successive owners for continuing nuisance.

After notice of a temporary restraining order, preliminary injunction, or permanent injunction, every successive owner of property who neglects to abate a continuing nuisance upon, or in the use of such property, created by a former owner, is liable therefor in the same manner as the one who first created it. (1977, c. 819, s. 3.)

§ 19-1.5. Abatement does not preclude action.

The abatement of a nuisance does not prejudice the right of any person to recover damages for its past existence. (1977, c. 819, s. 3.)

§ 19-2. Repealed by Session Laws 1977, c. 819, s. 4.

§ 19-2.1. Action for abatement; injunction.

Wherever a nuisance is kept, maintained, or exists, as defined in this Article, the Attorney General, district attorney, county, municipality, or any private citizen of the county may maintain a civil action in the name of the State of North Carolina to abate a nuisance under this Chapter, perpetually to enjoin all persons from maintaining the same, and to enjoin the use of any structure or thing adjudged to be a nuisance under this Chapter; provided, however, that no private citizen may maintain such action where the alleged nuisance involves the illegal possession or sale of obscene or lewd matter.

Upon request from the Attorney General, district attorney, county or municipality, including the sheriff or chief of police of any county or municipality, the Alcohol Law Enforcement Section of the Department of Public Safety or any other law enforcement agency with jurisdiction may investigate alleged public nuisances and make recommendations regarding actions to abate the public nuisances.

If an action is instituted by a private person, the complainant shall execute a bond prior to the issuance of a restraining order or a temporary injunction, with good and sufficient surety to be approved by the court or clerk thereof, in the sum of not less than one thousand dollars ($1,000), to secure to the party enjoined the damages he may sustain if such action is wrongfully brought, not prosecuted to final judgment, or is dismissed, or is not maintained, or if it is finally decided that the temporary restraining order or preliminary injunction ought not to have been granted. The party enjoined shall have recourse against said bond for all damages suffered, including damages to his property, person, or character and including reasonable attorney's fees incurred by him in making defense to said action. No bond shall be required of the prosecuting attorney, the Attorney General, county, or municipality, and no action shall be maintained against any public official or public entity, their employees, or agents for investigating or maintaining an action for abatement of a nuisance under the provisions of this Chapter. (1977, c. 819, s. 4; 1995, c. 528, s. 1; 1999-371, s. 5; 2011-145, s. 19.1(g), (n).)

§ 19-2.2. Pleadings; jurisdiction; venue; application for preliminary injunction.

The action, provided for in this Chapter, shall be brought in the superior court of the county in which the property is located. Such action shall be commenced by the filing of a verified complaint alleging the facts constituting the nuisance. After the filing of said complaint, application for a preliminary injunction may be made to the court in which the action is filed which court shall grant a hearing within 10 days after the filing of said application. (1977, c. 819, s. 4.)

§ 19-2.3. Temporary order restraining removal of personal property from premises; service; punishment.

Where such application for a preliminary injunction is made, the court may, on application of the complainant showing good cause, issue an ex parte temporary restraining order in accordance with G.S. 1A-1, Rule 65(b), preserving the status quo and restraining the defendant and all other persons from removing or in any manner interfering with any evidence specifically described, or in any manner removing or interfering with the personal property and contents of the place where such nuisance is alleged to exist, until the decision of the court granting or refusing such preliminary injunction and until further order of the court thereon. Nothing herein shall be interpreted to allow the prior restraint of the distribution of any matter or the sale of the stock in trade, but an inventory and full accounting of all business transactions involving alleged obscene or lewd matter thereafter shall be required. The inventory provisions provided by this section shall not apply to nuisances occurring at a private dwelling place unless the court finds the private dwelling place is used for profit.

Any person, firm, or corporation enjoined pursuant to this section may file with the court a motion to dissolve any temporary restraining order. Such a motion shall be heard within 24 hours of the time a copy of the motion is served on the complaining party, or on the next day the superior courts are open in the district, whichever is later. At such hearing the complaining party shall have the burden of showing why the restraining order should be continued.

In the event a temporary restraining order is issued, it may be served in accordance with the provisions of G.S. 1A-1, Rule 4, or may be served by handing to and leaving a copy of such order with any person in charge of such place or residing therein, or by posting a copy thereof in a conspicuous place at or upon one or more of the principal doors or entrances to such place, or by such service under said Rule 4, delivery and posting. The officer serving such temporary restraining order shall forthwith enter upon the property and make and return into court an inventory of the personal property and contents situated in and used in conducting or maintaining such nuisance.

Any violation of such temporary restraining order is a contempt of court, and where such order is posted, mutilation or removal thereof, while the same remains in force, is a contempt of court, provided such posted order contains therein a notice to that effect. (1977, c. 819, s. 4; 1999-371, s. 6.)

§ 19-2.4. Notice of hearing on preliminary injunction; consolidation.

A copy of the complaint, together with a notice of the time and place of the hearing of the application for a preliminary injunction, shall be served upon the defendant at least five days before such hearing. The place may also be served by posting such papers in the same manner as is provided for in G.S. 19-2.3 in the case of a temporary restraining order. If the hearing is then continued at the instance of any defendant, the temporary restraining order may be continued as a matter of course until the hearing.

Before or after the commencement of the hearing of an application for a preliminary injunction, the court, on application of either of the parties or on its own motion, may order the trial of the action on the merits to be advanced and consolidated with the hearing on the application for the preliminary injunction; provided, however, the defendant shall be entitled to a jury trial if requested. (1977, c. 819, s. 4.)

§ 19-2.5. Hearing on the preliminary injunction; issuance.

If upon hearing, the allegations of the complaint are sustained to the satisfaction of the court, the court shall issue a preliminary injunction restraining the defendant and any other person from continuing the nuisance and effectually enjoining its use thereafter for the purpose of conducting any such nuisance. The court may, in its discretion, order the closure of the property pending trial on the merits. (1977, c. 819, s. 4; 1999-371, s. 7.)

§ 19-3. Priority of action; evidence.

(a) The action provided for in this Chapter shall be set down for trial at the first term of the court and shall have precedence over all other cases except crimes, election contests, or injunctions.

(b) In such action, an admission or finding of guilt of any person under the criminal laws against lewdness, assignation, prostitution, gambling, breaches of the peace, the illegal possession or sale of alcoholic beverages, or the illegal possession or sale of substances proscribed by the North Carolina Controlled Substances Act, at any such place, is admissible for the purpose of proving the existence of said nuisance, and is evidence of such nuisance and of knowledge of, and of acquiescence and participation therein, on the part of the person charged with maintaining said nuisance.

(c) At all hearings upon the merits, evidence of the general reputation of the building or place constituting the alleged nuisance, of the inmates thereof, and of those resorting thereto, is admissible for the purpose of proving the existence of such nuisance. (Pub. Loc. 1913, c. 761, s. 27; 1919, c. 288; C.S., s. 3182; 1971, c. 528, s. 6; 1973, c. 47, s. 2; 1977, c. 819, s. 5; 1981, c. 412, s. 4; c. 747, s. 66; 1999-371, s. 8.)

§ 19-4. Violation of injunction; punishment.

In case of the violation of any injunction granted under the provisions of this Chapter, the court, or, in vacation, a judge thereof, may summarily try and punish the offender. A party found guilty of contempt under the provisions of this section shall be punished by a fine of not less than two hundred ($200.00) or more than one thousand dollars ($1,000), or by imprisonment in the county jail not less than three or more than six months, or by both fine and imprisonment. (Pub. Loc. 1913, c. 761, s. 28; 1919, c. 288; C.S., s. 3183.)

§ 19-5. Content of final judgment and order.

If the existence of a nuisance is admitted or established in an action as provided for in this Chapter an order of abatement shall be entered as a part of the judgment in the case, which judgment and order shall perpetually enjoin the defendant and any other person from further maintaining the nuisance at the place complained of, and the defendant from maintaining such nuisance elsewhere within the jurisdiction of this State. Lewd matter, illegal alcoholic beverages, gambling paraphernalia, or substances proscribed under the North Carolina Controlled Substances Act shall be destroyed and not be sold.

Such order may also require the effectual closing of the place against its use thereafter for the purpose of conducting any such nuisance.

The provisions of this Article, relating to the closing of a place with respect to obscene or lewd matter, shall not apply in any order of the court to any theatre or motion picture establishment which does not, in the regular, predominant, and ordinary course of its business, show or demonstrate lewd films or motion pictures, as defined in this Article, but any such establishment may be permanently enjoined from showing such film judicially determined to be obscene hereunder and such film or motion picture shall be destroyed and all proceeds and moneys received therefrom, after the issuance of a preliminary injunction, forfeited. (Pub. Loc. 1913, c. 761, s. 29; 1919, c. 288; C.S., s. 3184; 1977, c. 819, s. 6; 1981, c. 412, s. 4; c. 747, s. 66.)

§ 19-6. Civil penalty; forfeiture; accounting; lien as to expenses of abatement; invalidation of lease.

Lewd matter is contraband, and there are no property rights therein. All personal property, including all money and other considerations, declared to be a nuisance under the provisions of G.S. 19-1.3 and other sections of this Article, are subject to forfeiture to the local government and are recoverable as damages in the county wherein such matter is sold, exhibited or otherwise used. Such property including moneys may be traced to and shall be recoverable from persons who, under G.S. 19-2.4, have knowledge of the nuisance at the time such moneys are received by them.

Upon judgment against the defendant or defendants in legal proceedings brought pursuant to this Article, an accounting shall be made by such defendant or defendants of all moneys received by them which have been declared to be a nuisance under this Article. An amount equal to the sum of all moneys estimated to have been taken in as gross income from such unlawful commercial activity shall be forfeited to the general funds of the city and county governments wherein such activity took place, to be shared equally, as a forfeiture of the fruits of an unlawful enterprise, and as partial restitution for damages done to the public welfare; provided, however, that no provision of this Article shall authorize the recovery of any moneys or gross income received from the sale of any book, magazine, or exhibition of any motion picture prior to the issuance of a preliminary injunction. Where the action is brought pursuant to this Article, special injury need not be proven, and the costs of abatement are a lien on both the real and personal property used in maintaining the nuisance. Costs of abatement include, but are not limited to, reasonable attorney's fees and court costs.

Upon the filing of the action, the plaintiff may file a notice of lis pendens in the official records of the county where the property is located.

If it is judicially found after an adversary hearing pursuant to this Article that a tenant or occupant of a building or tenement, under a lawful title, uses such place for the purposes of lewdness, assignation, prostitution, gambling, sale or possession of illegal alcoholic beverages or substances proscribed under the North Carolina Controlled Substances Act, or repeated acts which create and constitute a breach of the peace, such use makes void the lease or other title under which he holds, at the option of the owner, and, without any act of the owner, causes the right of possession to revert and vest in such owner.

The clear proceeds of civil penalties and forfeitures provided for in this section, except for penalties and properties that accrue to local governments instead of the State, shall be remitted to the Civil Penalty and Forfeiture Fund in accordance with G.S. 115C-457.2. (Pub. Loc. 1913, c. 761, s. 30; 1919, c. 288; C.S., s. 3185; 1977, c. 819, s. 7; 1981, c. 412, s. 4; c. 747, s. 66; 1998-215, s. 106; 1999-371, s. 9.)

§ 19-6.1. Forfeiture of real property.

In all actions where a preliminary injunction, permanent injunction, or an order of abatement is issued pursuant to this Article in which the nuisance consists of or includes at least two prior occurrences within five years of the manufacture, possession with intent to sell, or sale of controlled substances as defined by the North Carolina Controlled Substances Act, two prior occurrences of the possession of any controlled substance included within Schedule I or II of that Act, or two prior convictions within five years of violation of G.S. 14-72.7, the real property on which the nuisance exists or is maintained is subject to forfeiture in accordance with this section. In the case of the two prior convictions of G.S. 14-72.7, the convictions shall not arise out of the same transaction or occurrence.

If all of the owners of the property are defendants in the action, the plaintiff, other than a plaintiff who is a private citizen, may request forfeiture of the real property as part of the relief sought. If forfeiture is requested, and if jurisdiction over all defendant owners is established, upon judgment against the defendant or defendants, the court shall order forfeiture as follows:

(1) If the court finds by clear and convincing evidence that all the owners either (i) have participated in maintaining the nuisance on the property, or (ii) prior to the action had written notice from the plaintiff, or any governmental agent or entity authorized to bring an action pursuant to this Chapter, that the nuisance existed or was maintained on the property and have not made good faith efforts to stop the nuisance from occurring or recurring, the court shall order that the property be forfeited;

(2) If the court finds that one or more of the owners did not participate in maintaining the nuisance on the property or did not have written notice from the plaintiff prior to the action that the nuisance existed or was maintained on the property, the court shall not order forfeiture of the property immediately upon judgment. However, if after judgment and an order directing the defendants to abate the nuisance, the nuisance either continues, begins again, or otherwise recurs within five years of the order and the defendants have not made good faith efforts to abate the nuisance, the plaintiff may petition the court for forfeiture. Upon such petition, the defendant owner or owners shall be given notice and an opportunity to appear and be heard at a hearing to determine the continuation or recurrence of the nuisance. If, in this hearing (i) the plaintiff establishes by clear and convincing evidence that the nuisance, with the owner's or owners' knowledge, has either continued, begun again, or otherwise recurred, and (ii) the defendants fail to establish that they have made and are continuing to make good faith efforts to abate the nuisance, the court shall order that the property be forfeited.

For the purposes of this section, factors which may evidence good faith by the defendant to abate the nuisance include but are not limited to (i) cooperation with law enforcement authorities to abate the nuisance; (ii) lease restrictions prohibiting the illegal possession or sale of narcotic drugs and an action to evict a tenant for any violations of the lease provision; (iii) a criminal record check of prospective tenants; and (iv) reference checks of prior residency of prospective tenants.

Upon an order of forfeiture, title to the property shall vest in the school board of the county in which the property is located. If at the time of forfeiture the property is subject to a lien or security interest of a person not participating in the maintenance of the nuisance, the school board shall either (i) pay an amount to that person satisfying the lien or security interest; or (ii) sell the property and satisfy the lien or security interest from the proceeds of the sale. If the property is not subject to any lien or security interest at the time of forfeiture, the school board may hold, maintain, lease, sell, or otherwise dispose of the property as it sees fit.

Upon the filing of the action, the plaintiff may file a notice of lis pendens in the official records of the county where the property is located. If the plaintiff files a notice of lis pendens, any person purchasing or obtaining an interest in the property thereafter shall be considered to have notice of the alleged nuisance, and shall forfeit his interest in the property upon a judgment of forfeiture in favor of the plaintiff.

If in the same action in which real property is forfeited the court finds that a tenant or occupant of the property participated in or maintained the nuisance, the lease or other title under which the tenant or occupant holds is void, and the right of possession vests in the new owner. Upon forfeiture, the rights of innocent tenants occupying separate units of the property who were not involved in the nuisance at the time the action was filed shall be in accordance with any relevant lease provisions in effect at the time or, in the absence of relevant lease provisions, in accordance with the law applying to other tenants or occupants of property that is sold, foreclosed upon, or otherwise obtained by new owners. (1995, c. 528, s. 2; 1999-371, s. 10; 2007-178, s. 4.)

§ 19-7. How order of abatement may be canceled.

If the owner appears and pays all cost of the proceeding and files a bond, with sureties to be approved by the clerk, in the full value of the property, to be ascertained by the court, or, in vacation, by the clerk of the superior court, conditioned that he will immediately abate said nuisance, and prevent the same from being established or kept within a period of one year thereafter, the court may, if satisfied of his good faith, order the premises closed under the order of abatement to be delivered to said owner, and said order of abatement canceled so far as same may relate to said property; and if the proceeding be a civil action, and said bond be given and costs therein paid before judgment and order of abatement, the action shall be thereby abated as to said building only. The release of the property under the provisions of this section shall not release it from any judgment, lien, penalty, or liability to which it may be subject by law. (Pub. Loc. 1913, c. 761, s. 31; 1919, c. 288; C.S., s. 3186.)

§ 19-8. Costs.

The prevailing party shall be entitled to his costs. The court shall tax as part of the costs in any action brought hereunder such fee for the attorney prosecuting or defending the action or proceedings as may in the court's discretion be reasonable remuneration for the services performed by such attorney. (Pub. Loc. 1913, c. 761, s. 32; 1919, c. 288; C.S., s. 3187; 1977, c. 819, s. 8.)

§ 19-8.1. Immunity.

The provisions of any criminal statutes with respect to the exhibition of, or the possession with the intent to exhibit, any obscene film shall not apply to a motion picture projectionist, usher, or ticket taker acting within the scope of his employment, provided that such projectionist, usher, or ticket taker: (i) Has no financial interest in the place wherein he is so employed, and (ii) freely and willingly gives testimony regarding such employment in any judicial proceedings brought under this Chapter, including pretrial discovery proceedings incident thereto, when and if such is requested, and upon being granted immunity by the trial judge sitting in such matters. (1977, c. 819, s. 9.)

§ 19-8.2. Right of entry.

Authorized representatives of the Commission for Public Health, any local health department or the Department of Health and Human Services, upon presenting appropriate credentials to the owner, operator, or agent in charge of a place described in G.S. 19-1.2, are authorized to enter without delay and at any reasonable time any such place in order to inspect and investigate during the regular hours of operation of such place. (1977, c. 819, s. 9; 1997-443, s. 11A.118(a); 2007-182, s. 2.)

§ 19-8.3. Severability.

If any section, subsection, sentence, or clause of this Article is adjudged to be unconstitutional or invalid, such adjudication shall not affect the validity of the remaining portion of this Article. It is hereby declared that this Article would have been passed, and each section, sentence, or clause thereof, irrespective of the fact that any one or more sections, subsections, sentences or clauses might be adjudged to be unconstitutional, or for any other reason invalid. (1977, c. 819, s. 10.)

Article 2.

Civil Remedy for Sales of Harmful Materials to Minors.

§ 19-9. Title.

This Article shall be known and cited as the North Carolina Law on the Protection of Minors from Harmful Materials. (1969, c. 1215, s. 1.)

§ 19-10. Purposes.

The purposes of this Article are to provide district attorneys with a speedy civil remedy for obtaining a judicial determination of the character and contents of publications, and with an effective power to enjoin promptly the sale of harmful materials to minors. (1969, c. 1215, s. 1; 1971, c. 528, s. 7; 1973, c. 47, s. 2.)

§ 19-11. Public policy.

The public policy of this State requires that all proceedings prescribed in this Article shall be examined, heard and disposed of with the maximum promptness and dispatch commensurate with constitutional requirements, including due process, freedom of the press and freedom of speech. (1969, c. 1215, s. 1.)

§ 19-12. Definitions.

As used within this Article, the following definitions shall apply:

(1) "Harmful Material".-

a. Any picture, photograph, drawing, or similar visual representation or image of a person or portion of the human body which depicts nudity, sexual conduct or sadomasochistic abuse, and which is harmful to minors, or

b. Any book, pamphlet, magazine, or printed matter however reproduced which contains any matter enumerated in subparagraph a of this subdivision or which contains explicit or detailed verbal descriptions or accounts of sexual excitement, sexual conduct or sadomasochistic abuse, and which, taken as a whole, is harmful to minors.

(2) "Harmful to minors". - That quality of any description or representation, in whatever form, of nudity, sexual conduct, sexual excitement, or sadomasochistic abuse, when it:

a. Predominantly appeals to the prurient, shameful or morbid interest of minors, and

b. Is patently offensive to prevailing standards in the adult community as a whole with respect to what is suitable materials for minors, and

c. Is utterly without redeeming social importance for minors.

(3) "Knowledge of the Minor's Age".-

a. Knowledge or information that the person is a minor, or

b. Reason to know, or a belief or ground for belief which warrants further inspection or inquiry as to, the age of the minor.

(4) "Knowledge of the Nature of the Material".-

a. Knowledge of the character and content of any material described herein, or

b. Knowledge or information that the material described herein has been adjudged to be harmful to minors in a proceeding instituted pursuant to this Article, or is the subject of a pending proceeding instituted pursuant to this Article.

(5) "Minor".-Any person under the age of 18 years.

(6) "Nudity".-The showing of the human male or female genitals, pubic area or buttocks with less than a full opaque covering, or the showing of the female breast with less than a full opaque covering of any portion thereof below the top of the nipple, or the depiction of covered male genitals in a discernibly turgid state.

(7) "Person".-Any individual, partnership, firm, association, corporation or other legal entity.

(8) "Sadomasochistic abuse".-Flagellation or torture by or upon a person clad in undergarments, a mask or a bizarre costume, or the condition of being fettered, bound or otherwise physically restrained on the part of one so clothed.

(9) "Sexual conduct".-Acts of masturbation, homosexuality, sexual intercourse, or physical contact with a person's clothed or unclothed genitals, pubic area, buttocks or, if such person be a female, breast.

(10) "Sexual excitement".-The condition of human male or female genitals when in a state of sexual stimulation or arousal. (1969, c. 1215, s. 1.)

§ 19-13. Commencement of civil proceeding.

(a) Whenever the district attorney for any prosecutorial district has reasonable cause to believe that any person is engaged in selling, distributing or disseminating in any manner harmful material to minors or may become engaged in selling, distributing or disseminating in any manner harmful material to minors, the district attorney for the prosecutorial district in which such material is so offered for sale shall institute an action in the district court for that district for adjudication of the question of whether such material is harmful to minors.

(b) The provisions of the Rules of Civil Procedure and all existing and future amendments of said Rules shall apply to all proceedings herein, except as otherwise provided in this Article. (1969, c. 1215, s. 1; 1971, c. 528, s. 8; 1973, c. 47, s. 2; 1987 (Reg. Sess., 1988), c. 1037, s. 73.)

§ 19-14. Filing and form of complaint.

The action authorized by this Article shall be commenced by the filing of a complaint to which shall be attached, as an exhibit, a true copy of the allegedly harmful material. The complaint shall:

(1) Be directed against such material by name, description, volume, and issue, as appropriate;

(2) Allege that such material is harmful to minors;

(3) Designate as respondents, and list the names and all known addresses of any person in this State preparing, selling, offering, commercially distributing or disseminating in any manner such material to minors, or possessing such material with the apparent intent to offer to sell or commercially distribute or disseminate in any manner such material to minors;

(4) Seek an adjudication that such material is harmful to minors; and

(5) Seek a permanent injunction against any respondent prohibiting him from selling, commercially distributing, or disseminating in any manner such material to minors or from permitting minors to inspect such material. (1969, c. 1215, s. 1.)

§ 19-15. Examination by the court; probable cause; service of summons.

(a) Upon the filing of a complaint pursuant to this Article, the district attorney shall present the same, together with attached exhibits, as soon as practicable to the court for its examination and reading.

(b) If, after such examination and reading, the court finds no probable cause to believe such material to be harmful to minors, the court shall cause an endorsement to that effect to be placed and dated upon the complaint and shall thereupon dismiss the action.

(c) If, after such examination and reading, the court finds probable cause to believe such material to be harmful to minors, the court shall enter an order to that effect whereupon it shall be the responsibility of the district attorney promptly to cause the clerk of the superior court to issue summonses together with copies of said order and said complaint as are needed for the service of the same upon respondents. Service of such summons, order and complaint shall be made upon each respondent thereto in any manner provided by law for the service of civil process. (1969, c. 1215, s. 1; 1971, c. 528, s. 8; 1973, c. 47, s. 2.)

§ 19-16. Appearance and answer; default judgment.

(a) On or before the return date specified in the summons issued pursuant to this Article, or within 15 days after the service of such summons, or within 15 days after receiving actual notice of the issuance of such summons, the author, publisher or any person interested in sending or causing to be sent, bringing or causing to be brought, into this State for sale or distribution or disseminating in any manner, or any person in this State preparing, selling, offering, exhibiting or commercially distributing, or disseminating in any manner or possessing with intent to sell, offer or commercially distribute or exhibit or disseminate in any manner the material attached as an exhibit to the endorsed complaint, may appear and may intervene as a respondent and file an answer.

(b) If, after service of summons has been effected upon all respondents, no person appears and files an answer on or before the return date specified in the summons, the court may forthwith adjudge whether the material so exhibited to the endorsed complaint is harmful to minors and enter an appropriate final judgment. (1969, c. 1215, s. 1.)

§ 19-17. Trial.

(a) Upon the expiration of the time for filing answers by all respondents, but not later than the return date specified in the summons, the court shall, upon its own motion, or upon the application of any party who has appeared and filed an answer, set a date for the trial of the issues joined.

(b) Any respondent named in the complaint, or any person who becomes a respondent by virtue of intervention pursuant to this Article, shall be entitled to a trial of the issues within one day after joinder of issue. A decision shall be rendered by the court or jury, as the case may be, within two days of the conclusion of the trial.

(c) Every person appearing and answering as a respondent shall be entitled, upon request, to a trial of any issue by a jury. If a jury is not requested by any such respondent, the issues shall be tried by the court without a jury. (1969, c. 1215, s. 1.)

§ 19-18. Judgment; limitation to district.

(a) In the event that the court or jury, as the case may be, fails to find the material attached as an exhibit to the complaint to be harmful to minors, the court shall enter judgment accordingly and shall dismiss the complaint.

(b) In the event that the court or jury, as the case may be, finds the material attached as an exhibit to the complaint to be harmful to minors, the court shall enter judgment to such effect and may, in such judgment or in subsequent orders of enforcement thereof, enter a permanent injunction against any respondent prohibiting him from selling, commercially distributing, or giving away such material to minors or from permitting minors to inspect such material.

(c) No interlocutory order, judgment, or subsequent order of enforcement thereof, entered pursuant to the provisions of this Article, shall be of any force and effect outside the district court district in which entered; and no such order or judgment shall be res judicata in any proceeding in any other district court district. (1969, c. 1215, s. 1; 1987 (Reg. Sess., 1988), c. 1037, s. 74.)

§ 19-19. Injunctions.

(a) If the court finds probable cause to believe the exhibited material to be harmful to minors, and so enters an order, the court may, upon the motion of the district attorney, issue a temporary restraining order against any respondent prohibiting him from offering, selling, commercially distributing or disseminating in any manner such material to minors or from permitting minors to inspect such material. No temporary restraining order shall be granted without notice to the respondents unless it clearly appears from specific facts shown by affidavit or by the verified complaint that one or more of the respondents are engaged in the sale, distribution or dissemination of harmful material to minors and that immediate and irreparable injury to the morals and general welfare of minors in this State will result before notice can be served and a hearing had thereon.

(b) Every temporary restraining order shall be endorsed with the date and hour of issuance; shall be filed forthwith in the clerk's office and entered of record; shall define the injury and state why it is irreparable and why the order was granted without notice; and shall expire by its own terms within such time after entry, not to exceed three days, as the court fixes unless within the time so fixed the respondent against whom the order is directed consents that it may be extended for a longer period.

(c) In the event that a temporary restraining order is granted without notice, a motion for a preliminary injunction shall be set down for hearing within two days after the granting of such order and shall take precedence over all matters except older matters of the same character; and when the motion comes on for hearing, the district attorney shall proceed with the application for a preliminary injunction and, if he does not do so, the court shall dissolve the restraining order.

(d) No preliminary injunction shall be issued without at least two days' notice to the respondents. (1969, c. 1215, s. 1; 1971, c. 528, s. 8; 1973, c. 47, s. 2.)

§ 19-20. Contempt; defenses; extradition.

(a) Any respondent, or any officer, agent, servant, employee or attorney of such respondent, or any person in active concert or participation by contract or arrangement with such respondent, who receives actual notice by personal service or otherwise of any restraining order or injunction entered pursuant to this Article, and who shall disobey any of the provisions thereof, shall be guilty of contempt of court and upon conviction after notice and hearing shall be sentenced as provided by law.

(b) No person shall be guilty of contempt pursuant to this section:

(1) For any sale, distribution or dissemination to a minor where such person had reasonable cause to believe that the minor involved was 18 years old or more, and such minor exhibited to such person a draft card, driver's license, birth certificate or other official or apparently official document purporting to establish that such minor was 18 years old or more;

(2) For any sale, distribution or dissemination where a minor is accompanied by a parent or guardian, or accompanied by an adult and such person has no reason to suspect that the adult accompanying the minor is not the minor's parent or guardian;

(3) Where such person is a bona fide school, museum or public library or is acting in his capacity as an employee of such organization or as a retail outlet affiliated with and serving the educational purposes of such organization.

(c) In the event that any person found guilty of contempt pursuant to this section cannot be found within this State, the executive authority of this State shall, unless such person shall have appealed from the judgment of contempt and such appeal has not been finally determined, demand his extradition from the executive authority of the state in which such person may be found, pursuant to the law of this State. (1969, c. 1215, s. 1.)

§ 19-21. Repealed by Session Laws 1971, c. 528, s. 9.

Chapter 19A.

Protection of Animals.

Article 1.

Civil Remedy for Protection of Animals.

§ 19A-1. Definitions.

The following definitions apply in this Article:

(1) The term "animals" includes every living vertebrate in the classes Amphibia, Reptilia, Aves, and Mammalia except human beings.

(2) The terms "cruelty" and "cruel treatment" include every act, omission, or neglect whereby unjustifiable physical pain, suffering, or death is caused or permitted.

(3) The term "person" has the same meaning as in G.S. 12-3. (1969, c. 831; 1979, c. 808, s. 2; 1995, c. 509, s. 19; 2003-208, s. 1.)

§ 19A-1.1. Exemptions.

This Article shall not apply to the following:

(1)   The lawful taking of animals under the jurisdiction and regulation of the Wildlife Resources Commission, except that this Article applies to those birds exempted by the Wildlife Resources Commission from its definition of "wild birds" pursuant to G.S. 113-129(15a).

(2)   Lawful activities conducted for purposes of biomedical research or training or for purposes of production of livestock, poultry, or aquatic species.

(3)   Lawful activities conducted for the primary purpose of providing food for human or animal consumption.

(4)   Activities conducted for lawful veterinary purposes.

(5)   The lawful destruction of any animal for the purposes of protecting the public, other animals, or the public health.

(6)   Lawful activities for sport.

(7)   The taking and holding in captivity of a wild animal by a licensed sportsman for use or display in an annual, seasonal, or cultural event, so long as the animal is captured from the wild and returned to the wild at or near the area where it was captured. (2003-208, s. 1; 2013-3, s. 3.)

§ 19A-2. Purpose.

It shall be the purpose of this Article to provide a civil remedy for the protection and humane treatment of animals in addition to any criminal remedies that are available and it shall be proper in any action to combine causes of action against one or more defendants for the protection of one or more animals. A real party in interest as plaintiff shall be held to include any person even though the person does not have a possessory or ownership right in an animal; a real party in interest as defendant shall include any person who owns or has possession of an animal. Venue for any action filed under this Article shall only be in the county where any violation is alleged to have occurred. (1969, c. 831; 1995, c. 509, s. 20; 2003-208, s. 1; 2013-3, s. 4; 2013-410, s. 4.1.)

§ 19A-3. Preliminary injunction; care of animal pending hearing on the merits.

(a) Upon the filing of a verified complaint in the district court in the county in which cruelty to an animal has allegedly occurred, the judge may, as a matter of discretion, issue a preliminary injunction in accordance with the procedures set forth in G.S. 1A-1, Rule 65. Every such preliminary injunction, if the plaintiff so requests, may give the plaintiff the right to provide suitable care for the animal. If it appears on the face of the complaint that the condition giving rise to the cruel treatment of an animal requires the animal to be removed from its owner or other person who possesses it, then it shall be proper for the court in the preliminary injunction to allow the plaintiff to take possession of the animal as custodian.

(b) The plaintiff as custodian may employ a veterinarian to provide necessary medical care for the animal without any additional court order. Prior to taking such action, the plaintiff as custodian shall consult with, or attempt to consult with, the defendant in the action, but the plaintiff as custodian may authorize such care without the defendant's consent. Notwithstanding the provisions of this subsection, the plaintiff as custodian may not have an animal euthanized without written consent of the defendant or a court order that authorizes euthanasia upon the court's finding that the animal is suffering due to terminal illness or terminal injury.

(c) The plaintiff as custodian may place an animal with a foster care provider. The foster care provider shall return the animal to the plaintiff as custodian on demand. (1969, c. 831; 1971, c. 528, s. 10; 1979, c. 808, s. 3; 2003-208, s. 1; 2006-113, s. 1.1.)

§ 19A-4. Permanent injunction.

(a) In accordance with G.S. 1A-1, Rule 65, a district court judge in the county in which the original action was brought shall determine the merits of the action by trial without a jury, and upon hearing such evidence as may be presented, shall enter orders as the court deems appropriate, including a permanent injunction and dismissal of the action along with dissolution of any preliminary injunction that had been issued.

(b)   If the plaintiff prevails, the court in its discretion may include the costs of food, water, shelter, and care, including medical care, provided to the animal, less any amounts deposited by the defendant under G.S. 19A-70, as part of the costs allowed to the plaintiff under G.S. 6-18. In addition, if the court finds by a preponderance of the evidence that even if a permanent injunction were issued there would exist a substantial risk that the animal would be subjected to further cruelty if returned to the possession of the defendant, the court may terminate the defendant's ownership and right of possession of the animal and transfer ownership and right of possession to the plaintiff or other appropriate successor owner. For good cause shown, the court may also enjoin the defendant from acquiring new animals for a specified period of time or limit the number of animals the defendant may own or possess during a specified period of time.

(c)   If the final judgment entitles the defendant to regain possession of the animal, the custodian shall return the animal, including taking any necessary steps to retrieve the animal from a foster care provider.

(d)   The court shall consider and may provide for custody and care of the animal until the time to appeal expires or all appeals have been exhausted. (1969, c. 831; 1971, c. 528, s. 10; 1979, c. 808, s. 4; 2003-208, s. 1; 2006-113, s. 1.2.)

§§ 19A-5 through 19A-9. Reserved for future codification purposes.

Article 2.

Protection of Black Bears.

§ 19A-10. Unlawful to buy, sell or enclose (except as provided) black bear.

Except as otherwise provided in applicable statutes, it shall be unlawful for any person to buy or sell black bears or for any person, firm or corporation to possess or keep any black bear (Ursus americanus) in any enclosure, pen, cage, or other place or means of captivity except as hereinafter provided. (1975, c. 56, s. 1.)

§ 19A-11. Inapplicable to bona fide zoos, etc.

The provisions of this Article shall not apply to bona fide zoos which are operated by federal, State, or local governmental agencies, or to educational institutions in which black bears are kept or exhibited as part of a bona fide course of training or research in the natural sciences, or to black bears held without caging under conditions simulating a natural habitat, the development of which is in accord with plans and specifications developed by the holder and approved by the Wildlife Resources Commission. (1975, c. 56, s. 2.)

§ 19A-12. Possession of black bear on July 1, 1975; surrender of bear; modification of facilities; forfeiture.

Any person, firm or corporation in possession of a black bear on July 1, 1975, under an existing permit issued by the Wildlife Resources Commission, where the conditions under which such black bear is held are in violation of this Article, may immediately surrender such black bear and such permit to the Wildlife Resources Commission which shall compensate such person, firm or corporation in the amount actually paid for such bear not to exceed the sum of one hundred dollars ($100.00) for any one bear. In lieu of surrendering such black bear and such permit, any such person, firm or corporation may give immediately written notice to the Wildlife Resources Commission that plans and specifications for facilities to hold such bear without caging under conditions simulating a natural habitat will be submitted to the Commission for approval within 30 days thereafter. In the event such plans and specifications are not submitted within the time thus limited, or they are disapproved by the Commission, or the facilities are not completed in accordance therewith within 60 days after approval by the Commission, continued possession of a black bear by such person, firm or corporation after any of such events shall constitute a violation of the provisions of this Article, and any such black bear shall be forfeited to the Wildlife Resources Commission without compensation. (1975, c. 56, s. 3.)

§ 19A-13. Violation of Article.

Violation of the provisions of this Article shall constitute a Class 2 misdemeanor. (1975, c. 56, s. 4; 1993, c. 539, s. 314; 1994, Ex. Sess., c. 24, s. 14(c).)

§ 19A-14. Enforcement of Article.

Law-enforcement officers of the Wildlife Resources Commission and all other peace officers are authorized and empowered to enforce the provisions of this Article. (1975, c. 56, s. 5.)

§§ 19A-15 through 19A-19. Reserved for future codification purposes.

Article 3.

Animal Welfare Act.

§ 19A-20. Title of Article.

This Article may be cited as the Animal Welfare Act. (1977, 2nd Sess., c. 1217, s. 1.)

§ 19A-21. Purposes.

The purposes of this Article are (i) to protect the owners of dogs and cats from the theft of such pets; (ii) to prevent the sale or use of stolen pets; (iii) to insure that animals, as items of commerce, are provided humane care and treatment by regulating the transportation, sale, purchase, housing, care, handling and treatment of such animals by persons or organizations engaged in transporting, buying, or selling them for such use; (iv) to insure that animals confined in pet shops, kennels, animal shelters and auction markets are provided humane care and treatment; (v) to prohibit the sale, trade or adoption of those animals which show physical signs of infection, communicable disease, or congenital abnormalities, unless veterinary care is assured subsequent to sale, trade or adoption. (1977, 2nd Sess., c. 1217, s. 2.)

§ 19A-22. Animal Welfare Section in Animal Health Division of Department of Agriculture and Consumer Services created; Director.

There is hereby created within the Animal Health Division of the North Carolina Department of Agriculture and Consumer Services, a new section thereof, to be known as the Animal Welfare Section of said division.

The Commissioner of Agriculture is hereby authorized to appoint a Director of said section whose duties and authority shall be determined by the Commissioner subject to the approval of the Board of Agriculture and subject to the provisions of this Article. (1977, 2nd Sess., c. 1217, s. 3; 1997-261, s. 1.)

§ 19A-23. Definitions.

For the purposes of this Article, the following terms, when used in the Article or the rules or orders made pursuant thereto, shall be construed respectively to mean:

(1)   "Adequate feed" means the provision at suitable intervals, not to exceed 24 hours, of a quantity of wholesome foodstuff suitable for the species and age, sufficient to maintain a reasonable level of nutrition in each animal. Such foodstuff shall be served in a sanitized receptacle, dish, or container.

(2)   "Adequate water" means a constant access to a supply of clean, fresh, potable water provided in a sanitary manner or provided at suitable intervals for the species and not to exceed 24 hours at any interval.

(3)   "Ambient temperature" means the temperature surrounding the animal.

(4)   "Animal" means any domestic dog (Canis familiaris), or domestic cat (Felis domestica).

(5)   "Animal shelter" means a facility which is used to house or contain seized, stray, homeless, quarantined, abandoned or unwanted animals and

which is under contract with, owned, operated, or maintained by a county, city, town, or other municipality, or by a duly incorporated humane society, animal welfare society, society for the prevention of cruelty to animals, or other nonprofit organization devoted to the welfare, protection, rehabilitation, or humane treatment of animals.

(5a)   "Approved foster care provider" means an individual, nonprofit corporation, or association that cares for stray animals that has been favorably assessed by the operator of the animal shelter through the application of written standards.

(5b)   "Approved rescue organization" means a nonprofit corporation or association that cares for stray animals that has been favorably assessed by the operator of the animal shelter through the application of written standards.

(5c)   "Boarding kennel" means a facility or establishment which regularly offers to the public the service of boarding dogs or cats or both for a fee. Such a facility or establishment may, in addition to providing shelter, food and water, offer grooming or other services for dogs and/or cats.

(6)   "Commissioner" means the Commissioner of Agriculture of the State of North Carolina.

(7)   "Dealer" means any person who sells, exchanges, or donates, or offers to sell, exchange, or donate animals to another dealer, pet shop, or research facility; provided, however, that an individual who breeds and raises on his own premises no more than the offspring of five canine or feline females per year, unless bred and raised specifically for research purposes shall not be considered to be a dealer for the purposes of this Article.

(8)   "Director" means the Director of the Animal Welfare Section of the Animal Health Division of the Department of Agriculture and Consumer Services.

(9)   "Euthanasia" means the humane destruction of an animal accomplished by a method that involves rapid unconsciousness and immediate death or by a method that involves anesthesia, produced by an agent which causes painless loss of consciousness, and death during such loss of consciousness.

(10)   "Housing facility" means any room, building, or area used to contain a primary enclosure or enclosures.

(11) "Person" means any individual, partnership, firm, joint-stock company, corporation, association, trust, estate, or other legal entity.

(12) "Pet shop" means a person or establishment that acquires for the purposes of resale animals bred by others whether as owner, agent, or on consignment, and that sells, trades or offers to sell or trade such animals to the general public at retail or wholesale.

(13) "Primary enclosure" means any structure used to immediately restrict an animal or animals to a limited amount of space, such as a room, pen, cage compartment or hutch.

(14) "Public auction" means any place or location where dogs or cats are sold at auction to the highest bidder regardless of whether such dogs or cats are offered as individuals, as a group, or by weight.

(15) "Research facility" means any place, laboratory, or institution at which scientific tests, experiments, or investigations involving the use of living animals are carried out, conducted, or attempted.

(16) "Sanitize" means to make physically clean and to remove and destroy to a practical minimum, agents injurious to health. (1977, 2nd Sess., c. 1217, s. 4; 1979, c. 734, s. 1; 1987, c. 827, s. 61; 1997-261, s. 2; 2005-276, s. 11.5(a); 2013-377, s. 1.)

§ 19A-24. Powers of Board of Agriculture.

(a) The Board of Agriculture shall:

(1) Establish standards for the care of animals at animal shelters, boarding kennels, pet shops, and public auctions. A boarding kennel that offers dog day care services and has a ratio of dogs to employees or supervisors, or both employees and supervisors, of not more than 10 to one, shall not as to such services be subject to any regulations that restrict the number of dogs that are permitted within any primary enclosure.

(2) Prescribe the manner in which animals may be transported to and from registered or licensed premises.

(3) Require licensees and holders of certificates to keep records of the purchase and sale of animals and to identify animals at their establishments.

(4) Adopt rules to implement this Article, including federal regulations promulgated under Title 7, Chapter 54, of the United States Code.

(5) Adopt rules on the euthanasia of animals in the possession or custody of any person required to obtain a certificate of registration under this Article. An animal shall only be put to death by a method and delivery of method approved by the American Veterinary Medical Association, the Humane Society of the United States, or the American Humane Association. The Department shall establish rules for the euthanasia process using any one or combination of methods and standards prescribed by the three aforementioned organizations. The rules shall address the equipment, the process, and the separation of animals, in addition to the animals' age and condition. If the gas method of euthanasia is approved, rules shall require (i) that only commercially compressed carbon monoxide gas is approved for use, and (ii) that the gas must be delivered in a commercially manufactured chamber that allows for the individual separation of animals. Rules shall also mandate training for any person who participates in the euthanasia process.

(b) In addition to rules on the euthanasia of animals adopted pursuant to subdivision (5) of subsection (a) of this section, the Board of Agriculture shall adopt rules for the certification of euthanasia technicians. The rules may provide for:

(1) Written and practical examinations for persons who perform euthanasia.

(2) Issuance of certification to persons who have successfully completed both training and examinations to become a euthanasia technician.

(3) Recertification of euthanasia technicians on a periodic basis.

(4) Standards and procedures for the approval of persons who conduct training of euthanasia technicians.

(5) Approval of materials for use in euthanasia technician training.

(6) Minimum certification criteria for persons seeking to become euthanasia technicians including, but not limited to: age; previous related experience;

criminal record; and other qualifications that are related to an applicant's fitness to perform euthanasia.

(7) Denial, suspension, or revocation of certification of euthanasia technicians who:

a. Violate any provision of this Article or rules adopted pursuant to this Article;

b. Have been convicted of or entered a plea of guilty or nolo contendere to:

1. Any felony;

2. Any misdemeanor or infraction involving animal abuse or neglect; or

3. Any other offense related to animal euthanasia, the duties or responsibilities of a euthanasia technician, or a euthanasia technician's fitness for certification;

c. Make any false statement, give false information, or omit material information in connection with an application for certification or for renewal or reinstatement of certification as a euthanasia technician; or

d. Otherwise are or become ineligible for certification.

(8) Provision of the names of persons who perform euthanasia at animal shelters and for the animal shelter to notify the Department when those persons are no longer affiliated, employed, or serving as a volunteer with the shelter.

(9) Certified euthanasia technicians to notify the Department when they are no longer employed by or are serving as a volunteer at an animal shelter.

(10) The duties, responsibilities, and standards of conduct for certified euthanasia technicians.

(c) Regardless of the extent to which the Board exercises its authority under subsection (b) of this section, the Department may deny, revoke, or suspend the certification of a euthanasia technician who has been convicted of or entered a plea of guilty or nolo contendere to a felony involving the illegal use, possession, sale, manufacture, distribution, or transportation of a controlled substance, drug, or narcotic.

(d) Persons seeking certification as euthanasia technicians, or a renewal of such certification, shall provide the Department a fingerprint card in a format acceptable to the Department, a form signed by the person consenting to a criminal record check and the use of the person's fingerprints, and such other identifying information as may be required by the State or national data banks. The Department may deny certification to persons who refuse to provide the fingerprint card or consent to the criminal background check. Fees required by the Department of Justice for conducting the criminal background check shall be collected by the Department and remitted to the Department of Justice along with the fingerprint card and consent form. (1977, 2nd Sess., c. 1217, s. 5; 1987, c. 827, s. 62; 2004-199, s. 12; 2005-276, s. 11.5(b); 2005-345, s. 22; 2008-198, s. 2(a); 2010-127, ss. 2, 3.)

§ 19A-25. Employees; investigations; right of entry.

For the enforcement of the provisions of this Article, the Director is authorized, subject to the approval of the Commissioner to appoint employees as are necessary in order to carry out and enforce the provisions of this Article, and to assign them interchangeably with other employees of the Animal Health Division. The Director shall cause the investigation of all reports of violations of the provisions of this Article, and the rules adopted pursuant to the provisions hereof; provided further, that if any person shall deny the Director or his representative admittance to his property, either person shall be entitled to secure from any superior court judge a court order granting such admittance. (1977, 2nd Sess., c. 1217, s. 6; 1987, c. 827, s. 63.)

§ 19A-26. Certificate of registration required for animal shelter.

No person shall operate an animal shelter unless a certificate of registration for such animal shelter shall have been granted by the Director. Application for such certificate shall be made in the manner provided by the Director. No fee shall be required for such application or certificate. Certificates of registration shall be valid for a period of one year or until suspended or revoked and may be renewed for like periods upon application in the manner provided. (1977, 2nd Sess., c. 1217, s. 7; 1987, c. 827, s. 64.)

§ 19A-27. License required for operation of pet shop.

No person shall operate a pet shop unless a license to operate such establishment shall have been granted by the Director. Application for such license shall be made in the manner provided by the Director. The license shall be for the fiscal year and the license fee shall be seventy-five dollars ($75.00) for each license period or part thereof beginning with the first day of the fiscal year. (1977, 2nd Sess., c. 1217, s. 8; 1987, c. 827, s. 65; 1989, c. 544, s. 17; 2011-145, s. 31.5(a).)

§ 19A-28. License required for public auction or boarding kennel.

No person shall operate a public auction or a boarding kennel unless a license to operate such establishment shall have been granted by the Director. Application for such license shall be made in the manner provided by the Director. The license period shall be the fiscal year and the license fee shall be seventy-five dollars ($75.00) for each license period or part thereof beginning with the first day of the fiscal year. (1977, 2nd Sess., c. 1217, s. 9; 1987, c. 827, s. 65; 1989, c. 544, s. 18; 2011-145, s. 31.5(b).)

§ 19A-29. License required for dealer.

No person shall be a dealer unless a license to deal shall have been granted by the Director to such person. Application for such license shall be in the manner provided by the Director. The license period shall be the fiscal year and the license fee shall be seventy-five dollars ($75.00) for each license period or part thereof, beginning with the first day of the fiscal year. (1977, 2nd Sess., c. 1217, s. 10; 1987, c. 827, s. 66; 1989, c. 544, s. 19; 2011-145, s. 31.5(c).)

§ 19A-30. Refusal, suspension or revocation of certificate or license.

The Director may refuse to issue or renew or may suspend or revoke a certificate of registration for any animal shelter or a license for any public auction, kennel, pet shop, or dealer, if after an impartial investigation as provided in this Article he determines that any one or more of the following grounds apply:

(1) Material misstatement in the application for the original certificate of registration or license or in the application for any renewal under this Article;

(2) Willful disregard or violation of this Article or any rules issued pursuant thereto;

(3) Failure to provide adequate housing facilities and/or primary enclosures for the purposes of this Article, or if the feeding, watering, sanitizing and housing practices at the animal shelter, public auction, pet shop, or kennel are not consistent with the intent of this Article or the rules adopted under this Article;

(4) Allowing one's license under this Article to be used by an unlicensed person;

(5) Conviction of any crime an essential element of which is misstatement, fraud, or dishonesty, or conviction of any felony;

(6) Making substantial misrepresentations or false promises of a character likely to influence, persuade, or induce in connection with the business of a public auction, commercial kennel, pet shop, or dealer;

(7) Pursuing a continued course of misrepresentation of or making false promises through advertising, salesmen, agents, or otherwise in connection with the business to be licensed;

(8) Failure to possess the necessary qualifications or to meet the requirements of this Article for the issuance or holding of a certificate of registration or license.

The Director shall, before refusing to issue or renew and before suspension or revocation of a certificate of registration or a license, give to the applicant or holder thereof a written notice containing a statement indicating in what respects the applicant or holder has failed to satisfy the requirements for the holding of a certificate of registration or a license. If a certificate of registration or a license is suspended or revoked under the provisions hereof, the holder shall have five days from such suspension or revocation to surrender all certificates of registration or licenses issued thereunder to the Director or his authorized representative.

A person to whom a certificate of registration or a license is denied, suspended, or revoked by the Director may contest the action by filing a petition under G.S. 150B-23 within five days after the denial, suspension, or revocation.

Any licensee whose license is revoked under the provisions of this Article shall not be eligible to apply for a new license hereunder until one year has elapsed from the date of the order revoking said license or if an appeal is taken from said order of revocation, one year from the date of the order or final judgment sustaining said revocation. Any person who has been an officer, agent, or employee of a licensee whose license has been revoked or suspended and who is responsible for or participated in the violation upon which the order of suspension or revocation was based, shall not be licensed within the period during which the order of suspension or revocation is in effect. (1977, 2nd Sess., c. 1217, s. 11; 1987, c. 827, s. 67.)

§ 19A-31. License not transferable; change in management, etc., of business or operation.

A license is not transferable. When there is a transfer of ownership, management, or operation of a business of a licensee hereunder, the new owner, manager, or operator, as the case may be, whether it be an individual, firm, partnership, corporation, or other entity shall have 10 days from such sale or transfer to secure a new license from the Director to operate said business. A licensee shall promptly notify the Director of any change in the name, address, management, or substantial control of his business or operation. (1977, 2nd Sess., c. 1217, s. 12.)

§ 19A-32. Procedure for review of Director's decisions.

A denial, suspension, or revocation of a certificate or license under this Article shall be made in accordance with Chapter 150B of the General Statutes. (1977, 2nd Sess., c. 1217, s. 13; 1987, c. 827, s. 68.)

§ 19A-32.1. Minimum holding period for animals in animal shelters; public viewing of animals in animal shelters; disposition of animals.

(a) Except as otherwise provided in this section, all animals received by an animal shelter or by an agent of an animal shelter shall be held for a minimum holding period of 72 hours, or for any longer minimum period established by a board of county commissioners, prior to being euthanized or otherwise disposed of.

(b) Before an animal may be euthanized or otherwise disposed of, it shall be made available for adoption under procedures that enable members of the public to inspect the animal, except in the following cases:

(1) The animal has been found by the operator of the shelter to be unadoptable due to injury or defects of health or temperament.

(2) The animal is seriously ill or injured, in which case the animal may be euthanized before the expiration of the minimum holding period if the manager of the animal shelter determines, in writing, that it is appropriate to do so. The writing shall include the reason for the determination.

(3) The animal is being held as evidence in a pending criminal case.

(c) Except as otherwise provided in this subsection, a person who comes to an animal shelter attempting to locate a lost pet is entitled to view every animal held at the shelter, subject to rules providing for such viewing during at least four hours a day, three days a week. If the shelter is housing animals that must be kept apart from the general public for health reasons, public safety concerns, or in order to preserve evidence for criminal proceedings, the shelter shall make reasonable arrangements that allow pet owners to determine whether their lost pets are among those animals.

(d) During the minimum holding period, an animal shelter may place an animal it is holding into foster care by transferring possession of the animal to an approved foster care provider, an approved rescue organization, or the person who found the animal. If an animal shelter transfers possession of an animal under this subsection, at least one photograph depicting the head and face of the animal shall be displayed at the shelter in a conspicuous location that is available to the general public during hours of operation, and that photograph shall remain posted until the animal is disposed of as provided in subsection (f) of this section.

(e)   If a shelter places an animal in foster care, the shelter may, in writing, appoint the person or organization possessing the animal to be an agent of the shelter. After the expiration of the minimum holding period, the shelter may (i) direct the agent possessing the animal to return it to the shelter, (ii) allow the agent to adopt the animal consistent with the shelter's adoption policies, or (iii) extend the period of time that the agent holds the animal on behalf of the shelter. A shelter may terminate an agency created under this subsection at any time by directing the agent to deliver the animal to the shelter. The local government or organization operating the shelter, as principal in the agency relationship, shall not be liable to reimburse the agent for the costs of care of the animal and shall not be liable to the owner of the animal for harm to the animal caused by the agent, absent a written contract providing otherwise.

(f)   An animal that is surrendered to an animal shelter by the animal's owner and not reclaimed by that owner during the minimum holding period may be disposed of in one of the following manners:

(1)   Returned to the owner.

(2)   Adopted as a pet by a new owner.

(3)   Euthanized by a procedure approved by rules adopted by the Department of Agriculture and Consumer Services or, in the absence of such rules, by a procedure approved by the American Veterinary Medical Association, the Humane Society of the United States, or the American Humane Association.

(g)   An animal that is surrendered to an animal shelter by the animal's owner may be disposed of before the expiration of the minimum holding period in a manner authorized under subsection (f) of this section if the owner provides to the shelter (i) some proof of ownership of the animal and (ii) a signed written consent to the disposition of the animal before the expiration of the minimum holding period.

(h)   If the owner of a dog surrenders the dog to an animal shelter, the owner shall state in writing whether the dog has bitten any individual within the 10 days preceding the date of surrender.

(i) An animal shelter shall require every person to whom an animal is released to present one of the following valid forms of government-issued photographic identification: (i) a drivers license, (ii) a special identification card issued under G.S. 20-37.7, (iii) a military identification card, or (iv) a passport. Upon presentation of the required photographic identification, the shelter shall document the name of the person, the type of photographic identification presented by the person, and the photographic identification number.

(j) Animal shelters shall maintain a record of all animals impounded at the shelter, shall retain those records for a period of at least three years from the date of impoundment, and shall make those records available for inspection during regular inspections pursuant to this Article or upon the request of a representative of the Animal Welfare Section. These records shall contain, at a minimum:

(1) The date of impoundment.

(2) The length of impoundment.

(3) The disposition of each animal, including the name and address of any person to whom the animal is released, any institution that person represents, and the identifying information required under subsection (i) of this section.

(4) Other information required by rules adopted by the Board of Agriculture. (2013-377, s. 2.)

§ 19A-33. Penalty for operation of pet shop, kennel or auction without license.

Operation of a pet shop, kennel, or public auction without a currently valid license shall constitute a Class 3 misdemeanor subject only to a penalty of not less than five dollars ($5.00) nor more than twenty-five dollars ($25.00), and each day of operation shall constitute a separate offense. (1977, 2nd Sess., c. 1217, s. 14; 1993, c. 539, s. 315; 1994, Ex. Sess., c. 24, s. 14(c).)

§ 19A-34. Penalty for acting as dealer without license; disposition of animals in custody of unlicensed dealer.

Acting as a dealer in animals as defined in this Article without a currently valid dealer's license shall constitute a Class 2 misdemeanor. Continued illegal operation after conviction shall constitute a separate offense. Animals found in possession or custody of an unlicensed dealer shall be subject to immediate seizure and impoundment and upon conviction of such unlicensed dealer shall become subject to sale or euthanasia in the discretion of the Director. (1977, 2nd Sess., c. 1217, s. 15; 1993, c. 539, s. 316; 1994, Ex. Sess., c. 24, s. 14(c).)

§ 19A-35. Penalty for failure to adequately care for animals; disposition of animals.

Failure of any person licensed or registered under this Article to adequately house, feed, and water animals in his possession or custody shall constitute a Class 3 misdemeanor, and such person shall be subject to a fine of not less than five dollars ($5.00) per animal or more than a total of one thousand dollars ($1,000). Such animals shall be subject to seizure and impoundment and upon conviction may be sold or euthanized at the discretion of the Director and such failure shall also constitute grounds for revocation of license after public hearing. (1977, 2nd Sess., c. 1217, s. 16; 1999-408, s. 4.)

§ 19A-36. Penalty for violation of Article by dog warden.

Violation of any provision of this Article which relates to the seizing, impoundment, and custody of an animal by a dog warden shall constitute a Class 3 misdemeanor and the person convicted thereof shall be subject to a fine of not less than fifty dollars ($50.00) and not more than one hundred dollars ($100.00), and each animal handled in violation shall constitute a separate offense. (1977, 2nd Sess., c. 1217, s. 17; 1993, c. 539, s. 317; 1994, Ex. Sess., c. 24, s. 14(c).)

§ 19A-37. Application of Article.

This Article shall not apply to a place or establishment which is operated under the immediate supervision of a duly licensed veterinarian as a hospital where animals are harbored, boarded, and cared for incidental to the treatment, prevention, or alleviation of disease processes during the routine practice of the profession of veterinary medicine. This Article shall not apply to any dealer, pet shop, public auction, commercial kennel or research facility during the period such dealer or research facility is in the possession of a valid license or registration granted by the Secretary of Agriculture pursuant to Title 7, Chapter 54, of the United States Code. This Article shall not apply to any individual who occasionally boards an animal on a noncommercial basis, although such individual may receive nominal sums to cover the cost of such boarding. (1977, 2nd Sess., c. 1217, s. 18; 1987, c. 827, s. 69.)

§ 19A-38. Use of license fees.

All license fees collected shall be used in enforcing and administering this Article. (1977, 2nd Sess., c. 1217, s. 19.)

§ 19A-39. Article inapplicable to establishments for training hunting dogs.

Nothing in this Article shall apply to those kennels or establishments operated primarily for the purpose of boarding or training hunting dogs. (1977, 2nd Sess., c. 1217, s. 21; 1979, c. 734, s. 2.)

§ 19A-40. Civil Penalties.

The Director may assess a civil penalty of not more than five thousand dollars ($5,000) against any person who violates a provision of this Article or any rule promulgated thereunder. In determining the amount of the penalty, the Director shall consider the degree and extent of harm caused by the violation. The clear proceeds of civil penalties assessed pursuant to this section shall be remitted to the Civil Penalty and Forfeiture Fund in accordance with G.S. 115C-457.2. (1995, c. 516, s. 6; 1998-215, s. 3.)

§ 19A-41. Legal representation by the Attorney General.

It shall be the duty of the Attorney General to represent the Commissioner of Agriculture and the Department of Agriculture and Consumer Services, or to designate some member of his staff to represent the Commissioner and the Department, in all actions or proceedings in connection with this Article. (2005-276, s. 11.5(c).)

§ 19A-42. Reserved for future codification purposes.

§ 19A-43. Reserved for future codification purposes.

§ 19A-44. Reserved for future codification purposes.

Article 4.

Animal Cruelty Investigators.

§ 19A-45. Appointment of animal cruelty investigators; term of office; removal; badge; oath; bond.

(a) The board of county commissioners is authorized to appoint one or more animal cruelty investigators to serve without any compensation or other employee benefits in his county. In making these appointments, the board may consider persons nominated by any society incorporated under North Carolina law for the prevention of cruelty to animals. Prior to making any such appointment, the board of county commissioners is authorized to enter into an agreement whereby any necessary expenses of caring for seized animals not collectable pursuant to G.S. 19A-47 may be paid by the animal cruelty investigator or by any society incorporated under North Carolina law for the prevention of cruelty to animals that is willing to bear such expense.

(b) Animal cruelty investigators shall serve a one-year term subject to removal for cause by the board of county commissioners. Animal cruelty investigators shall, while in the performance of their official duties, wear in plain view a badge of a design approved by the board identifying them as animal cruelty investigators, and provided at no cost to the county.

(c)   Animal cruelty investigators shall take and subscribe the oath of office required of public officials. The oath shall be filed with the clerk of superior court. Animal cruelty investigators shall not be required to post any bond.

(d)   Upon approval by the board of county commissioners, the animal cruelty investigator or investigators may be reimbursed for all necessary and actual expenses, to be paid by the county. (1979, c. 808, s. 1.)

§ 19A-46. Powers; magistrate's order; execution of order; petition; notice to owner.

(a)   Whenever any animal is being cruelly treated as defined in G.S. 19A-1(2), an animal cruelty investigator may file with a magistrate a sworn complaint requesting an order allowing the investigator to provide suitable care for and take immediate custody of the animal. The magistrate shall issue the order only when he finds probable cause to believe that the animal is being cruelly treated and that it is necessary for the investigator to immediately take custody of it. Any magistrate's order issued under this section shall be valid for only 24 hours after its issuance. After he executes the order, the animal cruelty investigator shall return it with a written inventory of the animals seized to the clerk of court in the county where the order was issued.

(b)   The animal cruelty investigator may request a law-enforcement officer or animal control officer to accompany him to help him seize the animal. An investigator may forcibly enter any premises or vehicle when necessary to execute the order only if he reasonably believes that the premises or vehicle is unoccupied by any person and that the animal is on the premises or in the vehicle. Forcible entry shall be used only when the animal cruelty investigator is accompanied by a law-enforcement officer. In any case, he must give notice of his identity and purpose to anyone who may be present before entering said premises. Forcible entry shall only be used during the daylight hours.

(c)   When he has taken custody of such an animal, the animal cruelty investigator shall file a complaint pursuant to Article 1 of this Chapter as soon as possible. When he seizes the animal, he shall leave with the owner, if known, or affixed to the premises or vehicle a copy of the magistrate's order and a written notice of a description of the animal, the place where the animal will be taken, the reason for taking the animal, and the investigator's intent to file a complaint in district court requesting custody of the animal pursuant to Article 1 of this Chapter.

(d) Notwithstanding the provisions of G.S. 7A-305(c), any person who commences a proceeding under this Article or Article 1 of this Chapter shall not be required to pay any court costs or fees prior to a final judicial determination as provided in G.S. 19A-4, at which time those costs shall be paid pursuant to the provisions of G.S. 6-18.

(e) Any judicial order authorizing forcible entry shall be issued by a district court judge. (1979, c. 808, s. 1.)

§ 19A-47. Care of seized animals.

The investigator must take any animal he seizes directly to some safe and secure place and provide suitable care for it. The necessary expenses of caring for seized animals, including necessary veterinary care, shall be a charge against the animal's owner and a lien on the animal to be enforced as provided by G.S. 44A-4. (1979, c. 808, s. 1.)

§ 19A-48. Interference unlawful.

It shall be a Class 1 misdemeanor, to interfere with an animal cruelty investigator in the performance of his official duties. (1979, c. 808, s. 1; 1993, c. 539, s. 318; 1994, Ex. Sess., c. 24, s. 14(c).)

§ 19A-49. Educational requirements.

Each animal cruelty investigator at his own expense must attend annually a course of at least six hours instruction offered by the North Carolina Humane Federation or some other agency. The course shall be designed to give the investigator expertise in the investigation of complaints relating to the care and treatment of animals. Failure to attend a course approved by the board of county commissioners shall be cause for removal from office. (1979, c. 808, s. 1.)

§§ 19A-50 through 19A-59. Reserved for future codification purposes.

ARTICLE 5.

Spay/Neuter Program.

§ 19A-60. Legislative findings.

The General Assembly finds that the uncontrolled breeding of cats and dogs in the State has led to unacceptable numbers of unwanted dogs, puppies and cats and kittens. These unwanted animals become strays and constitute a public nuisance and a public health hazard. The animals themselves suffer privation and death, are impounded, and most are destroyed at great expense to local governments. It is the intention of the General Assembly to provide a voluntary means of funding a spay/neuter program to provide financial assistance to local governments offering low-income persons reduced-cost spay/neuter services for their dogs and cats and to provide a statewide education program on the benefits of spaying and neutering pets. (2000-163, s. 1.)

§ 19A-61. Spay/Neuter Program established.

There is established in the Department of Agriculture and Consumer Services a voluntary statewide program to foster the spaying and neutering of dogs and cats for the purpose of reducing the population of unwanted animals in the State. The program shall consist of the following components:

(1) Education Program. - The Department shall establish a statewide program to educate the public about the benefits of having cats and dogs spayed and neutered. The Department may work cooperatively on the program with the North Carolina School of Veterinary Medicine, other State agencies and departments, county and city health departments and animal control agencies, and statewide and local humane organizations. The Department may employ outside consultants to assist with the education program.

(2) Local Spay/Neuter Assistance Program. - The Department shall administer the Spay/Neuter Account established in G.S. 19A-62. Monies deposited in the account shall be available to reimburse eligible counties and cities for the direct costs of spay/neuter surgeries for cats and dogs made available to low-income persons. (2000-163, s. 1; 2010-31, s. 11.4(b).)

§ 19A-62. Spay/Neuter Account established.

(a) Creation. - The Spay/Neuter Account is established as a nonreverting special revenue account in the Department of Agriculture and Consumer Services. The Account consists of the following:

(1) Repealed by Session Laws 2010-31, s. 11.4(c), effective October 1, 2010.

(2) Twenty dollars ($20.00) of the additional fee imposed by G.S. 20-79.7 for an Animal Lovers special license plate.

(3) Any other funds available from appropriations by the General Assembly or from contributions and grants from public or private sources.

(b) Use. - The revenue in the Account shall be used by the Department of Agriculture and Consumer Services as follows:

(1) Repealed by Session Laws 2010-31, s. 11.4(c), effective October 1, 2010.

(2) Up to twenty percent (20%) may be used to develop and implement the statewide education program component of the Spay/Neuter Program established in G.S. 19A-61(1).

(3) Up to twenty percent (20%) of the money in the Account may be used to defray the costs of administering the Spay/Neuter Program established in this Article.

(4) Funds remaining after deductions for the education program and administrative expenses shall be distributed quarterly to eligible counties and cities seeking reimbursement for reduced-cost spay/neuter surgeries performed during the previous calendar year. A county or city is ineligible to receive funds

under this subdivision unless it requires the owner to show proof of rabies vaccination at the time of the procedure or, if none, require vaccination at the time of the procedure.

(c) Report. - In February of each year, the Department must report to the Joint Legislative Commission on Governmental Operations and the Fiscal Research Division. The report must contain information regarding all revenues and expenditures of the Spay/Neuter Account. (2000-163, s. 1; 2007-487, ss. 2, 3; 2008-187, s. 8; 2010-31, s. 11.4(c); 2011-326, s. 4.)

§ 19A-63. Eligibility for distributions from Spay/Neuter Account.

(a) A county or city is eligible for reimbursement from the Spay/Neuter Account if it meets the following condition:

(1) The county or city offers one or more of the following programs to low-income persons on a year-round basis for the purpose of reducing the cost of spaying and neutering procedures for dogs and cats:

a. A spay/neuter clinic operated by the county or city.

b. A spay/neuter clinic operated by a private organization under contract or other arrangement with the county or city.

c. A contract or contracts with one or more veterinarians, whether or not located within the county, to provide reduced-cost spaying and neutering procedures.

d. Subvention of the spaying and neutering costs incurred by low-income pet owners through the use of vouchers or other procedure that provides a discount of the cost of the spaying or neutering procedure fixed by a participating veterinarian or other provider.

e. Subvention of the spaying and neutering costs incurred by persons who adopt a pet from an animal shelter operated by or under contract with the county or city.

(2) Reserved for future codification purposes.

(b) For purposes of this Article, the term "low-income person" shall mean an individual who qualifies for one or more of the programs of public assistance administered by the Department of Health and Human Services pursuant to Chapter 108A of the General Statutes or whose annual household income is under three hundred percent (300%) of the federal poverty level guidelines published by the United States Department of Health and Human Services.

(c) Each county shall make rules or publish guidelines that designate what proof a low-income person must submit to establish that the person qualifies for public assistance under subsection (b) of this section or has an annual household income lower than three hundred percent (300%) of the federal poverty level guidelines published by the United States Department of Health and Human Services. (2000-163, s. 1; 2010-31, s. 11.4(d).)

§ 19A-64. Distributions to counties and cities from Spay/Neuter Account.

(a) Reimbursable Costs. - Counties and cities eligible for distributions from the Spay/Neuter Account may receive reimbursement for the direct costs of a spay/neuter surgical procedure for a dog or cat owned by a low-income person as defined in G.S. 19A-63(b). Reimbursable costs shall include anesthesia, medication, and veterinary services. Counties and cities shall not be reimbursed for the administrative costs of providing reduced-cost spay/neuter services or capital expenditures for facilities and equipment associated with the provision of such services. The reimbursement amount for each surgical procedure for a female dog or cat shall be no more than one hundred fifty percent (150%) of the average reimbursement allowed for surgical procedures for female dogs and cats by the Spay/Neuter Program during the prior calendar year. The reimbursement amount for each surgical procedure for a male dog or cat shall be no more than one hundred fifty percent (150%) of the average reimbursement allowed for surgical procedures for male dogs and cats by the Spay/Neuter Program during the prior calendar year.

(b) Application. - A county or city eligible for reimbursement of spaying and neutering costs from the Spay/Neuter Account shall apply to the Department of Agriculture and Consumer Services by the last day of January, April, July, and October of each year to receive a distribution from the Account for that quarter. The application shall be submitted in the form required by the Department and shall include an itemized listing of the costs for which reimbursement is sought.

(c) Distribution. - The Department shall make payments from the Spay/Neuter Account to eligible counties and cities who have made timely application for reimbursement within 30 days of the closing date for receipt of applications for that quarter. In the event that total requests for reimbursement exceed the amounts available in the Spay/neuter Account for distribution, the monies available will be distributed as follows:

(1)   Fifty percent (50%) of the monies available in the Spay/Neuter Account shall be reserved for reimbursement for eligible applicants within development tier one areas as defined in G.S. 143B-437.08. The remaining fifty percent (50%) of the funds shall be used to fund reimbursement requests from eligible applicants in development tier two and three areas as defined in G.S. 143B-437.08.

(2)   Among the eligible counties and cities in development tier one areas, reimbursement shall be made to each eligible county or city in the proportion that the rate of spays and neuters per one thousand persons in that city or county compares to the total rate of spays and neuters per one thousand persons within the total tier one area. Population data shall be obtained from the most recent decennial census.

(3)   Among the eligible counties and cities in development tier two and three areas, reimbursement shall be made to each eligible county or city in the proportion that the rate of spays and neuters per one thousand persons in that city or county compares to the total rate of spays and neuters per one thousand persons within the total tier two and three area. Population data shall be obtained from the most recent decennial census.

(4)   Should funds remain available from the fifty percent (50%) of the Spay/Neuter Account designated for development tier one areas after reimbursement of all claims by eligible applicants in those areas, the remaining funds shall be made available to reimburse eligible applicants in development tier two and three areas. (2000-163, s. 1; 2006-252, s. 2.11; 2010-31, s. 11.4(e); 2013-377, s. 4.)

§ 19A-65. Annual Report Required From Every Animal Shelter in Receipt of State or Local Funding.

Every county or city animal shelter, or animal shelter operated under contract with a county or city or otherwise in receipt of State or local funding shall prepare an annual report in the form required by the Department of Agriculture and Consumer Services setting forth the numbers, by species, of animals received into the shelter, the number adopted out, the number returned to owner, and the number destroyed. The report shall also contain the total operating expenses of the shelter and the cost per animal handled. The report shall be filed with the Department of Agriculture and Consumer Services by March 1 of each year. A city or county that does not timely file the report required by this section is not eligible to receive reimbursement payments under G.S. 19A-64 during the calendar year in which the report was to be filed. (2000-163, s. 5; 2010-31, s. 11.4(f).)

§ 19A-66. Notification of available funding.

Prior to January 1 of each year, the Department of Agriculture and Consumer Services shall notify counties and cities that have, prior to that notification deadline, established eligibility for distribution of funds from the Spay/Neuter Account pursuant to G.S. 19A-63, of the following:

(1) The amount of funding in the Spay/Neuter Account that the Department will have available for distribution to each county or city receiving notification to pay reimbursement requests submitted by the county or city during the calendar year following the notification deadline; and

(2) The amount of additional funding, if any, the Department estimates, but does not guarantee, may be available to pay reimbursement requests submitted by the notified county or city to the Department during the calendar year following the notification deadline.

(3) The maximum amount that may be reimbursed for each surgical procedure for a female dog or cat during the upcoming calendar year.

(4) The maximum amount that may be reimbursed for each surgical procedure for a male dog or cat during the upcoming calendar year. (2010-31, s. 11.4(g); 2013-377, s. 5.)

§ 19A-67. Reserved for future codification purposes.

§ 19A-68. Reserved for future codification purposes.

§ 19A-69. Reserved for future codification purposes.

Article 6.

Care of Animal Subjected to Illegal Treatment.

§ 19A-70. Care of animal subjected to illegal treatment.

(a)   In every arrest under any provision of Article 47 of Chapter 14 of the General Statutes or under G.S. 67-4.3 or upon the commencement of an action under Article 1 of this Chapter by a county or municipality, by a county-approved animal cruelty investigator, by other county or municipal official, or by an organization operating a county or municipal shelter under contract, if an animal shelter takes custody of an animal, the operator of the shelter may file a petition with the court requesting that the defendant be ordered to deposit funds in an amount sufficient to secure payment of all the reasonable expenses expected to be incurred by the animal shelter in caring for and providing for the animal pending the disposition of the litigation. For purposes of this section, "reasonable expenses" includes the cost of providing food, water, shelter, and care, including medical care, for at least 30 days.

(b)   Upon receipt of a petition, the court shall set a hearing on the petition to determine the need to care for and provide for the animal pending the disposition of the litigation. The hearing shall be conducted no less than 10 and no more than 15 business days after the petition is filed. The operator of the animal shelter shall mail written notice of the hearing and a copy of the petition to the defendant at the address contained in the criminal charges or the complaint or summons by which a civil action was initiated. If the defendant is in a local detention facility at the time the petition is filed, the operator of the animal shelter shall also provide notice to the custodian of the detention facility.

(c)   The court shall set the amount of funds necessary for 30 days' care after taking into consideration all of the facts and circumstances of the case, including the need to care for and provide for the animal pending the disposition of the litigation, the recommendation of the operator of the animal shelter, the estimated cost of caring for and providing for the animal, and the defendant's ability to pay. If the court determines that the defendant is unable to deposit funds, the court may consider issuing an order under subsection (f) of this section.

Any order for funds to be deposited pursuant to this section shall state that if the operator of the animal shelter files an affidavit with the clerk of superior court, at least two business days prior to the expiration of a 30-day period, stating that, to the best of the affiant's knowledge, the case against the defendant has not yet been resolved, the order shall be automatically renewed every 30 days until the case is resolved.

(d) If the court orders that funds be deposited, the amount of funds necessary for 30 days shall be posted with the clerk of superior court. The defendant shall also deposit the same amount with the clerk of superior court every 30 days thereafter until the litigation is resolved, unless the defendant requests a hearing no less than five business days prior to the expiration of a 30-day period. If the defendant fails to deposit the funds within five business days of the initial hearing, or five business days of the expiration of a 30-day period, the animal is forfeited by operation of law. If funds have been deposited in accordance with this section, the operator of the animal shelter may draw from the funds the actual costs incurred in caring for the animal.

In the event of forfeiture, the animal shelter may determine whether the animal is suitable for adoption and whether adoption can be arranged for the animal. The animal may not be adopted by the defendant or by any person residing in the defendant's household. If the adopted animal is a dog used for fighting, the animal shelter shall notify any persons adopting the dog of the liability provisions for owners of dangerous dogs under Article 1A of Chapter 67 of the General Statutes. If no adoption can be arranged after the forfeiture, or the animal is unsuitable for adoption, the shelter shall humanely euthanize the animal.

(e) The deposit of funds shall not prevent the animal shelter from disposing of the animal prior to the expiration of the 30-day period covered by the deposit if the court makes a final determination of the charges or claims against the defendant. Upon determination, the defendant is entitled to a refund for any portion of the deposit not incurred as expenses by the animal shelter. A person who is acquitted of all criminal charges or not found to have committed animal cruelty in a civil action under Article 1 of this Chapter is entitled to a refund of the deposit remaining after any draws from the deposit in accordance with subsection (d) of this section.

(f) Pursuant to subsection (c) of this section, the court may order a defendant to provide necessary food, water, shelter, and care, including any necessary medical care, for any animal that is the basis of the charges or claims against the defendant without the removal of the animal from the existing location and until the charges or claims against the defendant are adjudicated. If the court issues such an order, the court shall provide for an animal control officer or other law enforcement officer to make regular visits to the location to ensure that the animal is receiving necessary food, water, shelter, and care, including any necessary medical care, and to impound the animal if it is not receiving those necessities. (2005-383, s. 1; 2006-113, s. 2.1.)

Vision Books Order Form

Fax Orders: 1-980-299-5965

Phone Orders: 1-704-898-0770

E-mail Orders: www.visionbooks.org

Mail Orders: Vision Books, LLC
P.O. Box 42406
Charlotte, NC 28215

Shipp To:
Name_____
Address_____
City_____State_____Zip_____
Phone_____Fax_____
Email_____@_____

Bill To: We can bill a third party on your behalf.
Name_____
Address_____
City_____State_____Zip_____
Phone___(_____)_____Fax_____
Email_____@_____

Pamphlet Number ($15.00 Each)	Qty	Total Cost
_____	_____	_____
_____	_____	_____
_____	_____	_____
_____	_____	_____
_____	_____	_____
_____	_____	_____
_____	_____	_____
_____	_____	_____
<u>Full Volume Set 1-92</u>	<u>92 Pamphlets</u>	<u>1,380.00</u>

Free Shipping Shipping & Handling on Full Volume Orders
Add $1.00 Shipping & Handling per pamphlet $_____

Total Cost $_____

Thany you for your support. Management!

DID YOU ENJOY THIS BOOK?

Vision Books, LLC would like to hear from you! If you or someone you know has been falsely imprisoned, we would like to hear your story. If the 'North Carolina Criminal Law and Procedure' has had an effect in your life or if you have suggestions, we would like to hear from you. Send your letters to:

Vision Books, LLC
Attn: Staff Writers
P.O. Box 42406
Charlotte, NC 28215
Email: staff@visionbooks.org

Order Additional Copies:

Fax Orders:	1-980-299-5965
Phone Orders:	1-704-898-0770
E-mail Orders:	www.visionbooks.org
Mail Orders:	Vision Books, LLC P.O. Box 42406 Charlotte, NC 28215

www.ingramcontent.com/pod-product-compliance
Lightning Source LLC
Chambersburg PA
CBHW071401170526
45165CB00001B/134